Weight Training Safely

The F.I.T.S. Way
(Free of Injury & Target-Specific)

A Reference Guide and Injury Prevention Program

Bruce Comstock, B.Sc., D.C.

Warwick Publishing
Toronto
www.warwickgp.com

WEIGHT TRAINING SAFELY THE F.I.T.S. WAY
Copyright ©2005 by Bruce Comstock, B.Sc., D.C.

We acknowledge the financial support of the Government of Canada through the Book Publishing Industry Development Program for our publishing activities.

ISBN: 1-894622-34-0

Published by Warwick Publishing Inc.
161 Frederick Street, Suite 200, Toronto, Ontario M5A 4P3 Canada
www.warwickgp.com

Distributed in Canada by
Canadian Book Network
c/o Georgetown Terminal Warehouses
34 Armstrong Avenue
Georgetown, Ontario L7G 4R9
www.canadianbooknetwork.com

Distributed in the United States by
CDS Books
193 Edwards Drive
Jackson TN 38301

Design: Kimberley Young
Exercise photos: Bruce Comstock
Anatomical illustrations: Roy Gardiner
Studio portraits: Murray Bray

Printed and bound in Canada

I AM DEDICATING this book to two people I met in late 1983, early 1984. It is a good bet that without their influence I would not have been capable of writing this book.

First is Bryan Rothenburger, who, within the first month after we opened an injury clinic at Gold's Gym in Toronto, sought help from me for a weight-training injury. I knew very little about serious weight training at that time, but thanks to his precise explanation of how much each exercise he did caused him pain, he planted in my head the notion that all exercises, in varying degrees, contribute to predictable and very specific injuries.

Second is Bob Ruffo, whom I met on the workout floor of Gold's Gym several months after meeting Bryan, as I embarked upon my own bodybuilding journey. For whatever reason, he took me under his wing and proceeded to show me the ropes of serious weight training. Through the breadth of his weight-training background, and the passion he holds for the sport, he taught me that specifically chosen exercises really do result in specifically chosen physique changes.

Thank you Bryan, for showing me the risks of weight training.

Thank you Bob, for showing me the benefits of weight training.

Bob Ruffo (left) and Bryan Rothenburger (right)
flank bodybuilders Christine Roth and Bob Weatherill.

Contents

Chapter 1

Essential F.I.T.S. Concepts

Chapter 2

F.I.T.S. Weight-Training Injury Concepts

Chapter 3
F.I.T.S. Weight-Training Exercise Concepts

Chapter 4
Integration of the F.I.T.S. Concepts

Appendix
Replacement Exercises

Acknowledgments

THROUGHOUT THE TWENTY years that have passed since the actual inception of *Weight Training the F.I.T.S. Way*, many different pieces of the concept/writing/publishing puzzle have had to fall into place. The solving of such a puzzle is unlikely to be achieved alone, and that is certainly true in this case. In chronological order I would like to acknowledge the contributions of the following individuals and establishment.:

Dr. Dan Proctor for offering me the first opportunity to be involved in the injury clinic associated with Gold's Gym, Toronto.

Marcia and **Eric Levine** for having the confidence in me to bring me back, in their plans to rejuvenate the injury clinic at Gold's Gym, Toronto.

Steven Moore for showing me how important it is to have a well informed and motivational personal trainer (such as him) at one's disposal.

Dr. David O'Brien for sharing with me the charge of operating the rejuvenated injury clinic at Gold's Gym, thus providing me with both the time and the means to develop my concept of weight-training exercises as a cause of injuries.

Tula Pazianas for being the best personal assistant imaginable — and for her handling of the formidable task of transcribing my long-hand manuscript into an electronic format.

Michael Levine for his early support of my book-writing pursuit, and later for his professional expertise when it was most needed and appreciated.

Maria Rudnick for her timely introduction, of me, to Jim Williamson of Warwick Communications.

Tony Bellissimo for his generous loan of the equipment that was needed during the exercise photography.

Bob Weatherill, **Christine Roth** and **Lorne King** for their time and energy in being photographed for this book.

Venice Gym, Toronto and **Club Markham** for granting me the access, and the freedom within their premises, to undertake photography of Christine and Lorne (respectively).

Roy Gardiner for his graphics expertise and technical advice regarding the final phases of photography and manuscript preparation.

Devon Comstock (my son) for his considerable effort in digitally enhancing my exercise photographs.

Murray Bray for his studio photography of Bob Weatherill.

Jenna Comstock (my daughter) for her singular effort in photographing me so she could have her name included here.

Peter Riolo for his extensive, and often timely, technical support.

Sue Comstock (my wife) for her indulgence and understanding during the often frenetic and time-consuming episodes of photography and manuscript completion.

My sincere thanks go to all of you.

Introduction

"No Pain — No Gain"

"NO PAIN — NO GAIN." This is, without a doubt, the most widely used and yet dangerous phrase in the world of weight training. As long as it remains the motto of the iron sport, participants will continue to suffer constant and, as this book will demonstrate, unnecessary pain.

The essential problem with this phrase is that it does not differentiate "good" pain from "bad" pain. "Good" pain is not only acceptable, for a weight-training athlete it is necessary for muscle development. "Bad" pain, however, represents actual tissue damage. We can distinguish "good" from "bad" pain by describing them like this:

***Good* pain =**
- the muscle "pump" during a workout
- the muscle "burn" during a workout
- the muscle soreness one to two days after a workout.

***Bad* pain =**   everything else!

When a weight-training athlete experiences *bad* pain, more often than not the subsequent visit to the family medical doctor or chiropractor is a frustrating experience. The usual advice is, "Stop your weight training," indicating that the doctor does not understand the overwhelming drive of the athlete, and thus underestimates the powerful reluctance to miss even a single workout. The athlete then rejects the advice, keeps working out, and no benefit comes from the visit. Minor injuries worsen to become debilitating, requiring extensive therapy, possibly even surgery.

A better-informed practitioner would suggest simple changes to the workouts that would allow the injured athlete to "train around the pain." But this can end up being just as futile because, until the writing of this book, no one has ever mapped out exactly how to "train around" the various *bad* pains associated with weight training.

Virtually all serious weight-training athletes are at one of the stages in the loop shown at right. The critical point for eliminating *bad* pain is when it must be decided whether to correct or not to correct the problem workout routine.

For an individual caught in this loop, the only way out is to either voluntarily withdraw from weight training, or decide to *correct* the workout routine, thus making it possible to train free of bad pain.

How to weight-train free of bad pain through improved exercise selection and execution, while maintaining the muscular development benefits of weight training, is what the F.I.T.S. way is all about — **F**ree of **I**njury and **T**arget-**S**pecific.

HOW TO USE THIS BOOK

This book has been put together with the intention of making it as user-friendly as possible to all potential readers. You have probably flipped through this book a few times and may have been tempted to move directly to the illustrated exercises in chapter three. But please try to hold that temptation at bay and read through chapters one and two. To make the F.I.T.S. way work for you, it is important to understand the underlying principles, which are explained in chapter one. To get the most from the exercise section, you need to understand the risk/benefit (R/B) ratios of each exercise and be alerted to the "injury zones"; these are fully explained in chapter two.

Once you have gained a solid understanding of the F.I.T.S. way, review the exercises in chapter three. Rather than change your present weight-training regimen, use the information in chapter four to chart out a new routine, based on what you have learned.

Figure 1: **The Weight-Training "Loop"**

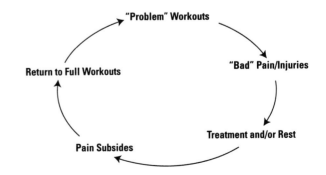

At this point you will be ready to weight-train the F.I.T.S. way. Have this book with you as you start your new program so that you can perform the exercises exactly as described.

If you read this book in its entirety, and carefully apply its message to your weight-training routine, you can look forward to many years of healthy and productive muscle development, without fear of serious or even permanent injury that too often accompanies traditional weight-training programs.

In order to make the most effective use of this book, follow the instructions below based on the category to which you belong. Please note that, regardless of your category instructions, you must read pages 13–36 to fully understand the principles behind the advice of this book.

(1) Individuals who weight-train as part of a broader fitness regimen

To best prepare for a lifetime of safe yet effective weight training, I suggest that you study the tables and figures at the beginning of each section devoted to a particular body part in Chapter 3. This will quite easily demonstrate how your usual selection of exercises fits into the R/B concept, and just how many different ways there are to perform a given exercise. It only makes sense to select exercises that will give you the desired benefit and are accompanied by a minimal risk of injury. Be sure to consult the section in Chapter 2 on your personal R/B value, based on your injury history and lifestyle, as well as the section called "Establishing Your Acceptable Workout Risks" in Chapter 3. Remember, good training amounts to continuous, repetitive training — which becomes impossible with injuries. The bottom line is *to avoid injuries at all costs* by using low-risk exercises.

(2) Injured weight-training athletes

First, refer to the appropriate injury region of Chapter 2 to locate and label your specific problem as accurately as possible on the illustration of that region. Second, look at the list of replacement and aggravating exercises in the Appendix, as they relate to your injury site. In most cases, you will know which exercises aggravate your pain, so simply begin to use the relevant replacement exercises within your workout to replace your original, aggravating exercises. You will also have to take into account your personal risks of injury (in Chapter 2). If you are not sure which of your current exercises aggravate your pain, I would advise that you replace all exercises listed as aggravating the injury zone.

(3) Novice bodybuilders

Look at the beginner's version of the "Sample F.I.T.S-ed Workout" in Chapter 4, and then familiarize yourself with all the exercises listed there by reading Chapter 3. Once you are comfortable executing these, you can use the tables associated with each body part in Chapter 3. Using the R/B values, you can continue to create your own workout programs suited to your advancing physique objectives, but guided by the personal risk tables of Chapter 2.

(4) Competitive bodybuilders

You will find that this book offers two distinct categories of important information for you. First, you have a set of completely accurate and target-specific training concepts, and second, you have deliberate and controlled injury avoidance. (If you are currently injured, please refer back to (2) — Injured Weight-Training Athletes.) As a competitor, you require, more than most, the ability to work on your "weak points." This need is easily met by using various target-specific modifications found throughout Chapter 3, learning to use the plane-of-action visualization principles, and familiarizing yourself with the precise purpose of every exercise in Chapter 3 (using the tables for each body part). For you, injuries are disastrous because you need a continuous training regimen. And, depending on what phase of training you are in (building, recuperation, competitive, off-season, etc.) your acceptable risk limits may change. I also strongly suggest that you take into account the personal risk ideas in Chapter 2 as you create your workouts. Regardless, Chapter 3 offers you the ability to select exercises for your program that are precise in their purpose, as well as to tailor the amount of risk you are willing to accept.

(5) Sport-specific athletes involved in "off-season" strength and conditioning programs

Refer to the "Sample F.I.T.S-ed Workout" in chapter 4, then study the illustrations and table for each body part in Chapter 3, and add or replace exercises best suited to your sport-specific physical objectives. However, when calculating the benefits or risks of a particular exercise, consider the types of injury that would be particularly devastating to your sport. Your prime objective is a full-body workout incorporating the least possible risk, especially to those crucial body components. This is accomplished using the tables of personal risk in Chapter 2, and the section called "Establishing Your Acceptable Workout Risks" in Chapter 3.

(6) Gym instructors, personal trainers, and phys-ed. teachers

Since there is much misinformation and myth-perpetration at the gym level, I urge you to study the Weight-Training Myths in Chapter 3, as well as every exercise of Chapter 3. This will teach you the many (often subtle) details of exercise execution, and more importantly, the purpose-shift and injury-risk that each detail creates. Most importantly, I urge you to become especially familiar with the personal risk tables of Chapter 2, such that you are able to tailor every client's workout for optimal injury prevention. You are the teachers, and thus are the most likely to be able to put an end to the myth-based weight-training *status quo* that this book reveals.

(7) Healthcare professionals involved in rehabilitative therapy (chiropractors, physio- and occupational therapists, athletic therapists, massage therapists and kinesiologists), especially regarding weight-training participants

Healthcare professionals who face the task of patient rehabilitation must realize that the rehabilitative task is dual in nature. The first and better established element is the use of exercises for strengthening. The second and more overlooked element is the ability to prescribe strengthening exercises that will neither aggravate the current injury nor add any risk of creating a new injury. To embrace this duality, I suggest that you (perhaps more than most) adopt the *Primum Non Nocere* principal as stated in Chapter 1. Then, to best follow it, become familiar with each injury region and its table of personal predisposition in Chapter 2 so that as you assign exercises for their therapeutic benefit (based on Chapter 3), you will be able to alter the assigned exercises according to your patient's current injury, his or her personal predisposition toward any other injuries, and the amount of risk associated with the exercise selected.

A suggested alternative use of this book for this group is to become completely familiar with all of the components of exercise performance that can cause injury at each site described in Chapter 2. Then you can ensure that they are only minimally involved within your prescribed therapy programs.

Note: For those practitioners who routinely treat injured weight-training participants, the aggravating and replacement exercise lists in the Appendix are a quick reference tool for altering your patients' workouts as you initiate their therapy. Remember: by not expecting your patients to stop working out while injured, you inspire trust and confidence in, as well as compliance with, your medical advice.

THE GENERALIZED APPROACH TO USING THIS BOOK

(1) Read all of pages 13–36 to fully understand and appreciate the principles behind the practical information.

(2) Make yourself familiar with the basic structure of the injury regions and the tables of personal risk in Chapter 2.

(3) Use Chapter 3 to create workouts that are based not only on exercise purpose, but also on their risk(s) of injury.

(4) Complete the workout-creating process by choosing and applying the appropriate parameters from Chapter 4 to your workout.

(5) Ensure that any variations to your workout follow the acceptable risk values as assigned for each exercise in the Appendix.

Chapter 1
Essential F.I.T.S. Concepts

THE WEIGHT-TRAINING DILEMMA

We know that weight training works. When properly pursued for a sufficient period of time, it results in bigger and stronger muscles. However, during the process of developing bigger and stronger muscles, it is all too common to experience considerable pain and injury.

As evidence of this I cite the fact that virtually all bodybuilding magazines feature regular advice columns about injury. Arnold Schwarzenegger's highly respected *Encyclopedia of Modern Bodybuilding* contains the details of many common weight-training injuries he and other legendary bodybuilders have incurred. Finally, my twenty years of clinical experience as a doctor of chiropractic, eight of them spent in an injury clinic adjacent to a major weight-training facility, have given me the opportunity to see the resulting injuries first-hand.

This is the weight-training dilemma: muscle development seems to carry a strong risk of pain and injury. The belief that this dilemma can and should be resolved has inspired me to write this book.

The essential premise of the book is that current weight-training methods lead to a dual outcome, one positive and one negative. Whether your outcome is predominantly positive or negative is determined by a balance of several components hidden within your workout. The intent of this book is to reveal, control, and even eliminate those components that contribute to the negative outcome (injury), thus shifting toward the more positive outcome, muscle development. I have called this the "F.I.T.S." way — **F**ree of **I**njury and **T**arget-**S**pecific. In this chapter I will explain the basis for the F.I.T.S. approach to weight training, and how it is applied

WEIGHT-TRAINING "INSURANCE"

Primum Non Nocere. This Latin phrase is best known as a component of the Hippocratic Oath to which all doctors pledge themselves upon their graduation. Translated, it reads, "First and above all else — do no harm."

I strongly urge you to adopt *Primum Non Nocere* as your prime directive as you create a weight-training program. It will guide you to select exercises that are safest (i.e., the least likely to injure) for the specific purpose

intended. This ensures your ability to train hard and heavy for many years with the least possible risk of sustaining an injury. The *Primum Non Nocere* principle essentially serves as a weight-training insurance policy of the very best kind — it has a maximum payout (no injuries) with a minimal premium (reading and using this book as reference.)

As already discussed, the primary principle of weight training has been "No Pain — No Gain." But in an ideal world, it would be replaced by *Primum Non Nocere*, giving rise to an era of injury-free weight training.

GOOD VS. BAD PAINS IN WEIGHT TRAINING

It would be unrealistic to expect the disappearance of a popular phrase just because I point out its shortcomings. Perhaps the more practical approach to the old phrase, "No Pain — No Gain," is to define the concept of weight-training pain.

First, we know already that in the weight-training process there are both *good* and *bad* types of pain. Second, we can assert that one must never "train through" *bad* pain. Third, we must remember that *good* pain is not only acceptable, it is necessary for muscle-building.

Bad pains occur primarily in connective/soft tissue (i.e., tendons, ligaments, bursae, joint capsules, joint cartilage, and fascia), and much less frequently within the muscles themselves. Such *bad* pains are

(1) apparent even during times of inactivity;
(2) exaggerated even by non-demanding exertion (like walking, sitting or carrying something); and
(3) worsened by continued weight-training.

These pains must be trained *around*, not *through*. Continued training in the face of intense, worsening pain, is weight-training "suicide."

Good pain, on the other hand, is the "pump" or "burn" experienced as a muscle is reaching a point of fatigue, well into your workout. It is also the soreness felt upon muscle flexing within two days of a hard workout. It is indicative of the controlled muscle breakdown that leads to muscle development — the positive (+) outcome.

Good pain can only lead to injury if the sore muscle is exercised again before it has fully recovered, that is, before the soreness subsides. If, however, the muscle pain has not subsided within three to four days of a workout, and especially if bruising appears, there was likely an actual tear in the muscle. In this case, the pain must be reassessed as *bad*, and treated accordingly.

With these definitions in mind, we can reconsider the old phrase to consist of two separate elements:

(1) No Muscle Pain — No Muscle Gain
(2) Any Other Pain — No Brain.

The *bad* pains have their origins in specific habits, beliefs and errors which, when isolated and infrequent, may be insignificant. But remember that weight training is about repetition, and it is the repetition of habits, errors and wrong beliefs that leads to *bad* pains.

REPETITIVE STRAIN SYNDROME

Repetitive strain injuries have become a common problem in the workplace. A worker who performs the same task, day in, day out, will suffer pain and disability, even if the task is not very physically demanding. The same is true of weight-training participants. If we think about it, weight training is by its nature forceful and repetitive, so it *should* result in repetitive strain injuries.

Unfortunately, the ever-present phrase, "No Pain — No Gain," not only ensures that the first bad pain felt during a workout is ignored (with the expected trade-off of muscle development), it also ensures that participants repeatedly "train through" their pain, thus converting mild tissue irritation into a full-fledged injury.

Remember: *everything counts when done in large amounts*. Even the smallest variations from ideal weight-training methods become magnified tremendously by the repetition necessary for effective weight training. Optimizing your workout choices so that this "repetition-magnification" effect cannot occur is the first aspect of eliminating the negative outcome of weight training.

WEIGHT-TRAINING MYTHOLOGY

I believe a powerfully held, but false, belief system is responsible for most of the injuries of weight training. It is a kind of weight-training mythology, not unlike the mythology of any culture. Weight-training culture does not concern itself as much with gods and their feats (although such imagery definitely exists), but with the set of rules about "how things are done." To belong in the culture is to accept wholeheartedly this set of rules.

Unfortunately, this blind acceptance of myth-based rules (or, as will be shown, untruths) has led to many unintentional, injury-producing methods and concepts. This *status quo* of weight training must change.

WEIGHT-TRAINING "TRUTHS" REVEALED

To counter the erroneous belief system that currently underlies the concepts and methods of weight training, a new framework is needed. Here are *my* universal truths of the weight-training process:

Weight-Training Truth #1 (WT #1):
Every exercise offers specific *benefit* to specific muscle(s).

Weight-Training Truth #2 (WT #2):
Every exercise, during its execution, puts those soft tissues that are either overstretched, compressed, or firmly grated against, at *risk* of injury.

Every weight-training exercise = benefit + risk
                                                    = WT #1 + WT #2

Choosing Maximum Benefit + Minimum Risk = **F.I.T.S.** (free of injury and target-specific)

As obvious as they seem, these weight-training truths are the critical support system behind the exercises described in this book. In assessing any weight-training exercise, there is always a dual outcome: WT #1 (+) and WT #2 (–). *Weight-training will break you down as it builds you up*. In other words, you cannot have one (the benefit) without some element of the other (the risk).

The main goal of this book is to show how to increase the (+) of your workout while decreasing its (–). You cannot eliminate the (+/–) duality of weight training, but you can certainly shift it in your favor.

THE RISK-TO-BENEFIT RATIO

In life, choosing a particular action always involves consideration of both the potential benefit to be gained and the amount of risk that can be accepted. Consider this risk-to-benefit (R/B) approach in relation to medical procedures or financial investments. Simply put, in examining the balance of risk versus benefit, if there is a greater risk of loss than possibility of gain, the proposed action is usually rejected. Weight-training exercises are no different — they also contain both (+) and (–) components (i.e., WT #1 and WT #2) and so should be viewed with the same kind of critical judgment.

The rest of this book depends heavily on the concept of R/B ratios for each individual exercise. As you will see, they are presented as values on a numerical range from one to ten. Of course, this scale of values is relative only to other exercises, since it would be impossible to assign an absolute value to the risk (or benefit) of a particular exercise. The assignment of values is based on the components of exercise performance that can cause injury as a particular body part is engaged in a given exercise. These injury zones are the subject of Chapter 2.

For every weight-training exercise, an R/B value has been assigned to each body part or region that is at risk of injury during the execution of that exercise. Reducing the number of moving parts used in an exercise will generally reduce the risk of injury.

The following ranges of R/B values can help you decide if a particular exercise fits into your workout. It is also a good general guideline for the R/B values that will be assigned more broadly (more on that later).

(1) R/B of 1 to 4: benefit > risk — considered safe
(2) R/B of 5 to 7: benefit = risk — can aggravate a prior condition
(3) R/B of 8 to 10: benefit < risk — will create an injury

Clearly, for exercises that have R/B values greater than seven, "the truth hurts." Applying the R/B concept to your workouts is the best way to make use of the old cliché that an ounce of prevention is worth a pound of cure.

THE INJURY-CAUSING ERRORS OF WEIGHT TRAINING

Earlier in this chapter, I referred to habits, beliefs, and errors committed by weight-training athletes. The significance of these errors is illustrated by their effect on the inherent, negative property of all exercises.

(1) *The lack of exercise variety* exaggerates the severity of WT #2 through "repetition magnification," meaning low-risk exercises develop into high-risk ones.
(2) *The bad execution of exercises* intensifies WT #2 for the target area and creates a strong potential to extend WT #2 to other injury zones not directly targeted.
(3) *The use of exercises that, by their nature, have a high risk of injury* maximizes the negative potential of WT #2.

A *lack of exercise variety* is easily corrected by reviewing the tables at the start of each body-part section in Chapter 3. Note that "exercise variety" not only involves continual shifting or "cycling" of exercises, but also the cycling of other elements, such as the amount of weight involved, the number of repetitions, and the order in which body parts are trained in your program. Mix, match, and be creative — this not only reduces the risk of pain and injuries but also improves muscle response.

The bad execution of exercises is all too common and usually based on myths. This is easily corrected and as such is unforgivable. The very least this book can do is show you how, simply by improving your execution, you can prevent much unnecessary pain. Bad execution may arise from fatigue. The first few reps may be performed well and risk-free, but subsequent reps become high-risk as form degenerates due to fatigue. If the reps cannot be

consistently performed as described by this book, the set must be stopped.

My designation of some exercises as high-risk may be difficult to accept, as many of them are assumed to have important muscle-developing elements. But if the ultimate outcome of such exercises is injury, what real value do they have? Should you decide that their value *is* real, at least acknowledge that they are risky and do not use them for a prolonged time. For the most part, I do not believe that high-risk exercises should *ever* be part of a workout routine. These exercises have R/B values of eight or more; take note of the ones you have routinely used in the past and replace them immediately.

THE WEIGHT-TRAINING "SEE-SAWS"

Remember: within every weight-training attempt to create muscle benefit (whether it be size, strength, or tone) there is a balancing act. Every weight-training athlete faces the potential dual outcome of muscle benefit and tissue injury. This can be represented as a kind of see-saw:

With the obviously desirable outcome being (+) muscle benefit, the challenge faced by weight-training athletes is to make choices that will lower the R/B values within their program, yet still fulfill their goals, ensuring muscle benefit outweighs the risk of tissue injury.

As a result, the selection of each exercise within a workout program is a balancing act between that exercise's (+) component (i.e., WT #1) and its (–) component (i.e., WT #2), as shown below, in the exercise see-saw:

Just as muscle benefit from an exercise requires much repetition and time to manifest, so too does tissue injury. Clearly, then, in relation to a potential injury site, the consistent use of exercises which tilt the exercise "see-saw" toward the (–) will result in the tipping of the outcome see-saw to (–), i.e., toward injury, as illustrated by the "outcome see-saw" below.

The exercises you choose for your workout determine the likelihood of becoming injured as a result of your

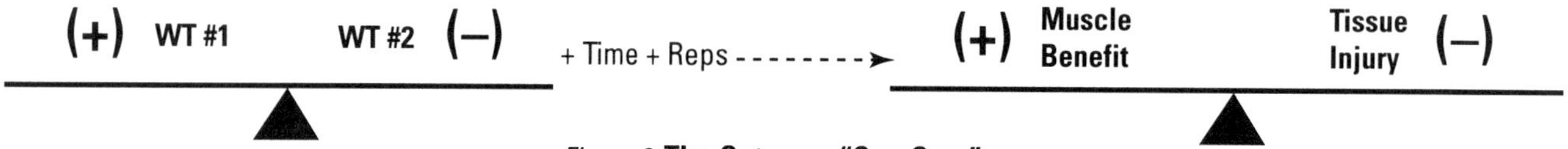

$$(+) \quad \text{WT \#1} \qquad \text{WT \#2} \quad (-) \qquad + \text{Time} + \text{Reps} \text{ - - - - - - - } \rightarrow \quad (+) \quad \begin{array}{l}\text{Muscle} \\ \text{Benefit}\end{array} \qquad \begin{array}{l}\text{Tissue} \\ \text{Injury}\end{array} \quad (-)$$

Figure 2: **The Outcome "See-Saw"**

weight-training efforts. This book will show you how to make better choices and thus control the outcome.

THE WEIGHT-TRAINER'S FLOWCHART

The weight-trainer's flowchart (opposite) shows how every weight-training participant will inevitably follow one of two paths, based entirely on their routine performance of either error-free workouts (i.e., free from bad pain) or myth-based workouts (i.e., leading to bad pain). The myth-based workouts contain any combination of bad exercise execution, high-risk exercises, and a lack of exercise variety. I believe that the vast majority of weight-training participants are routinely using such error-laden workouts, and therefore are either approaching or are already stuck in a "loop" of training, pain, resting, and resuming training.

The frustration of being stuck in a loop can only be eliminated by choosing the "corrected" workout option at the critical point in your decision-making process. While in a loop, participants will have periods during which their symptoms ease, but as soon as the uncorrected workout is resumed with full intensity, all of the previous pains return. The majority of this book is dedicated to illustrating how to correct the myth-based workouts, and thus prevent entry into or allow exit from an endless loop. Now, when we reformulate the bad habits listed above into positive steps to minimize WT #2 and reduce the "repetition-magnification" effect, a handy little mnemonic is the result.

Perfect Execution	eliminates the errors of execution that are responsible for unacceptable, high-stress body movements, and further eliminates any incorrect body motion that is not part of the proper exercise. Full awareness will ensure that proper (i.e., injury-free) exercise execution, as defined in Chapter 3, is not lost due to fatigue in the final rep(s) of your set.
Avoidance of high-risk exercises	as indicated throughout Chapter 3 by R/B values of 8 to 10, greatly decreases your risk of injury. Keep in mind that "high-risk" exercises for you can be assigned values below 8 if your personal R/B values, as explained in Chapter 2, are high.
Variation in Exercise Selection	if instituted on an approximately monthly basis, greatly reduces your risk of repetitive strain injury, by varying the sites of soft tissue strain.

P.E.A.V.E.S. is your reminder of how to prevent bad pain through **P**erfect **E**xecution, **A**voidance of high-risk exercises and **V**ariation in **E**xercise **S**election. With the routine use of all three of these guidelines, weight-training participants will remain in the only desirable part of the flowchart — the pain-free end point.

Please note that using a "corrected" workout does *not* heal damaged tissues. Such a workout does, however, remove the direct aggravating stresses from the pain site, allowing uninterrupted workouts. It is still vital to obtain proper injury treatment from a knowledgeable practitioner to accompany your use of a corrected workout.

VISUALIZATION AND THE PLANES OF ACTION

While good F.I.T.S. weight training will certainly be achieved by following the key premises of this book, the best will occur when a participant gains the ability to "see" what is involved in every exercise through visualization. Just as it improves the performance of a sport, visualization makes each rep of each set in weight training more accurate and effective. With complete focus and a clear "inner vision" of a muscle at work, you will optimize the results of every repetition.

Visualization applied to weight training involves a concept I call the "plane of action." Within the plane of action we find the target-specific muscle, the precise direction of muscle fiber contraction, the path followed by the weight, and even the tissue sites at risk of injury. The plane of action illustrates via our mind's inner vision the sites of both the risks and the benefits for every exercise. When you can routinely and effortlessly "see" an exercise's plane of action, you will have completely mastered that exercise's selection, application, and execution. Like any other skill, you must fully understand, then regularly practice, the process.

By definition, a plane consists of two basic features: a location and a direction. Every weight-training exercise also inherently possesses a location (a specific target) and a direction (a specific movement).

To visualize the plane of action, I suggest you "see" a pane of glass located along the length of a targeted muscle. There are then two options for the plane's direction. The first, which applies to free-weight (dumbbell and

Figure 3
The Weight-Trainer's Flowchart

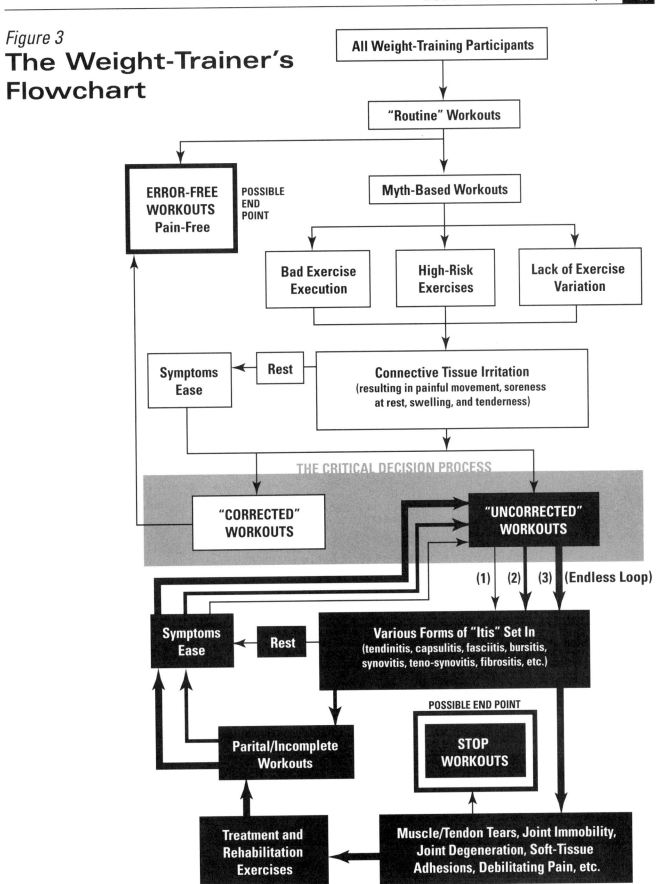

barbell) exercises, is the vertical plane. The second, which applies to machines and cables, has the direction of the plane following the length of the cable. The plane of action, so visualized, indicates the exact muscle target, the exact path of body movement (i.e., directly "through" the pane of glass), and the tissues at risk of injury (i.e., anywhere that body movement or soft tissue stretch or compression occurs within the plane, as the fully visualized pane of glass "passes through" the body).

In order to make this visualization process possible, every exercise in this book has its two plane-defining features applied and labeled. The location feature of the plane of action (PA) is labeled "PA-L" and the direction feature of the PA is labeled "PA-D." Each of these features is shown as a line in a photo for each exercise. The PA-D line also has an arrow to indicate the direction of force needed for the positive phase of a repetition.

As you learn the details of exercise execution as offered by this book, keep in mind the following summary:

PA-L = the target muscle

PA-D = the path of exercise movement

PA-L + PA-D = the plane of action for that exercise

The majority of weight-training exercises are easily labeled with these principles, but there are some exceptions to which I must draw your attention:

(1) Several exercises, due to their two equally active target muscles, have each of their "pure" PA-Ls illustrated by a dotted line overlying the specific muscle, while the resultant or "net" PA-L is indicated by a solid line. (For those who are interested in determining the "net" PA-L from two "pure" PA-Ls, it is the summation of the individual force vectors.)

(2) The performance of several exercises changes the true vertical PA-D into a slight arc. These situations are designated by PA-D★. Such exceptions do not change any other features of that exercise, and as a result you can simply overlook the anomaly.

The defining features of the plane of action (PA-L and PA-D) are illustrated as accurately as possible for every exercise in this book. Learn to visualize each exercise's plane of action to improve (1) your ability to understand and thus prevent injuries (i.e., **F**ree of **I**njury), and (2) your understanding of exercise purpose and execution (i.e., **T**arget-**S**pecific).

THE "3 Rs" OF EDUCATED WEIGHT-TRAINING

There are three activities you must engage in to become an educated weight-training athlete:

(1) **Reading**

(2) **Repping**

(3) **Reducing your risk.**

1. Reading

Injury prevention (not to mention muscle growth) requires a regular change or cycling of exercises, best learned by steadily re-reading, or at least reviewing, this book. The variety of ideas put forward in the array of bodybuilding magazines and books available also serves this purpose. However, I implore you to refer back to this book whenever you intend to add new exercises to your workout, so you will learn not only how to correctly perform them but also whether or not they add an excessive risk of injury. Keep in mind that any exercise done frequently enough over a long enough period of time can lead to repetitive injury strain. This is reason enough to periodically (approximately monthly) change the exercises in your workout routine. Reading is fundamental to growth, motivation and safety in weight-training.

2. Repping

Weight-training without "repping" is like a construction project without laborers. The raw materials, even with a carefully formulated plan, cannot achieve anything if the action of building is absent. As long as you are active (and the longer you are active) in the process of "bodybuilding" the more success you will have. Success, from this book's perspective, does not mean winning a bodybuilding contest. More important (and attainable by all) is successful living, by battling the forces of gravity and aging. To achieve this, a regular routine of "repping" — otherwise known as weight-training — is necessary, and an injury that stops the process is the only real failure.

3. Reducing your risk

Reducing your risks of injury begins by accepting WT#2 — that *every* exercise poses the risk of injury, and then using the principle of *Primum Non Nocere* to guide your new exercise selection process. Once this premise is accepted, you are actually obligated by common sense to investigate the degree of risk posed by each exercise, and how to eliminate it. You have the solution in your hands — *this book*! Don't let yourself fall victim to the myth-based untruths; always be in control of your workout choices and methods. The only way to fail in weight training is to be unable to continue because of injuries. Plan ahead — *prevent*!

Chapter 2

F.I.T.S. WEIGHT-TRAINING
INJURY CONCEPTS

ESSENTIAL PRINCIPLES

Before you begin this chapter, please review the principles on which the F.I.T.S. (free of injury and target-specific) method is based:

Weight-Training Truth #1 (WT #1):
Every exercise offers specific *benefit* to specific muscle(s).

Weight-Training Truth #2 (WT #2):
Every exercise, during its execution, puts those soft tissues that are either overstretched, compressed, or firmly grated against, at *risk* of injury.

Every weight-training exercise = benefit + risk
= WT #1 + WT #2

Choosing Maximum Benefit + Minimum Risk = **F.I.T.S.**

TRAUMATIC VERSUS NON-TRAUMATIC WEIGHT-TRAINING INJURIES

The vast majority of weight-training injuries are non-traumatic in origin. The very few weight-training injuries that are due to trauma are quite obvious when they do occur, and can be blamed on human error or equipment failure:

(1) human error
- dropping barbell plates onto toes,
- racking or unracking barbells without a proper spotter,
- swinging dumbbells into exercise position without a proper spotter, or
- unbalanced loading or unloading of a barbell on a rack;

(2) equipment failure
- break of a cable during lat pulldowns,
- break of a barbell during squat, deadlift, or shrug exercises (yes it can, and does, occur),
- collapse of a bench during flat, incline, decline, or shoulder press exercise.

The injuries sustained in any of the above are accidental, and are not what this book is about. Accidents can happen to anyone, at any time. This book is primarily concerned with non-traumatic injuries that occur due to repeated, *deliberately chosen* activities on the gym floor.

Preventing Traumatic Gym Injuries

Though they are not this book's focus, it is certainly worth noting ways to avoid traumatic injuries while weight training. They may seem basic, but most accident prevention techniques do.

(1) *Pay attention* whenever taking plates from racks, or loading/unloading barbells; foot gashes and fractured toes will certainly create some unnecessary "downtime" from your weight training.

(2) *Always use a spotter* in order to avoid various types of sprains and strains when racking or unracking a barbell; it is such awkward "forced" movements during exercise set-up that can traumatize; similarly, have dumbbells handed to you, rather than swinging them into position yourself.

(3) *Never load* more than one plate onto the end of a barbell without putting the same-sized plate onto the other end immediately — a disproportionately loaded bar can pivot on a rack with surprising speed, and with catastrophic results!

(4) *Always visually inspect* the apparatus you are about to use in order to spot potential equipment failure or breakage. A shredded cable, a loosely connected pulley, an excessively bent barbell, or a shaky, unstable bench — all signal danger. Do not use the apparatus; warn others of the potential danger and report it to the gym manager.

OBJECTIVES OF THIS CHAPTER

Returning to the central theme of this book, the objectives of this chapter are to delineate the non-traumatic weight-training injuries in general, and to show the cause-and-effect relationship between exercises and such injuries in particular. More specifically, they are to (1) identify the common injury sites associated with current weight training methods; and (2) provide a means to gauge the amount of risk regarding each possible injury site that is acceptable for each individual.

The material in this chapter works in close conjunction with the Appendix. The Appendix contains an exhaustive list of aggravating exercises according to injury site and their associated replacement exercises. Once you are familiar with the injury sites and you know your own personal risk factors, you can use the Appendix to replace aggravating exercises with ones that serve an identical purpose with a greatly reduced risk of injury. In this way the guess work of training around your injury can be eliminated.

WEIGHT-TRAINING SHORTCUTS

It is basic human nature to prefer to attain goals sooner rather than later. Within the realm of weight training, several shortcuts have been developed with the intent of achieving a more rapid or dramatic shift of the exercise see-saw toward the (+) muscle benefit side. Even those readers with only modest gym experience will recognize the terms *cheating, negatives,* and *forced reps.* These techniques are not only shortcuts to muscle benefit; they are also shortcuts to tissue injury. After all, it makes sense that if you magnify the outcome of an exercise, then both of its WT components will be similarly magnified.

Here are the definition and net effects of each shortcut:

1 — Cheating
Using body movement other than that originating from the target muscles (usually the torso) to enable the lifting of weights that are heavier than the target muscles are capable of lifting in strict form is called a *cheat.*
Effects:
(1) increases WT #1
(2) accentuates WT #2
(3) adds a new and unnecessary WT #2

2 — Negatives
The positive phase of a lift occurs during movement from the start position to the mid-phase position of an exercise, and the negative phase is the return of the weight from the mid-phase position to the finish position. *Negatives* or *negative reps* are performed after exhausting the target muscle's ability to perform the positive phase. At that point, a spotter helps lift the weight to the mid-phase position so the lifter can attempt to resist the return of the weight to the finish position.
Effects:
(1) increases WT #1
(2) accentuates WT #2

3 — Forced Reps
Fatiguing the target muscles of their ability to perform the positive phase of a lift and then having a spotter help just enough so that the lifter can move the weight through the positive phase is called a *forced rep.*
Effects:
(1) increases WT #1
(2) accentuates WT #2

Effect #1 of each shortcut shows that muscle benefit is indeed magnified, making them attractive for use in a weight-training program. However, if used with a myth-based workout, they are a *bad* idea. The shortcuts will accentuate the already high levels of WT #2 components, thus rendering a more pronounced shift of the exercise see-saw to the (–) tissue injury side. If, however, these shortcuts are applied to an exercise whose injury risk is low, then their use can be justified, at least occasionally.

But even following this rationale, the *cheating* shortcut is not approved for use at all because it actually adds another, unnecessary WT #2, which obviously runs counter to the *Primum Non Nocere* guideline.

THE COMMON INJURY SITES OF WEIGHT-TRAINING
Listed below are the injury regions of concern to weight-training participants, with more specific injury sites identified where appropriate. They are also labeled in figure 4.

Spine/Back Region
Zone I — Lower Back
Zone II — Upper Back
Shoulder Region
Zone I — Front
Zone II — Top
Zone III — at Chest
Elbow Region
Zone I — Inside
Zone II — Outside
Zone III — Front
Zone IV — Rear
Wrist
Knee
Hamstrings
Other
Zone I — Chest
Zone II — Ankle/Foot
Zone III — Achilles Heel
Zone IV — Groin

R/B-EXERCISE VALUES
Now we know the common injury sites, but what is the relationship between these injury sites and weight-training exercises? With the common injury sites identified and the specific biomechanics of injury-creation outlined, it is a relatively simple process to determine the risks of injury within every exercise. In the F.I.T.S. way, these "risk potentials," or R/B values, are based upon specific biomechanical components quantified on a scale of one to ten. The scale identifies the level that a given injury-causing biomechanical component is involved in the performance of that exercise. Or, more technically, this concept can be explained as follows:

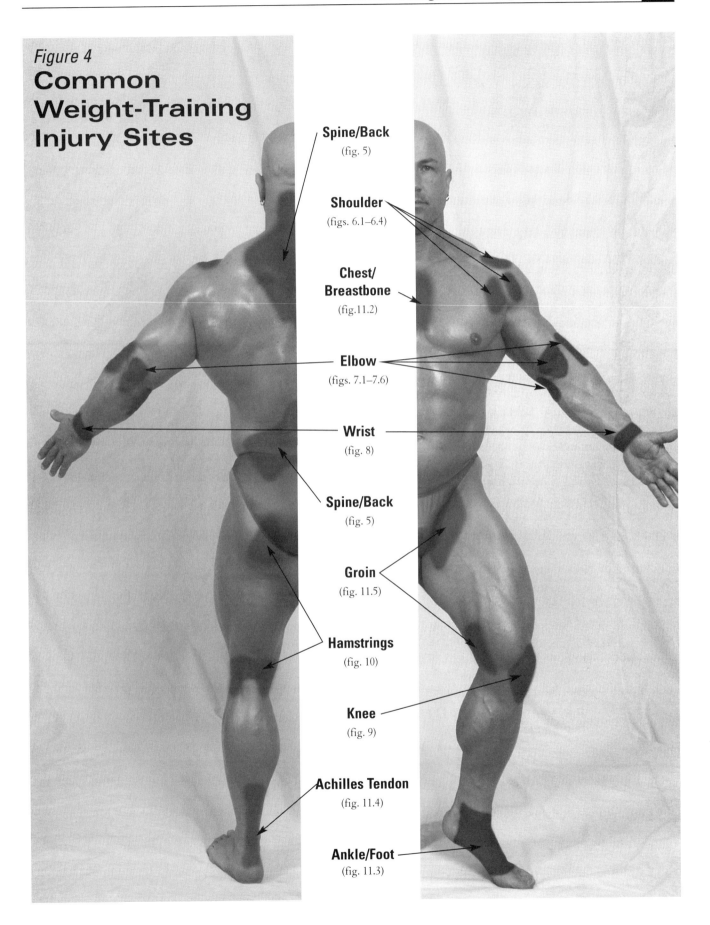

Figure 4
Common Weight-Training Injury Sites

Spine/Back
(fig. 5)

Shoulder
(figs. 6.1–6.4)

Chest/ Breastbone
(fig.11.2)

Elbow
(figs. 7.1–7.6)

Wrist
(fig. 8)

Spine/Back
(fig. 5)

Groin
(fig. 11.5)

Hamstrings
(fig. 10)

Knee
(fig. 9)

Achilles Tendon
(fig. 11.4)

Ankle/Foot
(fig. 11.3)

Deriving the cause(s) of pain in a given region is a matter of examining the principles of bio-mechanics as they apply to normal function, and then considering how excessive and repeated forces applied to that given region could injure any of the tissues known to be sources of pain in that given region.
—*Paraphrased from* Clinical Anatomy of the Lumbar Spine, *Bogduk and Twomey, Churchill and Livingston, 1991*

Accompanying each injury site is one or more specific biomechanical risk principle that causes that injury, based on the above premise. A total of thirty-two such biomechanical risk principles are outlined in this chapter. Understanding the medical jargon of these principles is not as important as applying the R/B values correctly, but some readers may want to know the technical basis for my assessments. (Please see the glossary on page 270 for explanations of the terminology.)

R/B-PERSONAL VALUES

We have seen that (1) there are predictable, common sites of weight-training injuries and (2) very specific injury-causing mechanisms are involved. There is a third crucial aspect of injury causation: your personal predisposition.

My years of clinical experience have made it abundantly clear that a person's history of prior injuries (even if no symptoms have been experienced for years), postural faults or habits, and occupation (often resulting in repetitive strain injuries), determine the likelihood that a specific injury will arise. The task in the remainder of this chapter is to create a way to factor this idea of "personal risk" into the intended program of injury prevention specifically for weight-training participants.

The term "R/B value," as described so far, refers strictly to the degree of risk posed by a given exercise to a particular injury site. This must now be referred to as the "R/B-exercise value," in order to distinguish it from the "R/B-personal value," which accounts for the contribution of your own predisposition to injuries.

The remainder of this chapter will give you a better understanding of the injury zone subsections outlined earlier by the use of labeled photographs. You will also be able to establish your own R/B-personal values using the table that accompanies each zone.

SPINE/BACK INJURIES

When considering weight-training-induced injuries of the spine/back region, there are two zones of concern:
　1. Zone I — Lower
　2. Zone II — Upper

Figure 5
Injury Zones of the Spine/Back

Spine/Back Zone II

Spine/Back Zone I

Region: Spine/Back
Zone: I — Lower (Figure 5)
Components of exercise performance that can injure this zone are as follows.

(1) Forceful torso exertion, when the lower back is either fully flexed or fully extended, can strain various ligaments, sprain facet joints, compress discs, and tear various muscle insertion points.

(2) Strengthening the hip-flexor muscles without a concurrent effort to stretch them can lead to their shortening and thus a state of ongoing lower-back compression that can damage discs and jam facet joints.

(3) Forceful lower-back rotation can traumatize the cartilage surfaces of the facet joints and strain joint capsules, discs and several small, deep lower-back inter-segmental muscles.

Personal R/B Values for Spine/Back Zone I		
Degree of Personal Risk	Descriptive Features of Your Personal Risk	Your R/B–Personal
SEVERE	you currently suffer with pain in your lower back	3
HIGH	you have suffered a previous episode of severe lower-back pain that lasted more than two days	2
MEDIUM	you tend to sit with your lower back curved outward (especially if you sit for long periods of time)	1
	you have performed a job that requires much bending over at the waist to push, pull, reach, lift, etc.	1
LOW	no current pain, and you don't fit the above risk categories	0

Region: Spine/Back
Zone: II – Upper (Figure 5)
Components of exercise performance that can injure this zone are as follows.

(1) Forceful lateral shoulder abduction or adduction above the horizontal plane while the neck is flexed can strain the levator muscle at its myotendinous region of origin.

(2) Forceful scapular elevation or retraction (from positions of full depression or protraction respectively) can strain the levator, trapezius, and rhomboid muscles at their myotendinous regions of origin.

(3) Forced flexion of the thoracic spine, while the cervical spine is in a flexed and/or rotated position, can strain the levator, trapezius, and rhomboid muscles at their myotendinous regions of origin.

(4) Forceful upper body exertion with the cervical spine fully extended can sprain the cervical facet joints.

(5) Forceful thoracic spine extension and scapular retraction from a position of thoracic spine flexion with full scapular protraction, can sprain intervertebral, costovertebral, and costotransverse joints, as well as strain various deep (ilicostalis cervicis, serratus posterior superior and scalene) muscles at their myotendinous regions.

(6) Forceful torso flexion while maintaining a position of full cervical spine flexion can sprain intervertebral, costovertebral, and costotransverse joints, as well as strain various deep (ilicostalis cervicis, serratus posterior superior and scalene) muscles at their myotendinous regions.

Personal R/B Values for Spine/Back Zone II		
Degree of Personal Risk	Descriptive Features of Your Personal Risk	Your R/B– Personal
SEVERE	you currently suffer with pain in your upper back/lower neck	3
HIGH	you have suffered a previous "whiplash" injury to your neck and upper back	2
MEDIUM	you tend to sit with your lower back curved backwards (especially if you sit for long periods)	1
	you tend to be round-shouldered or slump when you sit	1
LOW	no current pain, and you don't fit the above risk categories	0

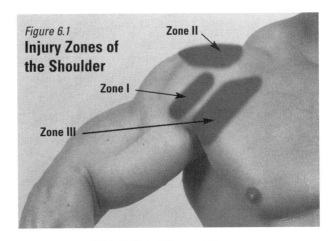

Figure 6.1
Injury Zones of the Shoulder

Zone II
Zone I
Zone III

SHOULDER INJURIES (Figure 6.1)
When considering weight-training-induced injuries of the shoulder region, there are three zones of concern:
1. Zone I — Front
2. Zone II — Top
3. Zone III — at Chest

Region: Shoulder
Zone: I — Front (Figure 6.2)
The component of exercise performance that can injure this zone is forceful upper body or arm movement that combines simultaneous elevation and inward rotation of the humerus. This can grate the lip of the bicipital groove against the bicipital tendon and its sheath.

Figure 6.2
Shoulder Injury Zone I – Front

Personal R/B Values for Shoulder Zone I		
Degree of Personal Risk	Descriptive Features of Your Personal Risk	Your R/B– Personal
SEVERE	you currently suffer pain in Zone I of your shoulder	3
HIGH	you have suffered previous "rotator cuff" damage	2
	you have a history of throwing or hand-overhead sports or work activities	2
MEDIUM	you frequently sleep in the fetal position or with one or both arms up under your pillow	1
	you tend to be round-shouldered or slumped when you sit	1
LOW	no current pain, and you don't fit the above risk categories	0

Personal R/B Values for Shoulder Zone II		
Degree of Personal Risk	Descriptive Features of Your Personal Risk	Your R/B– Personal
SEVERE	you currently suffer pain in Zone II of your shoulder	3
HIGH	you have previously suffered a shoulder separation	2
	you have previously suffered "rotator cuff" damage	2
	you have a history of involvement in throwing or hand-overhead sports/activities	2
MEDIUM	you frequently sleep in the fetal position, or with one or both arms up under your pillow	1
	you tend to round your shoulders/slump when you sit	1
LOW	no current pain, and you don't fit the above risk categories	0

Region: Shoulder
Zone: II — Top (Figure 6.3)

Any of the SITS tendons, the joint capsule, as well as several ligaments and bursae can be strained, compressed, or impinged beneath the acromio-clavicular joint during forceful shoulder elevation above the horizontal plane. This effect is magnified by the levator scapula muscle tension created through concurrent forced cervical spine flexion, and especially by inward rotation of the humerus.

Region: Shoulder
Zone: III — at Chest (Figure 6.4)

The component of exercise performance that can injure this zone is forceful horizontal shoulder adduction from a position of excessive horizontal shoulder abduction. This can strain the myotendinous region of the pectoralis major muscle at its insertion.

Figure 6.3
Shoulder Injury Zone II – Top

Figure 6.4
Shoulder Injury Zone III – Chest

Personal R/B Values for Shoulder Zone III		
Degree of Personal Risk	Descriptive Features of Your Personal Risk	Your R/B– Personal
SEVERE	you currently suffer pain in Zone III of your shoulder	3
HIGH	you have previously suffered a shoulder dislocation	2
MEDIUM	you tend to sleep in the fetal position, or with one or both arms up under your pillow	1
	you tend to round your shoulders or slump when sitting	1
LOW	no current pain, and you don't fit the above risk categories	0

ELBOW INJURIES

When considering weight-training induced injuries of the elbow region, there are four zones of concern. They are illustrated in figures 7.1 and 7.2.

1. Zone I — Inside
2. Zone II — Outside
3. Zone III — Front
4. Zone IV — Rear

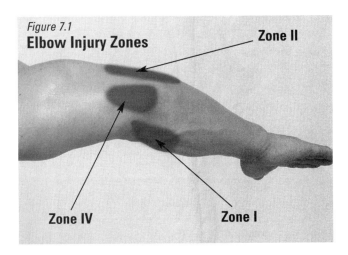

Figure 7.1
Elbow Injury Zones

Zone II

Zone IV   Zone I

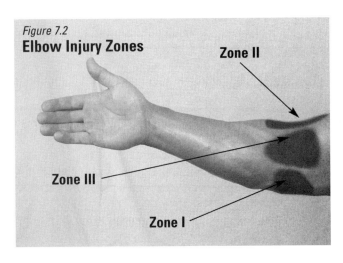

Figure 7.2
Elbow Injury Zones

Zone II

Zone III

Zone I

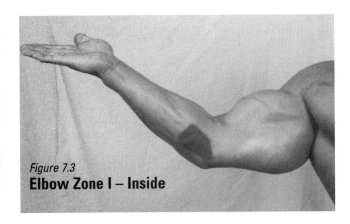

Figure 7.3
Elbow Zone I – Inside

Region: Elbow
Zone: I — Inside (Figure 7.3)
The components of exercise performance that can injure this zone are as follows.

(1) Forcefully flexing an elbow from a position of full extension, with full wrist flexion and hand supination, can strain the pronator teres and flexor carpi radialis muscles at the myotendinous region of their origins.

(2) Forcefully extending an elbow from a position of full elbow flexion, with full wrist flexion and hand pronation, can strain the pronator teres and flexor carpi radialis muscles at the myotendinous region of their origins.

(3) Forcefully flexing an elbow from a position of full elbow extension, with the elbow maintained in a forced valgus position, can strain or sprain the ulnar colateral ligaments.

Personal R/B Values for Elbow Zone I		
Degree of Personal Risk	Descriptive Features of Your Personal Risk	Your R/B– Personal
SEVERE	you currently suffer pain in Zone I of your elbow	3
HIGH	you have previously suffered from "golfer's elbow"	2
MEDIUM	your job requires that you frequently grasp and pull objects or machines toward you	1
LOW	no current pain, and you don't fit the above risk categories	0

Region: Elbow
Zone: II — Outside (Figure 7.4)
The components of exercise performance that can injure this zone are as follows.

(1) Forceful full wrist extension during forceful shoulder elevation, with the elbow fully extended and the

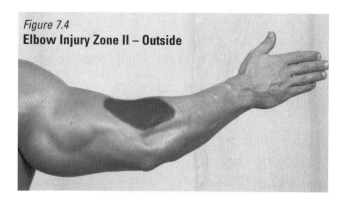

Figure 7.4
Elbow Injury Zone II – Outside

Personal R/B Values for Elbow Zone III

Degree of Personal Risk	Descriptive Features of Your Personal Risk	Your R/B–Personal
SEVERE	you currently suffer pain in Zone III of your elbow	3
HIGH	your elbows are hyper-extensible ("double-jointed")	2
MEDIUM	you have performed a job that requires frequent lifting of heavy objects with your arms down	1
LOW	no current pain, and you don't fit the above risk categories	0

hand fully pronated, can strain the extensor carpi radialis longus muscle at the myotendinous region of its origin.

(2) Forceful elbow flexion from a position of full elbow extension, with the hand fully pronated, can strain the brachioradialis muscle.

Personal R/B Values for Elbow Zone II

Degree of Personal Risk	Descriptive Features of Your Personal Risk	Your R/B–Personal
SEVERE	you currently suffer pain in Zone II of your elbow	3
HIGH	you have previously suffered from "tennis elbow"	2
MEDIUM	you have performed a job for years that requires much repetitive or forceful movements of the wrist and elbow	1
LOW	no current pain, and you don't fit the above risk categories	0

Region: Elbow
Zone: III — Front (Figure 7.5)

The component of exercise performance that can injure this zone is forceful elbow flexion from a position of full elbow extension, with the hand in full supination. This can strain the biceps brachii and/or the brachialis muscles at the myotendinous region of their insertions.

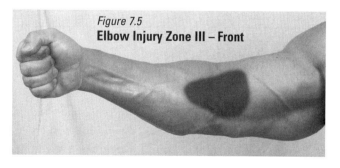

Figure 7.5
Elbow Injury Zone III – Front

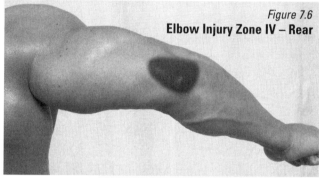

Figure 7.6
Elbow Injury Zone IV – Rear

Region: Elbow
Zone: IV — Rear (Figure 7.6)

The components of exercise performance that can injure this zone are as follows.

(1) Forcefully extending your elbow from a position of full elbow flexion (accentuated by positions of full shoulder elevation) can strain the myotendinous region at the insertion of the tricep muscle and/or the tendinous attachment of the tricep tendon into the olecranon periosteum (as a start/finish position).

(2) Forcefully extending your elbow drives the olecranon process into its fossa, which can compress or damage the articular cartilage, the synovial membranes or the fossa fat pad (at the mid-phase position).

Personal R/B Values for Elbow Zone IV

Degree of Personal Risk	Descriptive Features of Your Personal Risk	Your R/B–Personal
SEVERE	you currently suffer pain in Zone IV of your elbow	3
HIGH	you have previously suffered hyperextension trauma to your elbow	2
	you have previously chipped a bone in your elbow in a trauma	2
MEDIUM	you have been involved in high intensity overhead throwing sports or activities	1
LOW	no current pain, and you don't fit the above risk categories	0

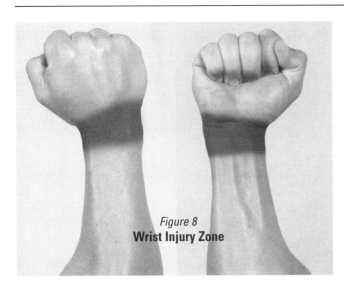

Figure 8
Wrist Injury Zone

WRIST INJURIES (Figure 8)

When considering weight-training-induced injuries of the wrist region, we can view it as a single zone. Components of exercise performance that can injure this zone are:

(1) Forceful arm "pushing" movements through wrists in close-packed carpal position (i.e., full wrist extension and forcefully flexed fingers) can compress and damage the articular joint surfaces of various carpals as well as their ligaments and synovia.

(2) Forceful flexion or extension of either the wrist or the elbow while the wrist is in either a forced varus or valgus position can compress and damage the articular joint surfaces of various carpals, along with their ligaments and synovia.

Personal R/B Values for Wrist

Degree of Personal Risk	Descriptive Features of Your Personal Risk	Your R/B– Personal
SEVERE	you currently suffer pain in one or both wrists	3
HIGH	you have had one or more episodes of falling onto your outstretched hands (with or without fractures)	2
	you have previously suffered from "carpal tunnel syndrome"	2
MEDIUM	your job requires constant activity at a computer terminal or keyboard	1
	you sleep with one or both wrists fully flexed under your chin or pillow	1
LOW	no current pain, and you don't fit the above risk categories	0

KNEE INJURIES (Figure 9)

When considering weight-training-induced injuries of the knee region, we can view it as a single zone. Components of exercise performance that can injure this zone are:

(1) Forceful knee extension from a position of full knee flexion while bearing weight can strain various peripatellar soft tissues and ultimately erode the articular cartilages of the patella (especially with an improperly tracking patella).

(2) Forceful knee extension from a position of full knee flexion, or vice versa, while the entire leg is rotated inward or outward, can strain a variety of peripatellar soft tissues, collateral ligaments and menisci.

Personal R/B Values for Knee

Degree of Personal Risk	Descriptive Features of Your Personal Risk	Your R/B– Personal
SEVERE	you currently suffer pain in your knee(s) (especially around the kneecap)	3
HIGH	you have suffered previous episodes of "jumper's knee" or condromalacia patellae	2
	you have previously suffered a torn ligament or torn meniscus in your knees	2
	you are visibly "knock-kneed"	2
MEDIUM	you have a history of non-injury based foot or knee pains	1
LOW	no current pain, and you don't fit the above risk categories	0

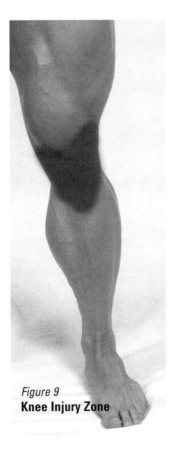

Figure 9
Knee Injury Zone

Figure 10
Hamstring Injury Zones
(see page 29)

Figure 11.1
"Other" Injury Zones

Zone I
Chest/Breastbone
(Figure 11.2)

Zone IV
Groin
(Figure 11.5)

Zone II
Ankle/Foot
(Figure 11.3)

Zone III
Achilles Tendon
(Figure 11.4)

HAMSTRING INJURIES (Figure 10)

When considering weight-training induced injuries of the hamstring region, we can regard it as a single zone.

The component of exercise performance that can injure this zone is forceful knee flexion from a position of maximum knee extension, which can strain the myotendinous regions of the hamstrings (accentuated by a fully flexed torso position).

Personal R/B Values for Hamstring

Degree of Personal Risk	Descriptive Features of Your Personal Risk	Your R/B– Personal
SEVERE	you currently suffer pain in your hamstrings	3
HIGH	you are unable to raise your straight leg (while lying on your back) more than sixty degrees above the ground due to tightness	2
	you have previously torn a hamstring	2
MEDIUM	your knees appear to be "double-jointed" (i.e., hyper-extensible)	1
LOW	no current pain, and you don't fit the above risk categories	0

"OTHER" INJURIES (Figure 11.1)

This region of weight-training induced injuries is actually a collection of less frequent injury sites that I have simply labelled as "other." Each zone of this "region" is illustrated and labelled in figure 11.1.

1. Zone I — Chest/Breastbone
2. Zone II — Foot/Ankle
3. Zone III — Achilles Heel
4. Zone IV — Groin

Region: "Other"
Zone: I — Chest/Breastbone (Figure 11.2)

Blunt compressive trauma to the central chest region can sprain the sternocostal joints and damage the costochondral junctions.

Personal R/B Values for Chest/Breastbone

Degree of Personal Risk	Descriptive Features of Your Personal Risk	Your R/B– Personal
SEVERE	you currently suffer with severe or steady pain in your breastbone or front ribcage area	3
HIGH	you have a history of trauma to the breastbone or front ribcage area from car accidents or contact sports	2
MEDIUM	nothing applicable	1
LOW	no current pain, and you don't fit the above risk categories	0

Figure 11.2
"Other" Injury Zone I
– Chest/Breastbone

Zone: II — Foot/Ankle (Figure 11.3)

The component of exercise performance that can injure this zone is forceful plantar flexion from a position of full ankle dorsi-flexion, while bearing weight on the toes rather than on the metatarsal heads (i.e., putting the foot/ankle in its loose-packed position). This can strain a variety of joint ligaments, synovia, and inter-osseous muscles.

Personal R/B Values for Foot/Ankle

Degree of Personal Risk	Descriptive Features of Your Personal Risk	Your R/B– Personal
SEVERE	you currently suffer severe daily pain in the feet or ankles	3
HIGH	you have a history of non-injury-based foot or ankle pain	2
	the arches of your feet have either visibly "dropped" or completely disappeared	2
MEDIUM	you have always worn tight-fitting shoes	1
	you frequently wear high-heeled shoes	1
	you have previously broken a bone in your foot/ankle	1
LOW	no current pain, and you don't fit the above risk categories	0

Zone: III — Achilles Tendon (Figure 11.4)

The component of exercise performance that can injure this zone is forceful plantar flexion from a position of full ankle dorsi-flexion. This can strain the myotendinous region of the soleus and gastrocnemius muscles, or the Achilles tendinous insertion into the calcaneal periosteurm. Also, the tendo-calcaneal bursae can be compressed or damaged between the Achilles tendon and the calcaneus.

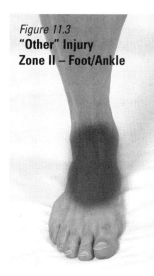

Figure 11.3
"Other" Injury Zone II – Foot/Ankle

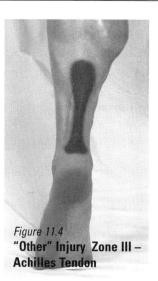

Figure 11.4
"Other" Injury Zone III – Achilles Tendon

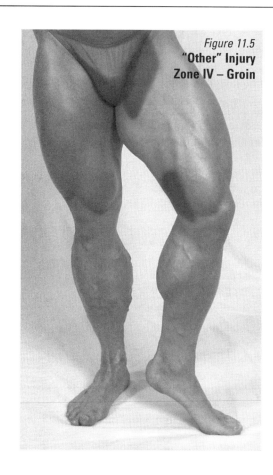

Figure 11.5
"Other" Injury Zone IV – Groin

Personal R/B Values for Achilles Tendon

Degree of Personal Risk	Descriptive Features of Your Personal Risk	Your R/B– Personal
SEVERE	you currently suffer with pain in your Achilles heel	3
HIGH	you have previously suffered a torn or strained Achilles tendon	2
MEDIUM	you suffer with cramping in your calf muscle(s)	1
	you have a history of non-injury-based foot/calf/knee pain	1
LOW	no current pain, and you don't fit the above risk categories	0

Region: "Other"
Zone: IV — Groin (Figure 11.5)
The component of exercise performance that can injure this zone is forceful hip adduction from a position of full hip abduction. This can strain the myotendinous regions of the hip adductor muscles.

Personal R/B Values for Groin

Degree of Personal Risk	Descriptive Features of Your Personal Risk	Your R/B– Personal
SEVERE	you currently suffer pain in the groin muscle region	3
HIGH	you have previously torn or "pulled" your groin muscle(s)	2
MEDIUM	nothing applicable	1
LOW	no current pain, and you don't fit the above risk categories	0

F.I.T.S. WEIGHT-TRAINING EXERCISE CONCEPTS

ESSENTIAL PRINCIPLES

Before you begin this chapter, please review the principles on which the F.I.T.S. (free of injury and target-specific) method is based:

Weight-Training Truth #1 (WT #1):
Every exercise offers specific *benefit* to specific muscle(s).

Weight-Training Truth #2 (WT #2):
Every exercise, during its execution, puts those soft tissues that are either overstretched, compressed, or firmly grated against, at *risk* of injury.

Every weight-training exercise = benefit + risk
= WT #1 + WT #2

Choosing Maximum Benefit + Minimum Risk = **F.I.T.S.**

OBJECTIVES OF CHAPTER 3

Weight-training exercises can, strangely enough, build and destroy simultaneously, as Weight-Training Truths #1 and #2 make clear. I hope you have already accepted this essential message.

As a result, you can now create your workout routine by balancing the purpose of each exercise with its risk of injury. This chapter will show you how to accomplish this feat that once seemed impossible.

The specific objectives of this chapter, based on the above two truths of weight-training, are

(1) to establish specific physique goals (to be reviewed and re-established about once a month),

(2) to create workout routines that are specific to your established physique goals,

(3) to prevent all the typical weight-training injuries by selecting exercises that are low-risk and specific to your established physique goals,

(4) to train around your injury by selecting exercises that do not aggravate it but still fulfill your specific physique goals, and

(5) to execute your selected exercises perfectly, thus eliminating the "unnecessary" injuries associated with sloppy or poor exercise performance.

ESTABLISHING YOUR WORKOUT GOALS

Your reasons for weight training can range from the obvious ones we have already discussed, such as competitive bodybuilding, off-season training, or injury rehabilitation, to more subtle and personal ones, such as improving your general health, longevity, and self-image, or reducing stress. It is up to you, your trainer, or your therapist to consider the exercise benefits described in this book and use them to meet your weight-training goals.

Within this section, the focus is strictly on selecting exercises whose benefits suit your goals. Remember, though, that a particular exercise benefit can only meet a weight-training goal if the appropriate implementation factors are used. In other words, remember that having goals is not the same thing as having the tools to get there (Chapter 4 will address these vital tools more closely).

Here is the five-step process for establishing your workout goals:

(1) Critically evaluate your physique to determine the muscles or muscle regions to be targeted by your workouts.

(2) Take note of the exact labels on the photographs of Chapter 3 that correlate to your target regions (see the figures at the beginning of each exercise section).

(3) Accept the premise that a complete and balanced workout routine must target every muscle, meaning that you must take note of at least one label for any muscle regions missing from step (2) (this is true except in particular cases where "incomplete" workouts are used for sport-specific or rehabilitation objectives — see Chapter 4 for more details).

(4) Using the table of exercises that follows each photograph (tables 1 through 12), locate the exercises that match your list of labels and suit your objectives — factoring in the muscle-benefit features (such as power, stretch and definition) that best match your goals for that muscle area.

(5) Make a list of all the possible exercises that suit your desired objectives for each muscle region and record the figure numbers accordingly.

Physique Evaluation

Step (1) above probably warrants further discussion. In the past, it has been all too common for weight-training participants to receive identical, generic workouts, regardless of their physical caliber. More recently, however, a greater effort toward "customized" workouts seems evident. These must, by necessity, begin with a critical physique evaluation. The individual under consideration should be dressed in a bathing suit or underwear. Here are the key criteria for evaluation:

(1) Note the muscles, or the regions of muscle, that appear to be in need of either strength or size development, relative to the same muscle or region on the other side of the body, or relative to its functionally opposite muscle (e.g., triceps versus biceps).

(2) Note the muscles, or the regions of muscle, that are disproportionately bulky, and thus require a tapering or defining approach.

(3) Note the muscles, or the regions of muscle, that have suffered disuse atrophy following surgery or a debilitating injury.

(4) Note the muscles, or the regions of muscle, that are in need of specific strengthening for the athlete's sport.

Criteria (2) through (4) are relatively easy to assess. Criterion (1) requires a good eye for detail but is the most often-used evaluation criterion on the list.

The list of possible exercises created following these steps is not yet a workout. In order to be transformed into a workout, the list must be cut down to a desirable number of exercises per body region (one to four, depending on your status — see Chapter 4 for status definitions). This selection process is achieved by considering your R/B-personal values and the R/B-exercise values of each exercise. The final step is to use the appropriate implementation factors, as presented in Chapter 4.

ESTABLISHING YOUR ACCEPTABLE WORKOUT RISKS

The injury-avoidance principle of *Primum Non Nocere* directs you to select exercises for your workout that not only suit your physique objectives, but more important, do not injure you. The key question during your exercise selection process is, "Is the potential benefit of this exercise worth the potential risk?"

You already have the tools necessary to answer this question and thus customize your exercise selections. They are

(1) Your R/B-personal values, as tabulated in Chapter 2.

(2) The principle of limiting the total R/B value for each exercise (and each injury site) to seven or lower (because eight and above will cause an injury). Recall the R/B guidelines given earlier:

R/B of 1 to 4 — BENEFIT > RISK

R/B of 5 to 7 — BENEFIT = RISK

R/B of 8 to 10 — RISK > BENEFIT

(3) The fact that the total R/B value for a given injury site is the sum of that exercise's R/B value plus your personal R/B value:

R/B-total = R/B-exercise + R/B-personal

Note that this equation can be re-arranged to allow you to calculate your maximum allowable R/B-exercise values, as below:

R/B-total – R/B-personal = R/B-exercise

Since I have previously set the limit for the R/B-total at seven, and you also have your R/B-personal values from Chapter 2, simple arithmetic completes the R/B-exercise limit-setting process.

The table below calculates for each of the designated degrees of risk (see Chapter 2) the maximum allowable R/B-exercise value. This must be repeated for every injury site given in Chapter 2 before you make your final selection of exercises from the list of those that suit your physique objectives.

Maximum R/B-Exercise per Degree of Risk			
Your degree of personal risk	Maximum Allowable R/B–Total	Your – R/B–Personal =	**Maximum R/B-Exercise**
SEVERE	7	– 3	= **4**
HIGH	7	– 2	= **5**
MEDIUM	7	– 1	= **6**
LOW	7	– 0	= **7**

Through this process, you will create a list of maximum R/B-exercise values that looks like the sample one below. The three columns reflect one final factor in determining maximum R/B values: your age. As the human body grows older, there is a slow but steady loss of connective (or soft) tissue elasticity that must be taken into consideration. The simple truth is, the less elasticity you have, the more vulnerable you are to injury.

So — if you are over 40 years old, reduce all your maximum R/B values by one. If you are over 60 years old, reduce all your maximum R/B values by two.

Sample List of Maximum R/B-Exercise Values			
Injury Site	Max R/B (under 40)	Max R/B (40–59)	Max R/B (60 +)
Back/Spine — Zone I	4	3	2
Back/Spine — Zone II	5	4	3
Shoulder — Zone I	6	5	4
Shoulder — Zone II	5	4	3
Shoulder — Zone III	7	6	5
Elbows — Zone I	5	4	3

. . . and so on.

Now, as you look through the exercises of Chapter 3 with your list of "potential" exercises handy, a simple glance at the R/B values provided for the exercises shown in Chapter 3 will enable you to decide whether or not you can include an exercise in your workout.

A shortcut to creating a customized, low-risk-of-injury workout is accomplished by assuming that you are at maximum risk of injury regarding every potential injury site (i.e., your R/B-personal is 3 for all injury sites). This automatically means that you can only use exercises that have R/B-exercise values of 4 or less.

Following the above procedure for every exercise you wish to use in your workout will ensure that the benefits outweigh the risks within your workout. In essence, you will have "F.I.T.S.-ed" your workout.

IDEAL EXERCISE EXECUTION

Even with your workout routine complete — as accurate and risk-free as it can be — you still are not quite ready to enter the gym. I urge you to, literally, *study* the details of exercise execution in the rest of this chapter. Frequently, these subtle execution details of exercise performance are what make the difference between a risky and a safe workout. The illustrations (with plane-of-action lines), the written instructions, and the many execution variations should make the typical injury-producing pitfalls evident to all.

For the beginner, this learning is a necessity before entering the gym. But my greater concern lies with the more experienced weight-training athletes who likely believe they already know how to perform any given exercise. Undoing bad gym habits (which I believe most bodybuilders do have) is a difficult task, but can be achieved by reading and learning all the details here.

WEIGHT-TRAINING MYTHS REVEALED

I have previously stated that much of the status quo approach to weight training is firmly rooted in a myth-based framework. There are numerous mindlessly repeated myths about the purpose and execution of exercises that are accepted as guidelines. In fact, they pose obvious risk of injury when examined in light of my weight-training truths.

Throughout the remainder of this chapter you will see "*Myth #*" in the top right corner of many of the exercise pages. This is my way of emphasizing the prevalence of this weight-training mythology. It does not mean that the so-labeled exercise must never be used, but I urge that your selection of exercises be based on the principle of keeping your total R/B values less than eight. There is a replacement exercise available for almost every myth-based exercise, as seen in the Appendix. If an exercise that you intend to include in your workout has a myth attached to it, I suggest that you re-check its purpose, look at the myth statement, and then, with your purpose clarified, select an appropriate exercise or execution variation whose total R/B values is less than eight.

Here is my list of the eighteen greatest weight-training myths. Each entry includes a brief explanation of why it is a myth and how it fails to meet the *Primum Non Nocere* principle.

MYTH #1:
You must do behind-the-neck shoulder presses.
The Truth: There is considerable risk of injuring the shoulder, neck, and upper back for the touted benefit (see exercises 21 and 23).
Excessive amounts and multiple sites of WT #2

MYTH #2:
Take the leg press to the bottom, but never lock out your knees.
The Truth: At the bottom there is extreme lower back strain and the target muscles actually become the gluteals. On the other hand, knee "lock-out," held briefly, poses little danger to healthy knees and actually benefits vastus medialis development (see exercises 121 and 135).
Insufficient WT #1 to justify the excessive WT #2

MYTH #3:
You must do traditional sit-ups, with your feet held down securely.
The Truth: This method of abdominal training uses too much hip-flexor muscle activity, which often contributes to lower back strain (see exercises 67 and 68).
Insufficient WT #1 to justify the excessive WT #2

MYTH #4:
You must do behind-the-neck pulldowns and chin-ups.

The Truth: There is considerable risk to the neck, shoulders, and elbows, considering that the benefit can be achieved much more safely (see exercises 51 and 54).
Excessive WT #2

MYTH #5:
A reverse-rolling of the shoulders while shrugging is a good variation of the standard method of shrugging.
The Truth: This actually detracts from the correct target muscles' benefit and, further, can strain the upper back and neck region (see exercise 60 and variation 61.e).
Excessive WT #2 and insufficient WT #1

MYTH #6:
Keep your back straight at all times.
The Truth: A straight lower back is a vulnerable lower back, and is also a weaker base of support for maximum exertion. A slight inward curve of the lower back is the correct, safe torso alignment. The wrong torso alignment is an outward curved lower back, which I call Round-Out. This creates the maximum risk for lower back injury (see all standing and seated exercises).
Excessive WT #2

MYTH #7:
Wearing a weight belt will protect your lower back from injury.
The Truth: The real function of the weight belt is to increase your intra-abdominal pressure, which greatly improves your capacity for heavy lifts by providing a firmer base of support. It does not protect your back.
Does not decrease WT #2

MYTH #8:
During dumbbell side raises, get your elbows higher than your hands.
The Truth: This creates a specific and rather severe risk of shoulder injuries (see exercises 26, 27).
Excessive WT #2

MYTH #9:
Don't lock out your knees during leg extensions and standing calf raises.
The Truth: Briefly locking your knees during leg extensions is very important for optimal development of the vastus medialis muscle. Similarly, fully (but not hyper-) extended knees are necessary in standing calf raises to fully stimulate the gastrocnemius muscles (see exercises 126 and 145–149).
Insufficient WT #1 and misunderstood WT #2

MYTH #10:
During seated cable rowing exercises, lean forward fully, then as you sit upright again, pull the grip fully into your chest.
The Truth: This method of execution poses considerable risk of injury to the upper and lower back regions, plus it is an inefficient means of benefiting the target muscles (see exercise 46).
Excessive WT #2 and insufficient WT #1

MYTH #11: Dumbbell pullovers are chest expanding.
The Truth: This exercise can certainly stretch the pecs and lats, but it is impossible to increase the size of a skeletal structure. Further, it is not a very accurate target-muscle exercise (see exercise 18).
Insufficient WT #1 with moderate WT #2

MYTH #12:
Lean your torso back when performing lat pulldowns.
The Truth: The backward torso lean changes the muscle target from the lats to the rhomboids, and with this mechanism you can strain your lower back (see exercises 55, 56, and variation 62.d). This is also considered a form of cheating (see Myth #17).
Excessive WT #2, adds a new WT #2, and insufficient WT #1

MYTH #13:
The straight-legged deadlift exercise is a good method of working the hamstrings.
The Truth: The hamstrings during this exercise are stretched into a position of passive insufficiency which makes them incapable of primary mover function, and further places the hamstrings and the entire lower back region at serious risk of injury (see exercise 128).
Excessive WT #2 and insufficient WT #1

MYTH #14:
Torso twisting is a good means of strengthening the lower back.
The Truth: Forceful, repeated torso twisting puts the tiny, deep, inter-segmental muscles of the lumbar spine at risk of injury. These muscles actually serve a more sensory function than a movement one (see exercise 71).
Excessive WT #2 and insufficient WT #1

MYTH #15:
Hyperextension exercises are great for lower back muscle development.
The Truth: The frequent use of momentum to perform

lower back exercises, unless stopped at the horizontal plane, puts the lower back at risk of facet joint compression and strain (see exercise 42).
Excessive WT #2

MYTH #16:
It is essential to do barbell bench presses as a primary means of building the chest.
The Truth: The considerable potential risks of injury (to the neck, elbows, wrists, and especially the shoulders), plus the effectiveness of other chest exercises, make this a high-risk-for-the-benefit exercise (see exercises 1, 2, and 4).
Excessive WT # 2

MYTH #17:
Incorporating cheating mechanisms into your workout improves your muscular development.
The Truth: The risk of injury within the exercise is often increased to unacceptable levels. (See Chapter 2, and variations 3.a–c, 31.i(i), 50.f, 62.d, 91.e, and 111.g).
Excessive WT #2, plus addition of new WT #2

MYTH #18:
High foot placement during deep leg-press exercises creates an improved hamstring workout.
The Truth: In the bottom position of the exercise, where the hamstring stretch and workload occur, only the glutes can actually perform any work. At the same time, the upper hamstring tendons and the lower back are put at considerable risk of injury (see Myth #2 and exer. 135).
Excessive WT #2 and insufficient WT #1

Just as the myth-based status quo described in Chapter 1 must be replaced with my weight-training truths, these eighteen weight-training myths must be replaced with some very specific truth guidelines, as follows.

THE TEN COMMANDMENTS OF SAFE WEIGHT-TRAINING

(1) Thou shalt believe that injury-free weight-training *is* possible.

(2) Thou shalt not cave in to any false myths.

(3) Thou shalt select all exercises based on weight-training truths #1 and #2.

(4) Thou shalt execute all exercises in a controlled and accurate fashion, based on the plane-of-action lines.

(5) Thou shalt alter thine own workout on a regular basis.

(6) Thou shalt not partake of any high-risk exercises.

(7) Thou shalt respect thy bodybuilding idols but disregard their false beliefs.

(8) Thou shalt only use well-maintained equipment and always have a proper spotter present.

(9) Thou shalt not train through pain, but around it.

(10) Thou shalt accept *Primum Non Nocere* as your primary directive for injury-free weight-training.

HOW TO USE THE REST OF THIS CHAPTER
The remainder of this chapter is divided into the following "body part" sections:

- Chest (Fig. 13 — page 38)
- Shoulders (Fig. 49 — page 60)
- Back (Fig. 83 — page 83)
- Abdominals (Fig. 129 — page 116)
- Biceps (Fig. 153 — page 136)
- Triceps (Fig. 180 — page 157)
- Forearms (Fig. 216 — page 184)
- Quadriceps (Fig. 226 — page 191)
- Hamstrings (Fig. 246 — page 206)
- Gluteals (Fig. 259 — page 215)
- Groin (Fig. 269 — page 225)
- Calves (Fig. 272 — page 228)

Each body-part section is introduced with a photograph of the muscle(s) under consideration, with coded labels for easy identification. Immediately following each labeled figure is a table showing all the exercises that are relevant to that body part. It is arranged to indicate how different muscles in that body part benefit (WT #1), how they risk being injured (WT #2), and the severity of those risks (the R/B values) as they are associated with each exercise. The codes regarding exercise benefit correlate directly with the previous page's photo, so that you can easily go from photo to label to table, thus facilitating the workout-creation process.

Please note the following when studying R/B values:

(1) a 0–10 scale is used, where 0 is no risk and 10 is severe risk of injury,

(2) multiple R/B values listed for a single exercise indicate that multiple sites are at risk of injury during the execution of that exercise,

(3) the use of (+) or (–) in front of an R/B value for a particular variation of execution indicates either an

increased (or new) risk, or a decreased risk of injury from the basic exercise.

The practical significance of the relationship between particular exercises and particular injuries is that they will demonstrate

(1) to what degree, and at what location(s), tissues can be injured by the execution of any given weight-training exercise,

(2) how a subtle exercise execution variation can or will change the muscle (or muscle region) that receives the primary benefit, and

(3) how a subtle exercise execution variation can or will change the site and/or the amount of injury risk.

Each exercise is described in the text on each page, step by step. One repetition is described from start to finish, where the start/finish position is the point from which concentric muscle contractions occur — creating the "positive" portion of the repetition — while the mid-phase position is the point from which eccentric muscle contractions occur — creating the "negative" portion of the repetition.

IMPORTANT NOTE

As you attempt to train around an injury, you must first identify the exercise(s) that have been the cause of your injury. However, in order for the F.I.T.S. R/B values to be accurate and valid for you, your previous execution of any given exercise must match the F.I.T.S. description exactly. This means that you must always check all of the possible execution variations relevant to the general, or basic, exercise. Only then can you make an accurate replacement exercise selection.

Figure 12

Weight-Training Targets

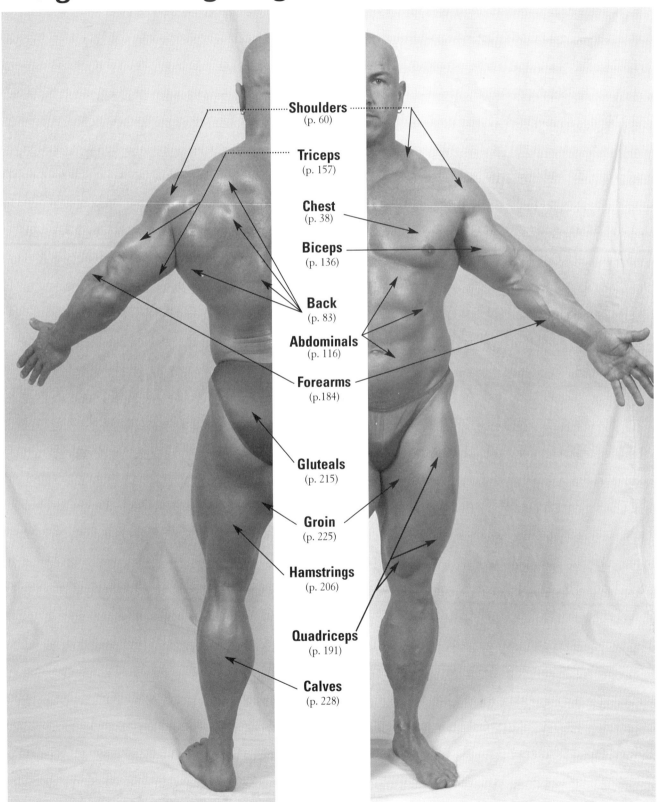

Shoulders
(p. 60)

Triceps
(p. 157)

Chest
(p. 38)

Biceps
(p. 136)

Back
(p. 83)

Abdominals
(p. 116)

Forearms
(p.184)

Gluteals
(p. 215)

Groin
(p. 225)

Hamstrings
(p. 206)

Quadriceps
(p. 191)

Calves
(p. 228)

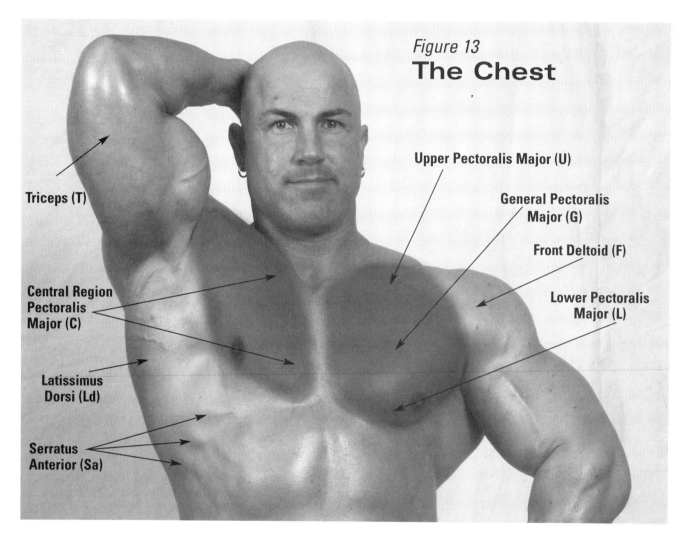

Figure 13
The Chest

Triceps (T)

Central Region Pectoralis Major (C)

Latissimus Dorsi (Ld)

Serratus Anterior (Sa)

Upper Pectoralis Major (U)

General Pectoralis Major (G)

Front Deltoid (F)

Lower Pectoralis Major (L)

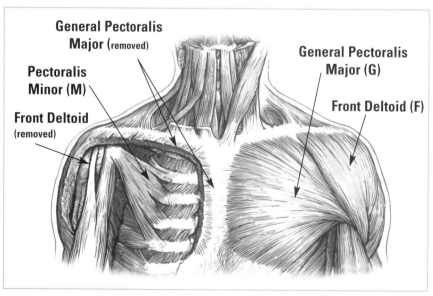

General Pectoralis Major (removed)

Pectoralis Minor (M)

Front Deltoid (removed)

General Pectoralis Major (G)

Front Deltoid (F)

Table 1: CHEST EXERCISES

Name of Exercise/Variation		Benefit (WT #1)	R/B Values (WT #2)	No.	Pg.
Flat Bench Press		G, Sa-P	7, 4	1	40
Narrow Grip Bench Press		T, C-P	8, 5, 4	96	160
Execution Variation:					
Toward the Neck		T, C-D	(+) 2, (+) 1	97	160
Incline Bench Press		U, F, Sa-P	6, 5	2	41
Execution Variations:					
Flat/Incline Bar	— Bounce "Cheat"		(+) 7	3.a	42
Bench Presses	— Back Arch "Cheat"		(+) 5	3.b	42
All Bench Presses	— Neck Arch "Cheat"		(+) 8	3.c	42
Decline Bench Press		L, Sa-P	8, 3	4	43
Flat Dumbbell Press		G, Sa-P	6, 4	5	44
Incline Dumbbell Press		U, Sa-P	5, 5	6	45
Decline Dumbbell Press		L, Sa-P	7, 3	7	46
Execution Variations:					
Barbell Presses	— Wide Grip		(−) 1, (−) 2	8.a	46
	— Shallow Depth		(−) 3	8.b	47
Dumbbell Presses	— Palms-Facing Grip		(−) 2	8.c	47
	— Shallow Depth		(−) 3	8.d	47
Bar & Dumbbell Presses	— Toward Neck		(+) 2, (+) 2	8.e	47
	— Wrist Extension		(+) 8	8.f	48
Pec-Deck Machine		G-S, D	4, 3, 4	9	48
Execution Variations:					
Low Hands		G, L-S, D	(−) 1, (−) 1	10.a	49
High Hands		G, U-S, D	(+) 1, (+) 1	10.b	49
Excessive Depth		G-S, D	(+) 4	10.c	49
Flat Dumbbell Flyes		G-S, D	4, 3, 4	11	50
Incline Dumbbell Flyes		U-S, D	3, 4, 5	12	51
Decline Dumbbell Flyes		L-S, D	5, 2, 3	13	52
Bent-over Cable Crossovers		G-S, D	4, 3, 4	14	53
Upright Cable Crossovers		L-S, D	5, 2, 3	15	54
Kneeling Cable Crossovers		U-S, D	3, 4, 5	16	55
Execution Variations:					
Dumbbell Flyes	— Excess Depth		(+) 4	17.a	55
Cable Crossovers	— Thumbs-Facing Grip		(+) 3	17.b	56
	— Excess Depth		(+) 4	17.c	56
	— Lower back Round-Out		(+) 5	17.d	56
Flyes & Crossovers	— Wrist Flex		(+) 5	17.e	56
	— Full Elbow Ext.		(+) 8	17.f	57
Pullovers — Dumbbell		M, Ld, G-S	7, 7, 7, 4	18	57
Execution Variations:					
Barbell (Narrow)		Ld, G-S, P	(−) 2, (−) 1, (−) 2	19.a	58
Barbell (Wide)		Ld-P, S	(−) 4, (−) 3, (−) 4	19.b	58
Modified Dumbbell Shoulder Press		U, F-P, D	6, 6	20	59
Body Dips	— Elbows Flared Outward	L, T-P, D	10, 6, 9	101.c	168

Key:

G = General Pectoralis Major
C = Central Pectoralis Major
Ld = Latissimus Dorsi *(see Table 3)*
P = Power/Size

U = Upper Pectoralis Major
M = Pectoralis Minor
T = Triceps *(see Table 6)*
S = Stretch

L = Lower Pectoralis Major
F = Front Deltoid *(see Table 2)*
Sa = Serratus Anterior
D = Definition

Exercise 1: FLAT BENCH PRESS

Myth #16

**Fig. 14.1
Start/Finish**

side view

↑ PA-D

top view

PA-L

[handwritten notes: bend keep ↑ feet up]

[handwritten note: don't drop elbows too deep]

Fig. 14.2   **Mid-Phase**

PA-L

BENEFIT (Weight Training Truth #1):

- This is a power-building exercise for the entire chest but the primary target (PA-L) is the middle portion of the pectoralis major muscle.

- There is considerable (although secondary) tricep and serratus anterior muscle activity.

HOW:

- Begin with the bar lightly touching your chest, just slightly above the sternum, with each hand placed two to six inches (five to fifteen cm) wider than shoulder width; this is the start/finish position (figure 14.1).

- Hold your wrists in line with your forearms (i.e., not bent backward).

- Following the plane of action (PA-D), smoothly raise the bar until your elbows are almost fully extended — pause briefly; this is the mid-phase position (figure 14.2).

- Keep your buttocks down, your back slightly arched and your feet flat on the floor.

- Smoothly return the bar to the start/finish position.

RISK (Weight Training Truth #2):

R/B	Injury Site
7	Shoulders (Zone I — Front)
4	Shoulders (Zone II — Top)

VARIATIONS OF EXECUTION: Please refer to exercises 3.a, 8.a, 8.b, 8.e, 8.f and 111.a.

[handwritten note: – do]

Exercise 2: INCLINE BENCH PRESS

Fig. 15.1   **Start/Finish**   *side view*

PA-D

top view

PA-L

Fig. 15.2   **Mid-Phase**

PA-L

BENEFIT (Weight Training Truth #1):

- This is a power-building exercise for the upper chest; the primary target (PA-L) is the upper pectoralis major muscle, just below the collar bones.

- There is considerable (but secondary) tricep, front deltoid, and serratus anterior muscle activity; this exercise is best done on a bench inclined thirty to forty-five degrees; if the incline is more than forty-five degrees, the target muscle becomes the front deltoid.

HOW:

- Begin with the bar lightly touching your chest at the junction of your collar bones and breast bone, with each hand placed approximately two to six inches (five to fifteen cm) wider than shoulder width; this is the start/finish position (figure 15.1).

- Hold your wrists in line with your forearms (i.e., not bent backward).

- Following the plane of action (PA-D), smoothly raise the bar until your elbows are almost fully extended — pause briefly; this is the mid-phase position (figure 15.2).

- Keep your buttocks down, your back slightly arched and your feet flat on the floor.

- Smoothly return the bar to the start/finish position.

RISK (Weight Training Truth #2):

R/B	Injury Site
6	Shoulders (Zone I — Front)
5	Shoulders (Zone II — Top)

VARIATIONS OF EXECUTION: Please refer to variations 3.a, 8.a, 8.b, 8.e, 8.f and 111.a.

FLAT AND INCLINE BARBELL BENCH PRESSES Execution Variations 3.a, 3.b, 3.c

Myth #17

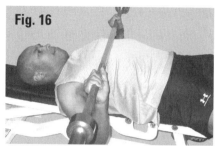

Fig. 16

3.a. Bounce "cheat"

Fig. 17

3.b. Lower back arch "cheat" (all bench presses)

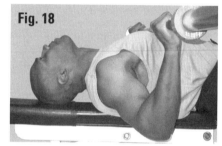

Fig. 18

3.c. Neck arch "cheat"

The three common methods of cheating during a flat or incline bench press are:

3.a. bouncing the bar off the rib cage instead of pausing at the bottom of the lift (figure16),

3.b. excessively arching the lower back during the upward press of the barbell (figure 17), and

3.c. arching the neck backward (figure 18).

All methods are to be discouraged because they create movement and excessive stress on body parts not involved with the actual lift, thus creating an unnecessary risk of injury. (Also, see the discussion of weight-training shortcuts in Chapter 2.)

RISK (Weight Training Truth #2):

"Cheats"	R/B	Injury Site
3.a Bounce cheat	(+) 7	"Other" (Chest)
3.b Lower back arch cheat	(+) 5	Back/Spine (Zone I — Lower)
3.c Neck arch cheat	(+) 8	Back/Spine (Zone II — Upper)

Exercise 4: DECLINE BENCH PRESS

Fig. 19.1   **Start/Finish**   *side view*

PA-D

top view

PA-L

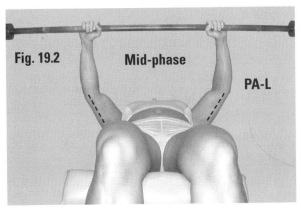

Fig. 19.2   **Mid-phase**

PA-L

BENEFIT (Weight Training Truth #1):

- This is a power-building exercise for the lower chest; the primary target (PA-L) is the lower portion of the pectoralis major muscle at and below the nipple-line.

- There is considerable (although secondary) tricep and serratus anterior muscle activity.

- This exercise can be done at any degree of decline, where the steeper the decline, the lower the target region of the pectoralis muscles.

HOW:

- Begin with the bar lightly touching your chest at the lowest edge of the pec muscles, with each hand placed approximately two to six inches (five to fifteen cm) wider than shoulder width; this is the start/finish position (figure 19.1).

- Hold your wrists in line with your forearms (i.e., not bent backward).

- Following the plane of action (PA-D), smoothly raise the bar until your elbows are almost fully extended — pause briefly; this is the mid-phase position (figure 19.2).

- Keep your buttocks down, your back slightly arched and your feet flat on the floor.

- Smoothly return the bar to the start/finish position.

RISK (Weight Training Truth #2):

R/B	Injury Site
8	Shoulders (Zone I — Front)
3	Shoulders (Zone II — Top)

VARIATIONS OF EXECUTION: Please refer to variations 8.a, 8.b, 8.e, 8.f and 111.a.

Exercise 5: FLAT DUMBBELL PRESS

Fig. 20.1   **Start/Finish**   *side view*

PA-D

top view

PA-L

Fig. 20.2

Mid-phase

PA-L

BENEFIT (Weight Training Truth #1):

- This is a power-building exercise for the entire chest but the primary target (PA-L) is the middle portion of the pectoralis major muscle.

- There is considerable (although secondary) tricep and serratus anterior muscle activity.

HOW:

- Begin with the dumbbells held at chest level, in line with your nipples, and your thumbs pointing at each other; this is the start/finish position (figure 20.1).

- Hold your wrists in line with your forearms (i.e., not bent backward).

- Keep your thumbs pointed at each other throughout.

- Following the plane of action (PA-D), raise the dumbbells until your elbows are almost fully extended — pause briefly; this is the mid-phase position (figure 20.2).

- Keep your buttocks down, your back slightly arched and your feet flat on the floor.

- Smoothly return the dumbbells to the start/finish position.

RISK (Weight Training Truth #2):

R/B	Injury Site
6	Shoulders (Zone I — Front)
4	Shoulders (Zone II — Top)

VARIATIONS OF EXECUTION: Please see variations 3.b, 3.c, 8.c–8.f and 111.a.

Exercise 6: INCLINE DUMBBELL PRESS

Fig. 21.1   Start/Finish   side view
PA-D

PA-L   top view

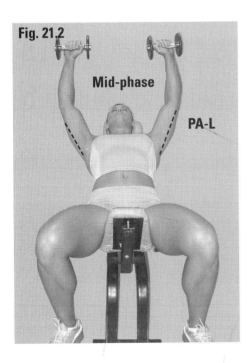

Fig. 21.2

Mid-phase

PA-L

BENEFIT (Weight Training Truth #1):

- This is a power-building exercise for the upper chest; the primary target (PA-L) is the upper pectoralis major muscle, just below the collar bone.
- There is considerable (although secondary) tricep and serratus anterior muscle activity.
- This exercise is best done on a bench inclined thirty to forty-five degrees; over forty-five degrees the target muscle becomes the front deltoid.

HOW:

- Begin with the dumbbells held at chest level, just above your sternum and with your thumbs pointing at each other; this is the start/finish position (figure 21.1).
- Hold your wrists in line with your forearms (i.e., not bent backward).
- Following the plane of action (PA-D), raise the dumbbells until your elbows are almost fully extended — pause briefly; this is the mid-phase position (figure 21.2).
- Keep your buttocks down, your back slightly arched and your feet flat on the floor.
- Smoothly return the dumbbells to the start/finish position.

RISK (Weight Training Truth #2):

R/B	Injury Site
5	Shoulders (Zone I — Front)
5	Shoulders (Zone II — Top)

VARIATIONS OF EXECUTION: Please see variations 3.b, 3.c, 8.c–8.f and 111.a.

Exercise 7: **DECLINE DUMBBELL PRESS**

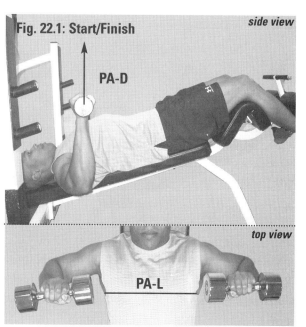

Fig. 22.1: Start/Finish   *side view*

PA-D

top view

PA-L

Fig. 22.2: Mid-phase

PA-L

ICAR

BENEFIT (Weight Training Truth #1):

- This is a power-building exercise for the lower chest; the primary target (PA-L) is the lower pectoralis major muscle at and below the sternum.

- There is considerable (although secondary) tricep and serratus anterior muscle activity.

- This exercise can be done at any degree of decline; the steeper the decline, the lower the target region of the pectoralis muscles.

HOW:

- Begin with the dumbbells held at chest level, in line with the lowest border of the pec muscles, and your thumbs pointing at each other; this is the start/finish position (figure 22.1).

- Hold your wrists in line with your forearms (i.e., not bent backward).

- Following the plane of action (PA-D), raise the dumbbells until your elbows are almost fully extended — pause briefly; this is the mid-phase position (figure 22.2).

- Keep your buttocks down, your back slightly arched, and your feet flat on the floor.

- Smoothly return the dumbbells to the start/finish position.

RISK (Weight Training Truth #2):

R/B	Injury Site
7	Shoulders (Zone I — Front)
3	Shoulders (Zone II — Top)

VARIATIONS OF EXECUTION: Please see exercises/variations 3.b, 8.c–8.f and 111.a for the variations of execution.

BARBELL PRESS Execution Variations

Fig. 23: Wide Grip

Variation 8.a — Wide Grip

Your choice of grip width is variable. Taking a wider grip (as shown in figure 23) increases the total work performed by the chest but shortens the range of total contraction. Secondarily, it reduces the potential for injury in zones I and II of the shoulder.

RISK (Weight Training Truth #2):

R/B	Injury Site
(–) 1	Shoulders (Zone I — Front)
(–) 2	Shoulders (Zone II — Top)

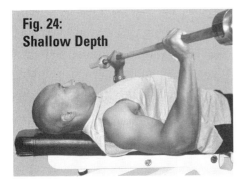

**Fig. 24:
Shallow Depth**

Variation 8.b — Shallow Depth
As the bar is being lowered toward the chest, stop the movement above your chest such that your upper arms do not break parallel to the floor. This reduces the risk of injury in zone I of the shoulder.

RISK (Weight Training Truth #2):

R/B	Injury Site
(−) 3	Shoulders (Zone I — Front)

The other R/B value for this exercise remains unchanged.

DUMBBELL PRESS Execution Variations

**Fig. 25:
Palms
Facing**

Variation 8.c — Palms-Facing Grip
Dumbbell presses as described in exercises 5, 6, and 7 but performed with your palms facing each other reduce the risk of injury in zone I of the shoulder.

RISK (Weight Training Truth #2):

R/B	Injury Site
(−) 2	Shoulders (Zone I — Front)

The other R/B value for this exercise remains unchanged.

**Fig. 26:
Shallow Depth**

Variation 8.d — Shallow Depth
As the dumbbells are being lowered, stop the motion as your elbows reach a ninety-degree angle. This reduces the risk of injury in zone I of the shoulder.

RISK (Weight Training Truth #2):

R/B	Injury Site
(−) 3	Shoulders (Zone I — Front)

The other R/B value for this exercise remains unchanged.

NOTE: Combining the shallow depth variation (8.d) with the palms-facing grip variation (8.c) reduces the R/B value for the shoulders (Zone I — front) by a total of (−) 5.

BARBELL AND DUMBBELL PRESS Execution Variations

**Fig. 27:
Toward Neck**

Variation 8.e — Toward Neck
When performing barbell or dumbbell presses with any of the bench inclinations, be aware that if the path of the weight nears your chin, there is a notably increased risk of injury to the shoulder in zones I and II.

RISK (Weight Training Truth #2):

R/B	Injury Site
(+) 2	Shoulders (Zone I — Front)
(+) 2	Shoulders (Zone II — Top)

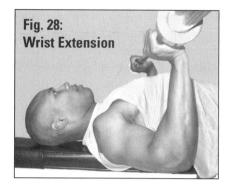

**Fig. 28:
Wrist Extension**

Variation 8.f — Wrist Extension

When performing barbell or dumbbell presses with any of the inclinations, there is a common tendency to extend the wrists (i.e., bend them backward, as shown in figure 28). This mechanism creates a rather high risk of injury within the wrist region.

RISK (Weight Training Truth #2):

R/B	Injury Site
(+) 8	Wrists

All other R/B values remain unchanged for that exercise.

Exercise 9: PEC-DECK MACHINE

**Fig. 29.1:
Start/Finish**

PA-L

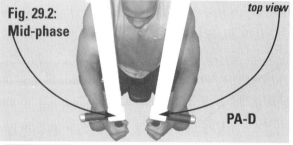

**Fig. 29.2:
Mid-phase**

top view

PA-D

side view

Fig. 29.3: *Using forearm press pads*

BENEFIT (Weight Training Truth #1):

- This is a general exercise for the entire chest that combines strengthening with stretching; the primary target (PA-L) is the middle portion of the pectoralis major muscle.

- There is good pectoralis contraction through the entire range of motion but the stretch involved reduces the strength gains.

HOW:

- Adjust the seat elevation of the pec-deck machine so that your upper arm is parallel to the floor as you grasp the handle-bar grips.

- Sit with your feet on the floor and your back firmly against the support.

- Grasp the handle-bar grips (as shown) so your elbows are bent at a twenty-degree angle and your wrists are locked in the neutral position; this is the start/finish position Figure 29.1).

- Following the plane of action (PA-D), squeeze your hands toward each other until they touch — pause briefly; this is the mid-phase position (figure 29.2).

- Keep your head and buttocks against the seat, with your back slightly arched throughout.

- Smoothly return to the start/finish position.

RISK (Weight Training Truth #2):

R/B	Injury Site
4	Shoulders (Zone I — Front)
3	Shoulders (Zone II — Top)
4	Shoulders (Zone III — at Chest)

NOTE: If you are using a pec-deck machine that has forearm press pads rather than handle-bar grips, be sure that your forearms are placed on the pads so that your elbows are on the same horizontal plane as your target muscle chest region (fig. 29.3).

PEC-DECK MACHINE Execution Variations

Fig. 30: Low Hands

PA-L

Variation 10.a — Low Hands

In order to decrease the risk of injury in the shoulders, your hands can be lowered, relative to your shoulders by raising the seat (as shown in figure 30). As the relative hand position is lowered, the target region (PA-L), of the pectoralis major shifts downward.

RISK (Weight Training Truth #2):

R/B	Injury Site
(–) 1	Shoulders (Zone II — Top)
(–) 1	Shoulders (Zone III — at Chest)

The other R/B value for the exercise remains unchanged.

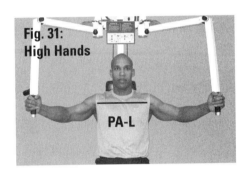

Fig. 31: High Hands

PA-L

Variation 10.b — High Hands

If you have inadvertently selected a low seat position (as shown in figure 31), your hand position relative to your shoulder height puts the shoulders at a higher risk of injury. As the relative hand position is raised, the target region (PA-L) of the pectoralis shifts upward.

RISK (Weight Training Truth #2):

R/B	Injury Site
(+) 1	Shoulders (Zone II — Top)
(+) 1	Shoulders (Zone III — at Chest)

All other R/B values remain unchanged for that exercise.

Fig. 32: Excessive Depth

Variation 10.c — Excessive Depth

If the hands are allowed to pull back too deeply (as shown in figure 32), zone III of the shoulder will be subjected to extreme tension, thus increasing the risk of injury.

RISK (Weight Training Truth #2):

R/B	Injury Site
(+) 4	Shoulders (Zone III — at Chest)

All other R/B values remain unchanged for that exercise.

Exercise 11: FLAT DUMBBELL FLYES

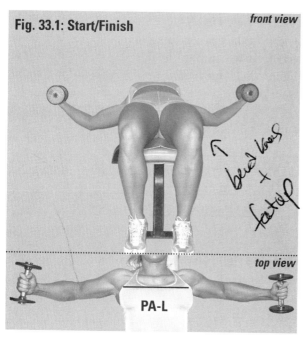

Fig. 33.1: Start/Finish *front view*

top view

PA-L

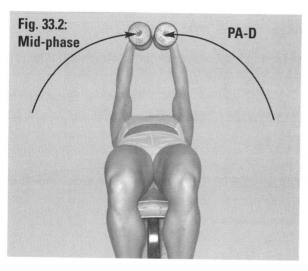

Fig. 33.2: Mid-phase **PA-D**

BENEFIT (Weight Training Truth #1):

This is a general exercise for the entire chest that stretches and defines; the primary target (PA-L) is the middle portion of the pectoralis major muscle.

HOW:

- Begin with your arms out-stretched from your chest, with your elbows bent approximately twenty degrees (i.e., not fully extended), and the dumbbells level with your chest.
- Hold your wrists in line with your forearms, (i.e., not curled upward).
- Keep your feet flat on the floor, buttocks down, and back slightly arched.
- Keep your palms facing each other, throughout; this is the start/finish position (figure 33.1).
- Following the plane of action (PA-D) with your elbows locked in slight flexion, smoothly squeeze the dumbbells upward until they touch in the midline — pause briefly; this is the mid-phase position (figure 33.2).
- Smoothly return the dumbbells to the start/finish position.

RISK (Weight Training Truth #2):

R/B	Injury Site
4	Shoulders (Zone I — Front)
3	Shoulders (Zone II — Top)
4	Shoulders (Zone III — at Chest)

VARIATIONS OF EXECUTION: Please see variations 17.a, 17.e and 17.f.

Exercise 12: INCLINE DUMBBELL FLYES

Fig. 34.1: Start/Finish — *side view*

top view

PA-L

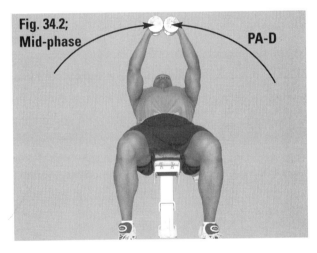

Fig. 34.2; Mid-phase — PA-D

BENEFIT (Weight Training Truth#1):

- This is a general exercise for the upper chest that stretches and defines; the primary target (PA-L) is the upper portion of the pectoralis major muscle, just below the collar bones.

- This exercise is best done on a bench inclined thirty to forty-five degrees, to best target the upper pectoralis region.

HOW:

- Begin with your arms out-stretched from your chest, with your elbows bent approximately twenty degrees (i.e., not fully extended), and the dumbbells level with your shoulders.

- Hold your wrists in line with your forearms (i.e., not curled upward); this is the start/finish position (figure 34.1).

- Keep your feet flat on the floor, buttocks down, and your back slightly arched.

- Keep your palms facing each other throughout.

- Following the plane of action (PA-D) with your elbows locked in slight flexion, smoothly squeeze the dumbbells upward until they touch in the midline — pause briefly; this is the mid-phase position figure 34.2).

- Smoothly return the dumbbells to the start/finish position.

RISK (Weight Training Truth #2):

R/B	Injury Site
3	Shoulders (Zone I — Front)
4	Shoulders (Zone II — Top)
5	Shoulders (Zone III — at Chest)

VARIATIONS OF EXECUTION: Please see variations 17.a, 17.e and 17.f.

Exercise 13: DECLINE DUMBBELL FLYES

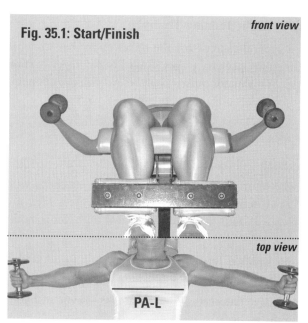

Fig. 35.1: Start/Finish

front view

top view

PA-L

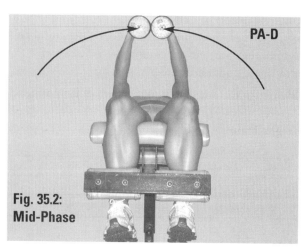

PA-D

Fig. 35.2: Mid-Phase

BENEFIT (Weight Training Truth #1):

This is a general exercise for the lower chest that stretches and defines; the primary target (PA-L) is the lower portion of the pectoralis major muscles at and below the sternum.

This exercise can be done at any angle of decline; the steeper the decline, the lower the target region of the pectoralis major.

HOW:

- Begin with your arms out-stretched from your chest, with your elbows bent approximately twenty degrees (i.e., not fully extended), and the dumbbells level with your lower chest.

- Hold your wrists in line with your forearms, (i.e., not curled upward); this is the start/finish position (figure 35.1).

- Keep your feet flat on the floor, buttocks down, and your back slightly arched.

- Keep your palms facing each other throughout.

- Following the plane of action (PA-D) with your elbows locked in slight flexion, smoothly squeeze the dumbbells upward until they touch in the midline — pause briefly; this is the mid-phase position (figure 35.2).

- Smoothly return the dumbbells to the start/finish position

RISK (Weight Training Truth #2):

R/B	Injury Site
5	Shoulders (Zone I — Front)
2	Shoulders (Zone II — Top)
3	Shoulders (Zone III — at Chest)

VARIATIONS OF EXECUTION: Please see variations 17.a, 17.e and 17.f.

Exercise 14: BENT-OVER CABLE CROSSOVERS

Myth #6

Fig. 36.1: Start/Finish

PA-L

Fig. 36.2: Mid-Phase

PA-D

BENEFIT (Weight Training Truth #1):

This is a general exercise for the chest that stretches and defines; the primary target (PA-L) is the middle portion of the pectoralis major muscle.

HOW:

- Begin with your torso flexed forward, between forty and sixty degrees, with your arms out-stretched from your body, your elbows bent approximately twenty degrees (i.e., not fully extended), and the cable grips held even with your chest.

- Slightly arch your lower back, and hold it firmly throughout.

- Hold your wrists in line with your forearms (i.e., not flexed forward); this is the start/finish position (figure 36.1).

- Keep your palms facing each other throughout.

- Following the plane of action (PA-D) with your elbows locked in slight flexion, smoothly squeeze the cable grips together until they touch in the midline — pause briefly; this is the mid-phase position (figure 36.2).

- Smoothly return the cable grips to the start/finish position.

RISK (Weight Training Truth #2):

R/B	Injury Site
4	Shoulders (Zone I — Front)
3	Shoulders (Zone II — Top)
4	Shoulders (Zone III — at Chest)

VARIATIONS OF EXECUTION: Please see variations 17.b–17.f.

Exercise 15: UPRIGHT CABLE CROSSOVERS

Myth #6

Fig. 37.1: Start/Finish

PA-L

Fig. 37.2: Mid-Phase

PA-D

BENEFIT (Weight Training Truth #1):

This is a general exercise for the lower chest that stretches and defines; the primary target (PA-L) is the lower pectoralis major muscle at and below the sternum.

HOW:

- Begin with your torso upright (but with a slight lower back arch), your arms out-stretched from your body, your elbows bent approximately twenty degrees (i.e., not fully extended), and the cable grips held even with your chest.

- Hold your wrists in line with your forearms (i.e., not curled forward); this is the start/finish position (figure 37.1).

- Keep your palms facing each other throughout.

- Following the plane of action (PA-D) with your elbows locked in slight flexion, smoothly squeeze the cable grips together until they touch in the midline — pause briefly; this is the mid-phase position (figure 37.2).

- Smoothly return the cable grips to the start/finish position.

RISK (Weight Training Truth #2):

R/B	Injury Site
5	Shoulders (Zone I — Front)
2	Shoulders (Zone II — Top)
3	Shoulders (Zone III — at Chest)

VARIATIONS OF EXECUTION: See variations 17.b–17.f.

Exercise 16: KNEELING CABLE CROSSOVERS

Myth #6

Fig. 38.1: Start/Finish

PA-L

Fig. 38.2: Mid-Phase

PA-D

No!
— Seated pec dec.

BENEFIT (Weight Training Truth #1):

This is a general exercise for the chest that stretches and defines; the primary target (PA-L) is the upper pectoralis major muscle, just below the collar bones.

HOW:

- Kneel on the floor, with your torso leaning forward about twenty degrees (with a slight lower back arch), your arms outstretched from your body, your elbows bent approximately twenty degrees (i.e., not fully extended), and the cable grips held even with, or slightly below, your head.
- Hold your wrists in line with your forearms (i.e., not curled forward); this is the start/finish position (figure 38.1).
- Keep your palms facing each other throughout.
- Following the plane of action (PA-D) with your elbows locked in slight flexion, smoothly squeeze the cable grips together until they touch in the midline — pause briefly; this is the mid-phase position (figure 38.2).
- Smoothly return the cable grips to the start/finish position

RISK (Weight Training Truth #2):

R/B	Injury Site
3	Shoulders (Zone I — Front)
4	Shoulders (Zone II — Top)
5	Shoulders (Zone III — at Chest)

VARIATIONS OF EXECUTION: See variations 17.b –17.f.

ALL DUMBBELL FLYES Execution Variation 17.a — Excessive Depth

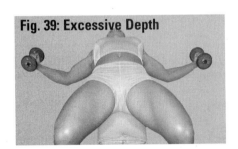

Fig. 39: Excessive Depth

If the dumbbells are allowed to drop below the bench, as shown in figure 39, zone III of the shoulder is placed under extreme tension, increasing the risk of injury.

RISK (Weight Training Truth #2):

R/B	Injury Site
(+) 4	Shoulders (Zone III — at Chest)

The other R/B values for the exercise remain unchanged.

CABLE CROSSOVER Execution Variations

Fig. 40: Thumbs-facing grip

Variation 17.b — Thumbs-Facing Grip

Cable crossovers performed as described in exercises 14, 15, and 16 but with the thumbs facing each other throughout increase the risk of injury to zone II of the shoulders.

RISK (Weight Training Truth #2):

R/B	Injury Site
(+) 3	Shoulders (Zone II — Front)

All other R/B values remain unchanged for that exercise.

Fig. 41: Excessive Depth

Variation 17.c — Excessive Depth

When cable crossovers are executed with the palms-facing grip, there is the possibility of the cable grips pulling backward too far, creating extreme tension within zone III of the shoulders, thus increasing the risk of injury.

RISK (Weight Training Truth #2):

R/B	Injury Site
(+) 4	Shoulders (Zone III — at Chest)

All other R/B values remain unchanged for that exercise.

Fig. 42: Lower Back Round-Out

Variation 17.d — Lower Back Round-Out   *Myth #6*

If you allow your lower back to curve outward during cable crossovers (as shown in figure 42), there is a notable increase in the risk of injury to your lower back. This is called "round-out." Also see variation 50.g for further information on this important execution variable.

RISK (Weight Training Truth #2):

R/B	Injury Site
(+) 5	Spine/Back (Zone I — Lower)

All other R/B values remain unchanged for that exercise.

FLYES AND CROSSOVERS Execution Variations

Fig. 43: Wrist Flexion

17.e Wrist flexion variation

Variation 17.e — Wrist Flexion

During the execution of any flye or crossover exercise, if your wrists are forcibly flexed during the range of motion (as shown in figure 43), there is an added and unnecessary risk of straining or tearing in zone I of the elbow.

RISK (Weight Training Truth #2):

R/B	Injury Site
(+) 5	Elbows (Zone I — Inside)

All other R/B values remain unchanged for that exercise.

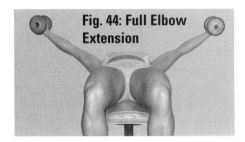
Fig. 44: Full Elbow Extension

Variation 17.f — Full Elbow Extension

During the execution of any flye or crossover exercise, if your elbows are allowed to fully extend (as shown in figure 44) during the range of motion, there is an added and unnecessary risk of straining or tearing in zone III of the elbow.

RISK (Weight Training Truth #2):

R/B	Injury Site
(+) 8	Elbows (Zone III — Front)

The other R/B values, for the exercise, remain unchanged.

Exercise 18: PULLOVERS (DUMBBELLS)

Myth #11

Fig. 45.1: Start/Finish *side view*
PA-D

top view
PA-L

BENEFIT (Weight Training Truth #1):

This is essentially a stretching exercise; the primary targets (PA-L) are the pectoralis minor, the latissimus dorsi and the pectoralis major muscles.

HOW:

• Set your feet firmly on the floor, with your head and upper back lying on the edge of a bench.

• Grasp a dumbbell with both hands. Hold it behind your head, with your hands at bench level, and with slightly flexed elbows; this is the start/finish position (figure 45.1).

• Following the plane of action (PA-D), keep your hips stationary (just below bench height) and your elbows at a constant angle of about twenty degrees of flex and pull the dumbbell up as high as possible above your face — pause briefly; this is the mid-phase position (figure 45.2).

• Smoothly return the dumbbell to the start/finish position.

RISK (Weight Training Truth #2):

R/B	Injury Site
7	Shoulders (Zone I — Front)
7	Shoulders (Zone II — Top)
7	Shoulders (Zone III — at Chest)
4	Elbows (Zone I — Inside)

Fig. 45.2: Mid-Phase

BARBELL PULLOVER Execution Variations

Fig. 46: Narrow Grip

PA-L

Variation 19.a Narrow Grip

The use of a barbell and a narrow grip (with eight to twelve inches/twenty to thirty cm between your hands — see Figure 46) diminishes the stretch of the pectoralis minor and increases the strengthening capacity for the latissimus dorsi muscles.

RISK (Weight Training Truth #2):

R/B	Injury Site
(–) 2	Shoulders (Zone I — Front)
(–) 1	Shoulders (Zone II — Top)
(–) 2	Shoulders (Zone III — at Chest)

The other R/B value, for the exercise, remains unchanged.

Fig. 47: Wide Grip

PA-L

Variation 19.b — Wide Grip

The use of a barbell and a wide grip (more than fourteen inches/thirty-six cm between your hands — see Figure 47) makes the exercise almost strictly for latissimus dorsi strength and stretch.

RISK (Weight Training Truth #2):

R/B	Injury Site
(–) 4	Shoulders (Zone I — Front)
(–) 3	Shoulders (Zone II — Top)
(–) 4	Shoulders (Zone III — at Chest)

The other R/B value, for the exercise, remains unchanged.

Exercise 20: MODIFIED DUMBBELL SHOULDER PRESS

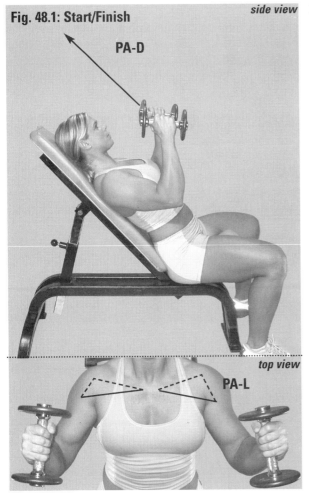

Fig. 48.1: Start/Finish

side view

PA-D

top view

PA-L

Fig. 48.2: Mid-Phase

BENEFIT (Weight Training Truth #1):

- This exercise strengthens and defines the uppermost region of the chest and also "ties in" the chest with the shoulders.
- The target muscles (PA-L) are the upper most pectoralis major and the anterior deltoid muscles.
- The triceps are also involved, secondarily.

HOW:

- Sit on an adjustable bench set at forty-five to sixty degrees of incline.
- Hold the dumbbells as if to do a dumbbell shoulder press (i.e., with hands held halfway between a palms-facing and a thumbs-facing grip, dumbbells at ear level) but point your elbows slightly forward — about forty-five degrees from a true shoulder press position; this is the start/finish position (figure 48.1).
- Following the plane of action (PA-D), smoothly press the dumbbells upward in front of your face. As your elbows straighten, squeeze your pecs firmly together, in order to draw your upper arms toward the midline until the dumbbells make contact — pause briefly; this is the mid-phase position (figure 48.2).
- Smoothly return the dumbbells to the start/finish position.

RISK (Weight Training Truth #2):

R/B	Injury Site
6	Shoulders (Zone I — Front)
6	Shoulders (Zone II — Top)

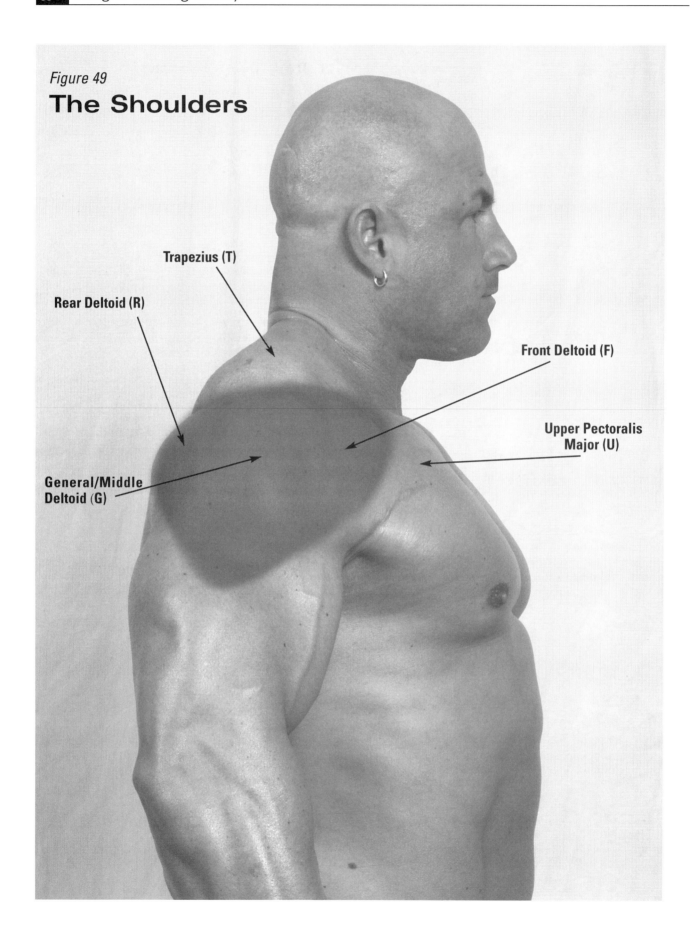

Figure 49

The Shoulders

Trapezius (T)

Rear Deltoid (R)

Front Deltoid (F)

Upper Pectoralis Major (U)

General/Middle Deltoid (G)

Table 2 – SHOULDER EXERCISES

Name of Exercise/Variation		Benefit (WT #1)	R/B Values (WT #2)	No.	Pg.
Behind Head Press	— Standing	G-P	9, 5, 4, 6, 5	21	62
Front Press	— Standing	F-P	7, 5, 5	22	63
Behind Head Press	— Seated	G-P	9, 5, 4, 6	23	64
Front Press	— Seated	F-P	7, 5	24	65
Dumbbell Press		G-D, P	7, 5	25	66
Modified Dumbbell Press		U, F-D	6, 6	20	59
Dumbbell Lateral Raises	— Upright	G-D	6, 5	26	67
Dumbbell Lateral Raises	— Bent-Over	R-D	7, 5	27	68
Cable Lateral Raises	— Upright	G-D	6, 4	28	69
Cable Lateral Raises	— Bent-Over	R-D	7, 4	29	70
Cable Lateral Raises	— Behind Back	R-D	8, 9, 6	30	71
Execution Variations:					
Barbell Presses	— Wide Grip		(–) 3	31.a	72
Bar/Dumbbell Presses	— Wrist Extension		(+) 8	31.b	72
Dumbbell Presses	— Palms-facing Grip		(–) 1	31.c	72
Bar/Dumbbell Presses	— Shallow Depth		(–) 2	31.d	72
Dumb. & Cable Lat. Raises	— One-arm		(+) 1	31.e	73
	— Elbow Elevation		(+) 2, (+) 9	31.f(i)	73
Behind-Back Cab. Lat Raises	— Elbow Elevation		(+) 2, (+) 2	31.f(ii)	73
Cable Lat. Raises	— Open Hand/Wrist Strap		(–) 3	31.g	74
All Presses & Raises	— Lower Back Round-Out		(+) 5	31.h	74
Standing Presses	— "Cheating"		(+) 2	31.i(i)	74
Lateral Raises	— "Cheating"		(+) 5	31.i(ii)	74
Front Raises	— Barbell	F-D	5, 6, 7	32	75
Execution Variations:					
Wide Grip		F-D	(+) 1, (–) 2	33.a	76
Narrow Grip		F-D	(–) 1, (+) 2	33.b	76
Front Raises	— Dumbbells	F-D	5, 6, 6	34	77
Execution Variations:					
Angled to the Side		F, G-D	(+) 1, (–) 2	35.a	78
Elbow Elevation		F-D	(+) 2, (+) 3	35.b	78
Upright Rowing		G, F, T-D	8, 10, 6, 5, 6, 6	36	79
Execution Variations:					
Wide Grip		G, F, T-D	(+) 2, (–) 2, (–) 2, (+) 1	37.a	80
Narrow Grip		T, G, F-D	(–) 2, (+) 2, (+) 2, (–) 1	37.b	80
Partial-range		G, F-D	(–) 4, (–) 4, (–) 4 (–) 4, (–) 4, (–) 4	37.c	80
Target-specific		G, F, T-D	(–) 4, (–) 4, (–) 4 (–) 2, (–) 4, (–) 4	37.d	81
Lateral Dumbbell "Flares"		R-D, P	6, 4, 5	38	82

KEY:

G = General/Mid Deltoid   T = Trapezius *(see Table 3)*   F = Front Deltoid

R = Rear Deltoid   U = Upper Pec Major *(see Table 1)*

P = Power/Size   D = Definition

Exercise 21: BEHIND-THE-HEAD PRESS (STANDING)

Myths #1 & #7

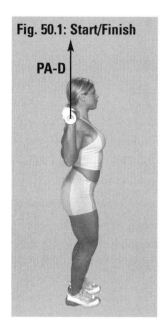

Fig. 50.1: Start/Finish

PA-D

No

Fig. 50.2: Mid-Phase

front view

top view

PA-L

BENEFIT (Weight Training Truth #1):

• This is a general shoulder power-building exercise; the primary target (PA-L) is the mid deltoid muscle.

• The standing position allows for slightly heavier weights than a similar seated exercise.

HOW:

• Stand with your feet ten to twelve inches (twenty-five to thirty cm) apart and your knees slightly bent.

• Hold a barbell behind your neck, resting it lightly across your shoulders, and angle your head slightly forward.

• Hold your wrists in line with your forearms (i.e., not bent backward), each hand placed approximately two to four-inches (five to ten cm) wider than shoulder width; this is the start/finish position (figure 50.1).

• Maintain a slight arch in your lower back throughout.

• Following the plane of action (PA-D), smoothly press the bar straight upward until your elbows are almost fully extended — pause briefly; this is the mid-phase position (figure 50.2).

• Smoothly return the barbell to the start/finish position.

RISK (Weight Training Truth #2):

R/B	Injury Site
9	Shoulders (Zone II — Top)
5	Shoulders (Zone III — at Chest)
4	Shoulders (Zone I — Front)
6	Spine/Back (Zone II — Upper)
5	Spine/Back (Zone I — Lower)

NOTE:

A "staggered stance" (one foot placed half a stride ahead of the other) can be used for better balance and power, with no change to either the benefit or the risks.

VARIATIONS OF EXECUTION: Please refer to variations 31.a, 31.b, 31.d, 31.i(i), and 111.a.

Exercise 22: FRONT PRESS (STANDING)

Myth #7

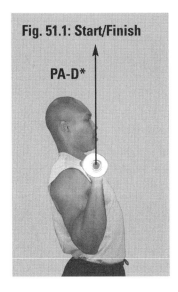

Fig. 51.1: Start/Finish

PA-D*

front view

Fig. 51.2: Mid-Phase

top view

PA-L

BENEFIT (Weight Training Truth #1):

• This is a general shoulder power exercise; the primary target (PA-L) is the front deltoid muscle.

• The standing position allows for slightly heavier weights than a similar seated exercise.

HOW:

• Stand with your feet placed ten to twelve inches (twenty-five to thirty cm) apart and your knees slightly bent.

• Hold a barbell in front of your neck, just above the top of your sternum.

• Hold your wrists in line with your forearms (i.e., not bent backward), each hand placed approximately two to four inches (five to ten cm) wider than shoulder width; this is the start/finish position (figure 51.1).

• Maintain a slight arch in your lower back throughout.

• Following the plane of action (PA-D), smoothly press the bar straight upward until your elbows are almost fully extended — pause briefly; this is the mid-phase position (figure 51.2).

• Smoothly return the bar to the start/finish position.

RISK (Weight Training Truth #2):

R/B	Injury Site
7	Shoulders (Zone II — Top)
5	Shoulders (Zone I — Front)
5	Spine/Back (Zone I — Lower)

NOTE:

A staggered stance (one foot placed half a stride ahead of the other) can be used, for better balance and power, with no change to either the benefit or the risks.

* The mid-phase position (figure 51.2 — top view) implies a slightly curved PA-D (the bar is being held directly above the head). This slight deviation from PA-D does not affect the R/B values or purpose of the exercise.

VARIATIONS OF EXECUTION: Please see variations 31.a, 31.b, 31.d, 31.i(i), and 111.a.

Exercise 23: BEHIND-THE-HEAD PRESS (SEATED)

Myth #1

Fig. 52.1: Start/Finish *side view*

PA-D

top view

PA-L

Fig. 52.2: Mid-Phase

BENEFIT (Weight Training Truth #1):
This is a general shoulder power exercise; the primary target (PA-L) is the mid-deltoid muscle.

HOW:

- Hold the bar behind your neck, just above shoulder height.

- Hold your wrists in line with your forearms (i.e., not bent backward), each hand placed approximately two to four-inches (five to ten cm) wider than shoulder width; this is the start/finish position (figure 52.1).

- Keep your feet flat on the floor, keep your buttocks down and your back slightly arched throughout.

- Following the plane of action (PA-D), smoothly press the bar straight upward until your elbows are almost fully extended — pause briefly; this is the mid-phase position (figure 52.2).

- Smoothly return the bar to the start/finish position.

RISK (Weight Training Truth #2):

R/B	Injury Site
9	Shoulders (Zone II — Top)
5	Shoulders (Zone III — at Chest)
4	Shoulders (Zone I — Front)
6	Spine/Back (Zone II — Upper)

VARIATIONS OF EXECUTION: Please see variations 31.a, 31.b, 31.d, 31.h and 111.a.

Exercise 24: FRONT PRESS (SEATED)

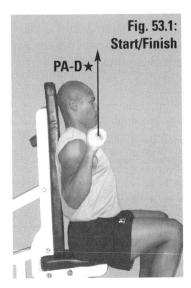

**Fig. 53.1:
Start/Finish**

PA-D★

front view

**Fig. 53.2:
Mid-Phase**

PA-L   *top view*

BENEFIT (Weight Training Truth #1):
This is a general shoulder power exercise; the primary target (PA-L) is the front deltoid muscle.

HOW:

- Hold the bar in front of your neck, just above the top of your sternum.

- Hold your wrists in line with your forearms (i.e., not bent backward), each hand placed approximately two to four-inches (five to ten cm) wider than shoulder width; this is the start/finish position (figure 53.1).

- Keep your feet flat on the floor.

- Keep your buttocks down and your back slightly arched throughout.

- Following the plane of action (PA-D), smoothly press the bar straight upward until your elbows are almost fully extended — pause briefly; this is the mid-phase position (figure 53.2).

- Smoothly return the bar to the start/finish position.

RISK (Weight Training Truth #2):

R/B	Injury Site
7	Shoulders (Zone II — Top)
5	Shoulders (Zone I — Front)

★ The mid-phase position shown in the top view of figure 53.2 implies a slightly curved PA-D (the bar is being held directly above the head). This slight deviation from PA-D does not affect the R/B values or purpose of the exercise.

VARIATIONS OF EXECUTION: Please see variations 31.a, 31.b, 31.d, 31.h and 111.a.

Exercise 25: DUMBBELL PRESS

Fig. 54.1: Start/Finish — side view
PA-D

top view
PA-L

Fig. 54.2: Mid-Phase

BENEFIT (Weight Training Truth #1):

- This is a general shoulder strengthening exercise; the primary target (PA-L) is the mid region of the deltoid muscle.

- This is also a good exercise for improving deltoid definition.

HOW:

- Sitting, hold the dumbbells at ear level, with your palms facing forward and your elbows pointed outward.

- Hold your wrists in line with your forearms (i.e., not bent backward); this is the start/finish position (figure 54.1).

- Keep your buttocks down and your back slightly arched throughout.

- Keep your palms facing forward throughout the exercise.

- Following the plane of action (PA-D), smoothly press the dumbbells straight up overhead, until your elbows are almost fully extended — pause briefly; this is the mid-phase position (figure 54.2).

- Smoothly return the bar to the start/finish position.

RISK (Weight Training Truth #2):

R/B	Injury Site
7	Shoulders (Zone II — Top)
5	Shoulders (Zone I -Front)

VARIATIONS OF EXECUTION: Please refer to variations 31.b, 31.c, 31.d, 31.h and 111.a.

← with straight Back bench for support.

Exercise 26: DUMBBELL LATERAL RAISES (UPRIGHT)

Myth #6

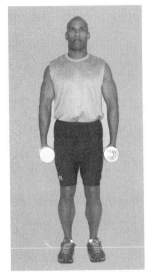

**Fig. 55.1:
Start/Finish**

front view

PA-D

**Fig. 55.2:
Mid-Phase**

top view

PA-L

BENEFIT (Weight Training Truth #1):

This is a thickening and defining shoulder exercise; the primary target (PA-L) is the mid region of the deltoid muscle.

HOW:

• Standing or sitting, hold the dumbbells at your sides, with your elbows flexed ten to fifteen degrees.

• Slightly arch your lower back and hold it firmly throughout.

• Hold your wrists in line with your forearms (i.e., not bent forward or backward); this is the start/finish position (figure 55.1).

• Keep your palms facing downward and your elbow angle constant throughout the exercise.

• Following the plane of action (PA-D), smoothly raise the dumbbells sideways until they are at ear level — pause briefly; this is the mid-phase position (figure 55.2).

• Ensure that your hands are slightly higher than your elbows at the top of the exercise.

• Smoothly return the dumbbells to the start/finish position.

RISK (Weight Training Truth #2):

R/B	Injury Site
6	Shoulders (Zone II — Top)
5	Elbows (Zone II — Outside)

NOTES:

• This exercise can be performed standing or sitting with no change to either the benefit or the risks.

• Please see variations 31.e, 31.f(i), 31.h and 31.i(ii).

Exercise 27: DUMBBELL LATERAL RAISES (BENT-OVER)

Myths #6 & #8

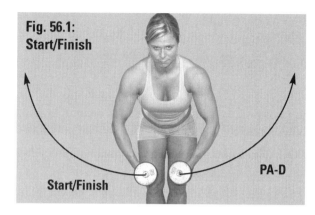

Fig. 56.1: Start/Finish

Start/Finish

PA-D

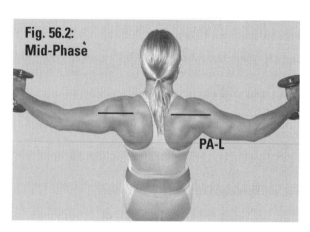

Fig. 56.2: Mid-Phase

PA-L

BENEFIT (Weight Training Truth #1):

This is a thickening and defining shoulder exercise; the primary target (PA-L) is the rear region of the deltoid muscle.

HOW:

- Standing or sitting, hold the dumbbells in front of your thighs with your elbows flexed ten to fifteen degrees, your torso flexed forward twenty to thirty degrees and your palms facing each other.

- Maintain a slight arch in your lower back throughout.

- Hold your wrists in line with your forearms (i.e., not bent forward or backward); this is the start/finish position (figure 56.1).

- Keep your palms facing downward and your elbow angle constant throughout the exercise.

- Following the plane of action (PA-D), smoothly raise the dumbbells in a vertical plane until they are at ear level — pause briefly; this is the mid-phase position (figure 56.2).

- Ensure that your hands are slightly higher than your elbows at the top of the exercise.

- Smoothly return the bar to the start/finish position.

RISK (Weight Training Truth #2):

R/B	Injury Site
7	Shoulders (Zone II — Top)
5	Elbows (Zone II — Outside)

NOTES:

- To accurately target the rear deltoid muscles, the amount of forward torso flex must be limited to the point where the plane of action (PA-L) overlies the rear deltoids exactly. Too much forward torso flex puts the plane of action over the mid and outer scapular muscles. Conversely, not enough forward torso flex puts the PA-L through the mid-deltoid region.

- This exercise can be performed standing or sitting with no change to either the benefit or the risks.

- Please see variations 31.e, 31.f(i), 31.h and 31.i(ii).

Exercise 28: CABLE LATERAL RAISES (UPRIGHT)

Myths #6 & #8

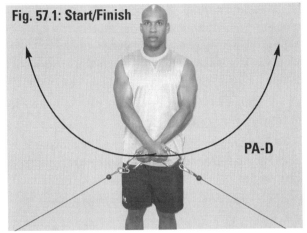

Fig. 57.1: Start/Finish

PA-D

Fig. 57.2: Mid-Phase — *front view*

top view

PA-L

BENEFIT (Weight Training Truth #1):
This is a thickening and defining shoulder exercise; the primary target (PA-L) is the mid region of the deltoid muscle.

HOW:

- Standing or sitting, hold the cable grips in front of your hips, with your elbows flexed ten to fifteen degrees; this is the start/finish position (figure 57.1).

- Slightly arch your lower back and hold it firmly throughout.

- Keep your palms facing downward and your elbow angle constant throughout the exercise.

- Following the plane of action (PA-D), smoothly raise the cable grips sideways until they are at ear level — pause briefly; this is the mid-phase position (figure 57.2).

- Ensure that your hands are slightly higher than your elbows at the top of the exercise.

- Smoothly return the grips to the start/finish position.

RISK (Weight Training Truth #2):

R/B	Injury Site
6	Shoulders (Zone II — Top)
4	Elbows (Zone II — Outside)

VARIATIONS OF EXECUTION: Please see variations 31.e, 31.f(i), 31.g, 31.h and 31.i(ii).

Exercise 29: CABLE LATERAL RAISES (BENT-OVER)

Myth #6

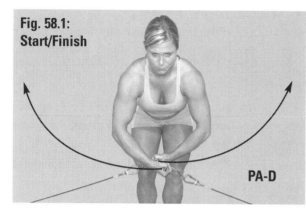

Fig. 58.1: Start/Finish

PA-D

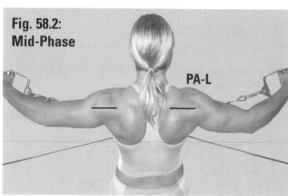

Fig. 58.2: Mid-Phase

PA-L

BENEFIT (Weight Training Truth #1):
This is a thickening and defining shoulder exercise; the primary target (PA-L) is the rear region of the deltoid muscle

HOW:

- Standing or sitting, hold the cable grips, palms facing each other, in front of your thighs.

- Flex your elbows ten to fifteen degrees and bend your torso forward twenty to thirty degrees; this is the start/finish position (figure 58.1).

- Maintain a slight arch in your lower back throughout.

- Hold your wrists in line with your forearms (i.e., not bent forward or backward).

- Keep your palms facing downward and your elbow angle constant throughout the exercise.

- Following the plane of action (PA-D), smoothly raise the cable grips in a vertical plane until they are at ear level — pause briefly; this is the mid-phase position (figure 58.2).

- Ensure that your hands are slightly higher than your elbows at the top of the exercise.

- Smoothly return the grips to the start/finish position.

RISK (Weight Training Truth #2):

R/B	Injury Site
7	Shoulders (Zone II — Top)
4	Elbows (Zone II — Outside)

NOTES:

- To accurately target the rear deltoid muscles, the amount of forward torso flex must be limited to the point where the plane of action (PA-L) overlies the rear deltoids exactly. Too much forward torso flex puts the PA-L over the mid and outer scapular muscles. Conversely, not enough forward torso flex puts the plane of action over the mid-deltoid region.

- Please see variations 31.e, 31.f(i), 31.g, 31.h and 31.i(ii).

Exercise 30: CABLE LATERAL RAISES (BEHIND THE BACK)

Myth #6

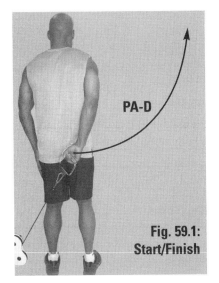

PA-D

**Fig. 59.1:
Start/Finish**

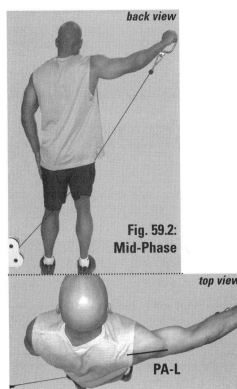

back view

**Fig. 59.2:
Mid-Phase**

top view

PA-L

BENEFIT (Weight Training Truth #1):
This is a thickening and defining shoulder exercise; the primary target (PA-L) is the rear region of the deltoid muscle.

HOW:

- Standing or sitting, hold a cable grip behind your back (almost touching your buttocks), with your elbow flexed ten to fifteen degrees.

- Lean your torso forward about ten degrees and slightly arch your lower back; this is the start/finish position (figure 59.1) — hold both firmly throughout the exercise.

- Hold your wrist in line with your forearm (i.e., not bent forward or backward).

- Keep your palm facing downward and your elbow angle constant throughout the exercise.

- Following the plane of action (PA-D), smoothly raise the cable grip sideways until it is at ear level — pause briefly; this is the mid-phase position (figure 59.2).

- Ensure that your hand finishes higher than your elbow at the top of the exercise.

- Smoothly return the grip to the start/finish position.

RISK (Weight Training Truth #2):

R/B	Injury Site
8	Shoulders (Zone II — Top)
9	Shoulders (Zone I — Front)
6	Elbows (Zone II — Outside)

VARIATIONS OF EXECUTION: Please see variations 31.f(ii), 31.g, 31.h and 31.i(ii).

BARBELL PRESSES Execution Variation

**Fig. 60:
Wide Grip**

Variation 31.a — Wide Grip

Taking a wide grip (as shown) shortens the range of total movement, which reduces the risk of injury to zone II of the shoulder.

RISK (Weight Training Truth #2):

R/B	Injury Site
(–) 3	Shoulders (Zone II — Top)

All other R/B values remain unchanged for that exercise.

ALL SHOULDER PRESSES Execution Variation

**Fig. 61:
Wrist
Hyperextension**

Variation 31.b — Wrist Hyperextension

In the performance of any of the shoulder press exercises (exercises 21–25), full wrist extension as shown in figure 61 creates an unnecessary, severe risk of wrist injury.

RISK (Weight Training Truth #2):

R/B	Injury Site
(+) 8	Wrists

All other R/B values remain unchanged for that exercise.

DUMBBELL PRESSES Execution Variation

**Fig. 62:
Palms-Facing
Grip**

Variation 31.c — Palms-Facing Grip

Dumbbell presses performed as described in exercise 25 but with palms facing each other reduce the risk of injury in zone I of the shoulder.

RISK (Weight Training Truth #2):

R/B	Injury Site
(–) 1	Shoulders (Zone I — Front)

All other R/B values remain unchanged for that exercise.

BARBELL AND DUMBBELL PRESSES Execution Variation

**Fig. 63:
Shallow
Depth**

Variation 31.d — Shallow Depth

During barbell or dumbbell presses, as the weight is being lowered toward the base of your neck, stop the movement such that your upper arms just reach parallel to the floor. This reduces the risk of injury in zone I of shoulders.

RISK (Weight Training Truth #2):

R/B	Injury Site
(–) 2	Shoulders (Zone I — Front)

The other R/B value remains unchanged.

NOTE: For dumbbell presses, combining the shallow depth variation (31.d) and the palms-facing grip variation (31.c) alters the R/B value for zone I of the shoulders by a total of (–) 3.

DUMBBELL AND CABLE LATERAL RAISE Execution Variations

**Fig. 64:
One Arm
at a Time**

**Fig. 65:
Elbow
Elevation**

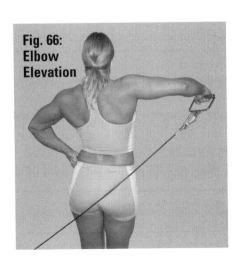

**Fig. 66:
Elbow
Elevation**

Variation 31.e — One Arm at a Time

Any of the lateral raise exercises (26–29) can be performed one arm at a time. To do so, your free hand grasps a stationary object or braces against your hip for balance. This technique allows for a more complete range of motion, thus offering the deltoid muscle (PA-L) a deeper contraction. The drawback, however, is an increased risk of injury in zone II of the shoulders.

RISK (Weight Training Truth #2):

R/B	Injury Site
(+) 1	Shoulders (Zone II -Top)

All other R/B values remain unchanged for that exercise.

NOTE: If one-arm-at-a-time variation 31.e is combined with elbow-elevation variation 31.f(i) (below), the R/B value for zone II of the shoulders is altered by (+) 3.

Variation 31.f(i) — Elbow Elevation   *Myth #8*

In dumbbell or cable lateral raise exercises (26–29), forcibly elevate your elbow so that your hand drops forward (much like pouring water from a pitcher). This "peaks" the deltoid (PA-L) contraction, but also increases the risk of injury at two shoulder regions (zones I and II).

RISK (Weight Training Truth #2):

R/B	Injury Site
(+) 2	Shoulders (Zone II -Top)
(+) 9	Shoulders (Zone I — Front)

All other R/B values remain unchanged for that exercise.

NOTE: If elbow-elevation variation 31.f(i) is used with one-arm-at-a-time variation 31.e, the R/B value for zone II of the shoulders is altered by (+) 3.

Variation 31.f(ii) — Elbow Elevation   *Myth #8*

In behind-the-back cable lateral raises (exercise 30), forcibly elevate your elbow so that your hand drops forward (like pouring water from a pitcher). This "peaks" the deltoid (PA-L) contraction, but also increases the risk of injury at two shoulder regions (zones I and II).

RISK (Weight Training Truth #2):

R/B	Injury Site
(+) 2	Shoulders (Zone II — Top)
(+) 2	Shoulders (Zone I — Front)

All other R/B values remain unchanged for that exercise.

CABLE LATERAL RAISES Execution Variation

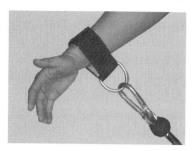

**Fig. 67:
Open Hand,
Wrist Strap**

Variation 31.g — Open Hand, Wrist Strap
The use of a wrist strap (as shown in fig. 67) with an open, relaxed hand reduces the risk of injury to zone II of the elbow.

RISK (Weight Training Truth #2):

R/B	Injury Site
(–) 3	Elbows (Zone II — Outer)

All other R/B values remain unchanged for that exercise.

ALL PRESSES AND LATERAL RAISES Execution Variation

**Fig. 68: Lower
Back Round-Out**

Variation 31.h — Lower Back Round-Out
If lower back round-out (as shown) occurs during any of the shoulder press or lateral raise exercises, an unnecessary and severe risk of lower back injury is created. See variation 50.g for further information on this important execution variable.

RISK (Weight Training Truth #2):

R/B	Injury Site
(+) 5	Back/Spine (Zone I — Lower)

All other R/B values remain unchanged for that exercise.

STANDING PRESSES Execution Variation

Fig. 69: "Cheating"

Variation 31.i(i) — "Cheating"
Cheating in standing shoulder presses occurs by the use of a torso "bounce" just as the weights begin the upward movement. This creates momentum, allowing the deltoids to lift heavier weight, but puts the lower back at higher risk of injury. (Also see the discussion of weight-training shortcuts in Chapter 2.)

RISK (Weight Training Truth #2):

R/B	Injury Site
(+) 2	Back/Spine (Zone I — Lower)

All other R/B values remain unchanged for that exercise.

LATERAL RAISES Execution Variation

Fig. 70: "Cheating"

Variation 31.i(ii) — "Cheating"
Cheating in lateral raise exercises occurs by using a sideways torso "bounce" just as the weights begin the upward movement. This creates momentum, allowing the deltoids to lift heavier weight, but puts the lower back at higher risk of injury. (Also see the discussion of weight-training shortcuts in Chapter 2.)

RISK (Weight Training Truth #2):

R/B	Injury Site
(+) 5	Back/Spine (Zone I — Lower)

All other R/B values remain unchanged for that exercise.

Exercise 32: FRONT RAISES (BARBELL)

Fig. 71.1: Start/Finish

side view

PA-D

Fig. 71.2: Mid-Phase

top view

PA-L

BENEFIT (Weight Training Truth #1):

This is a thickening and defining shoulder exercise; the primary target (PA-L) is the front region of the deltoid muscle.

HOW:

- Grasp the bar (palms down) with each hand about two inches (5 cm) wider than shoulder width.

- Hold the bar in front of your thighs, keeping your elbows flexed about five to ten degrees.

- Hold your wrists in line with your forearms (i.e., not bent up or down); this is the start/finish position (figure 71.1).

- Slightly arch your lower back and hold firmly throughout.

- Following the plane of action (PA-D), smoothly raise the bar until it is just above shoulder height — pause briefly; this is the mid-phase position (figures 71.2).

- Smoothly lower the bar to the start/finish position.

RISK (Weight Training Truth #2):

R/B	Injury Site
5	Shoulders (Zone II — Top)
6	Shoulders (Zone I — Front)
7	Elbows (Zone II — Outside)

FRONT RAISES (BARBELL) Execution Variations

**Fig. 72
Wide Grip**

Variation 33.a — Wide Grip

Taking a wider grip (as shown in figure 72) reduces the risk of injury in zone I of the shoulder but increases the risk of injury in zone II of the shoulder.

RISK (Weight Training Truth #2):

R/B	Injury Site
(+) 1	Shoulders (Zone II — Top)
(–) 2	Shoulders (Zone I — Front)

The other R/B value remains unchanged.

**Fig. 73
Narrow Grip**

Variation 33.b — Narrow Grip

Taking a narrower grip (as shown in figure 73) reduces the risk of injury in zone II of the shoulder but increases the risk of injury in zone I of the shoulder.

RISK (Weight Training Truth #2):

R/B	Injury Site
(–) 1	Shoulders (Zone II — Top)
(+) 2	Shoulders (Zone I — Front)

The other R/B value remains unchanged.

Exercise 34: FRONT RAISES (DUMBBELLS)

Myth #8

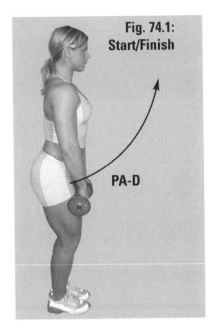

**Fig. 74.1:
Start/Finish**

PA-D

front view | *top view*

PA-L

**Fig. 74.2:
Mid-Phase**

BENEFIT (Weight Training Truth #1):
This is a thickening and defining shoulder exercise; the primary target (PA-L) is the front region of the deltoid muscle.

HOW:

- Grasp the dumbbells (palms down) and hold them in front of your thighs, keeping your elbows flexed about five to ten degrees.

- Keep your wrists in line with your forearms (i.e., not bent up or down).

- Slightly arch your lower back and hold firmly throughout; this is the start/finish position (figure 74.1).

- Following the plane of action (PA-D), smoothly raise the dumbbells directly in front of your torso until the weight is just above shoulder height — pause briefly; this is the mid-phase position (figure 74.2).

- Keep the dumbbells higher than your elbows at the top of the exercise.

- Smoothly lower the weights to the start/finish position.

RISK (Weight Training Truth #2):

R/B	Injury Site
5	Shoulders (Zone II — Top)
6	Shoulders (Zone I — Front)
6	Elbows (Zone II — Outside)

FRONT RAISE (DUMBBELLS) Execution Variations

Fig. 75: Angled to the Side

Variation 35.a — Angled to the Side
BENEFIT (Weight Training Truth #1):
Rather than raise the dumbbells directly to the front, a slight angle to the side (as shown) will change the primary target to the mid-deltoid (PA-L). This concurrently decreases the risk of injury in zone I of the shoulder and increases the risk of injury in zone II of the shoulder. An even wider angle to the side further alters the target and the R/B values until the exercise becomes a dumbbell side lateral raise.

RISK (Weight Training Truth #2):

R/B	Injury Site
(+) 1	Shoulders (Zone II — Top)
(−) 2	Shoulders (Zone I — Front)

The other R/B value remains unchanged.

Fig. 76 Elbow Elevation

Variation 35.b — Elbow Elevation *Myth #8*
BENEFIT (Weight Training Truth #1):
As the dumbbell is lifted, keep your elbow higher than your hand (as shown in fig. 76), in order to accentuate the deltoid (PA-L) contraction. This increases the injury potentials for zones I and II of the shoulder.

RISK (Weight Training Truth #2):

R/B	Injury Site
(+) 2	Shoulders (Zone II — Top)
(+) 3	Shoulders (Zone I — Front)

The other R/B value remains unchanged.

NOTE: If the elbow elevation variation (35.b) is combined with the angled-to-the-side variation (35.a) the R/B value for zone II of the shoulder is altered by (+) 3 and the R/B value for zone I of the shoulder is altered by (+) 1.

Exercise 36: UPRIGHT ROWING

Myth #6

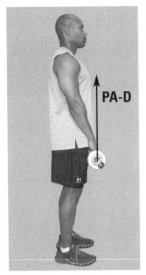

**Fig. 77.1:
Start/Finish**

PA-D

front view

top view

PA-L

**Fig. 77.2:
Mid-Phase**

BENEFIT (Weight Training Truth #1):
This exercise is best used for defining and "tying in" the shoulders and upper back; the primary targets (PA-L) are the mid and front regions of the deltoid and the upper trapezius muscles.

HOW:

- Hold a barbell in front of your thighs (palms down), with your hands eight inches (fifteen cm) apart.
- Keep your torso erect throughout the exercise, with a slight lower back arch; this is the start/finish position (fig. 77.1).
- Following the plane of action (PA-D), smoothly pull the bar up to chin height, squeezing your elbows up and back at the top — pause briefly; this is the mid-phase position (fig. 77.2).
- Do not snap the bar upward.
- Smoothly lower the bar to the start/finish position.

RISK (Weight Training Truth #2):

R/B	Injury Site	
8	Shoulders	(Zone II — Top)
10	Shoulders	(Zone II — Front)
6	Wrist	
5	Spine/Back	(Zone II — Upper)
6	Elbows	(Zone I — Inside)
6	Elbows	(Zone II — Outside)

VARIATIONS OF EXECUTION: See variations 37.a–37.d.

UPRIGHT ROWING Execution Variations

Fig. 78
Wide Grip

Fig. 79:
Narrow
Grip

Fig. 80:
Partial
Range

Variation 37.a — Wide Grip
BENEFIT (Weight Training Truth #1):
Using a wider grip, of twelve to fourteen inches (thirty to thirty-five cm), as shown, shifts the emphasis from the trapezius to the deltoids (PA-L), while also altering most of the risks of injury.

RISK (Weight Training Truth #2):

R/B	Injury Site
(+) 2	Shoulders (Zone II — Top)
(–) 2	Shoulders (Zone I — Front)
(–) 2	Wrist
(+) 1	Elbows (Zone II — Outside)

The other R/B values remain as in exercise 36.

Variation 37.b — Narrow Grip
BENEFIT (Weight Training Truth #1):
Using a narrower grip of four to six inches (ten to fifteen cm), as shown, shifts the emphasis from the deltoids to the trapezius (PA-L) and alters most of the risks of injury.

RISK (Weight Training Truth #2):

R/B	Injury Site
(–) 2	Shoulders (Zone II — Top)
(+) 2	Shoulders (Zone I — Front)
(+) 2	Wrist
(–) 1	Elbows (Zone II — Outside)

The other R/B values remain as in exercise 36.

Variation 37.c — Partial Range
BENEFIT (Weight Training Truth #1):
Rather than lifting the bar up to your chin (as in ex. 36), stopping the bar at your lower chest level will change both the benefit and the risks of the exercise. The reduced bar elevation (as shown) reduces the trapezius muscle activity, thus changing its primary benefit (PA-L) to strictly deltoid development. All risks of injury are notably reduced by this execution variation.

RISK (Weight Training Truth #2):

R/B	Injury Site
(–) 4	Shoulders (Zone II — Top)
(–) 4	Shoulders (Zone I — Front)
(–) 4	Wrist
(–) 4	Spine/Back (Zone II — Upper)
(–) 4	Elbows (Zone I — Inside)
(–) 4	Elbows (Zone II — Outside)

Variation 37.c — Partial Range (cont'd)

Fig. 81: Target-Specific

NOTES:

- If the partial-range variation 37.c is combined with the wide-grip variation 37.a, the R/B values change as follows: shoulder (zone II) is (–)2, shoulder (zone I) is (–)6, wrist is (–)6, spine/back (zone II) is (–)4, elbow (zone I) is (–)4 and elbow (zone II) is (–)3.

- If the partial-range variation 37.c is combined with the narrow-grip variation 37.b, the R/B values change as follows: shoulder (zone II) is (–) 6, shoulder (zone I) is (–) 2, wrist is (–) 2, spine/back (zone II) is (–) 4, elbow (zone I) is (–) 4 and elbow (zone II) is (–) 5.

Variation. 37.d — Target-Specific
BENEFIT (Weight Training Truth #1):
The addition of a shrug movement to the partial-range variation of the upright row (as shown) targets the deltoid and trapezius muscles (PA-L) in equal proportions. Thus, the benefits of exercise 36 remain the same, but all the risks of injury are significantly reduced.

RISK (Weight Training Truth #2):

R/B	Injury Site
(–) 4	Shoulders (Zone II — Top)
(–) 4	Shoulders (Zone I — Front)
(–) 4	Wrist
(–) 2	Spine/Back (Zone II -Upper)
(–) 4	Elbows (Zone I — Inside)
(–) 4	Elbows (Zone II — Outside)

NOTES:

- If the target-specific variation 37.d is combined with the wide-grip variation 37.a, the R/B values change as follows: shoulder (zone II) is (–) 2, shoulder (zone I) is (–) 6, wrist is (–) 6, spine/back (zone II) is (–) 2, elbow (zone I) is (–) 4 and elbow (zone II) is (–) 3.

- If the target-specific variation 37.d is used with the narrow-grip variation 37.b, the R/B values change as follows: shoulder (zone II) is (–) 6, shoulder (zone I) is (–) 2, wrist is (–) 2, spine/back (zone II) is(–) 2, elbow (zone I) is (–) 4 and elbow (zone II) is (–) 5.

Exercise 38: DUMBBELL LATERAL "FLARES"

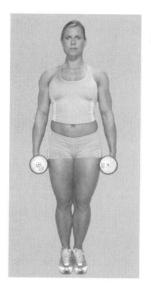

**Fig. 82.1:
Start/Finish**

BENEFIT (Weight Training Truth #1):
This is a defining exercise for the shoulders; the primary target (PA-L) is the rear region of the deltoid muscle.

HOW:

- Standing or sitting, hold the dumbbells vertically downward, with your palms facing each other.

- Maintain a slight arch in your lower back throughout; this is the start/finish position (figure 82.1).

- Following the plane of action (PA-D), without using any trapezius shrugging, lift your elbows up, back, and out simultaneously, such that the dumbbell path is vertical — pause briefly; this is the mid-phase position (figure 82.2).

- Smoothly return the dumbbells to the start/finish position.

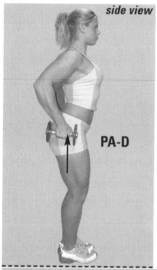

side view **Fig. 82.2:
Mid-Phase**

PA-D

RISK (Weight Training Truth #2):

R/B	Injury Site
6	Shoulders (Zone I -Front)
4	Shoulders (Zone II — Top)
5	Elbows (Zone II — Outside)

PA-L   *top view*

Figure 83
The Back

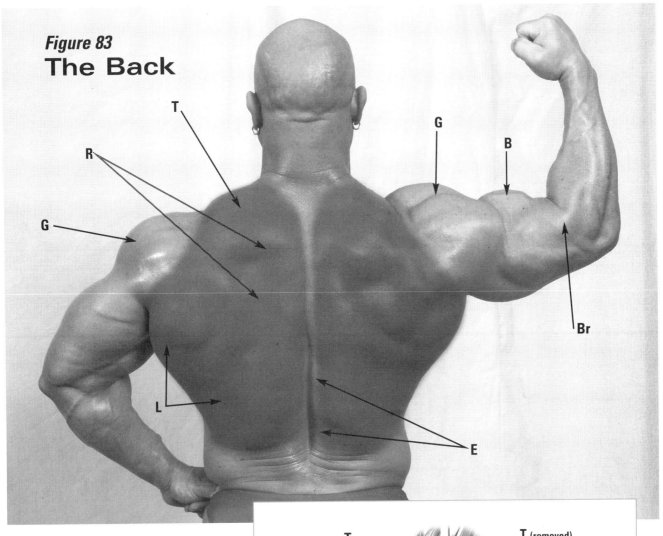

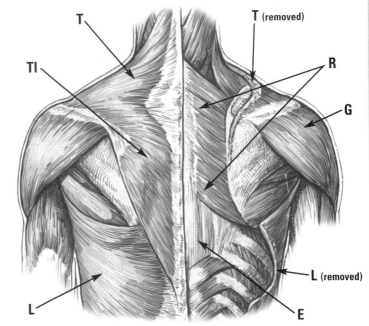

KEY:
E = Erector Spinales
L = Latissimus Dorsi
R = Rhomboid Muscles
T = Trapezius (Upper Region)
Tl = Trapezius (Lower Region)
G = General Deltoid
B = Biceps
Br = Brachioradialis

Table 3 — BACK EXERCISES

Name of Exercise/Variation	Benefit (WT #1)	R/B Values (WT #2)	No.	Pg.
Bent-Leg Deadlift (Barbell)	E, G-P	5, 6, 4, 4, 3	39	86
Bent-Leg Deadlift (Dumbbells)	E, G-P	6, 3, 4, 3	40	87
"Good Mornings"	E-Th, P	6	41	88
Lower Back Extensions ("Hyper")	E-Th, D	7, 6	42	89
Execution Variations:				
Half Range	E-Th, D	(−) 2	43.a	89
On Floor	E-Th, D	(−) 4, (−) 6	43.b	90
Machine Resistance	E-P, D	(−) 3, (−) 6	43.c	90
Bent-Over Rowing (Barbell)	R, L, T-P, Th	6, 5, 5, 4, 3, 7	44	91
Execution Variations:				
T-Bar	R, L, T-P, Th	(+) 1, (+) 1, (−) 1	45.a	92
Supported, T-Bar	R, L, T-P, Th	(−) 6, (−) 1, (−) 1	45.b	92
Seated Cable Rowing (Bar, Wide)	R, L-P, Th	6, 6, 4, 4, 3, 7	46	93
Execution Variation:				
"V" Grip	R, L-P, Th, S	(−) 1, (−) 1	47	94
Dumbbell Rowing	L, R-Th	4, 4, 3, 4, 3, 4	48	94
Execution Variation:				
Elbow Flare	R-P, Th	(+) 2	49	95
Execution Variations:				
All Bent-Over and Straight-Bar Seated Rows — Narrow Grip		(+) 1, (+) 2, (−) 2	50.a	96
All Bent-Over and Seated Rows — Toward Neck		(+) 2	50.b	96
Wide T-Bar and Seated Rowing — Palms-Facing Grip		(−) 3, (−) 2	50.c	96
Seated Rowing — Upright Torso		(−) 4, (−) 2	50.d	97
All Rowing Exercises — Target-Specific		(−) 5, (−) 7	50.e	97
Barbell and T-Bar Rowing — "Cheating"		(+) 2	50.f	98
"Good Mornings" and Standing Stiff-Arm Pulldowns — Lower Back Round-Out		(+) 4	50.g	98
Deadlifts and All Rowing Exercises — Full Spine Round-Out		(+) 4, (+) 3	50.h	99
The Single Deadly Sin of Weight Training				99
Deadlifts, "Good Mornings" and all Rowing Exercises — Locked Knees		(+) 8	50.i	100
Behind-Head Chin-ups	L-P, W	6, 6, 3, 4, 7, 5	51	101
Front Chin-ups	L-P, W	3, 3, 4, 7, 3	52	102
Reverse-Grip Chin-ups	B, L-P, S	5, 6, 6	53	103
Behind-Head Pulldowns	L-P, W	6, 6, 3, 4, 7, 5	54	104
Front Pulldowns	L-P, W	3, 3, 4, 7, 3	55	105
Reverse-Grip Pulldowns	B, L-P, S	5, 6, 6	56	106
Execution Variations:				
Behind-Head, Palms-Forward Chin-ups and Pulldowns — Narrow Grip		(+) 2, (+ 1), (−) 1, (−) 5	57.a	107
Front, Palms-Forward, Chin-ups and Pulldowns — Narrow Grip		(+) 2, (−) 1, (−) 3	57.b	107
Reverse-Grip Chin-ups and Pulldowns — Narrow Grip		(−) 2	57.c	107
Standing Stiff-Arm Pulldowns	L-P, Th	2, 5, 4	58	108
Execution Variation:				
Narrow Grip	L-S, Th	(+) 3	59	109
Shrugs — Barbell	T-P, Th	4, 3	60	110

Name of Exercise/Variation		Benefit (WT #1)	R/B Values (WT #2)	No.	Pg.
Execution Variations:					
Behind-the-Back		T, Tl-P, Th	(+) 7	61.a	111
Behind-the-Back, Narrow Grip		T-P, Th	(+) 9	61.b	111
One Palm Up and One Palm Down			(+) 4	61.c	111
Dumbbells		T-Th		61.d	112
Shoulder Rolling		R, T-Th	(+) 3	61.e	112
Upright Rowing		T, G-D	8, 10, 6, 5, 6, 6	36	79
Execution Variations:					
Narrow Grip		T, De-D	(−) 2, (+) 2, (+) 2, (−) 1	37.b	80
Execution Variations:					
All Deadlifts, Rowing,	— Hook Grip/Wrist Straps		(−) 3	62.a	113
Chin-ups, Pulldowns					
and Shrugs	— Elbow Flexion		(−) 4	62.b	113
Front Palms-Forward Chin-ups					
and Pulldowns	— Target-Specific		(−) 2, (−) 3	62.c(i)	114
Behind-Head, Palms-Forward					
Chin-ups and Pulldowns	— Target-Specific		(−) 2, (−) 2, (−) 3	62.c(ii)	114
Front Pulldowns (Palms-Forward					
and Reverse Grip)	— "Cheating"		(+) 7	62.d	115

KEY:

E = Erector Spinales

T = Trapezius (Upper Region)

B = Biceps *(see Table 5)*

W = Widen

S = Stretch

L = Latissimus Dorsi

Tl = Trapezius (Lower Region)

Br = Brachioradialis *(see Table 5)*

Th = Thicken

D = Define

R = Rhomboid Muscles

De = Deltoid *(see Table 2)*

P = Power

G = Gluteal

Exercise 39: BENT-LEG DEADLIFT (BARBELL)

Myths #6 & #7

Fig. 84.1: Start/Finish

PA-D

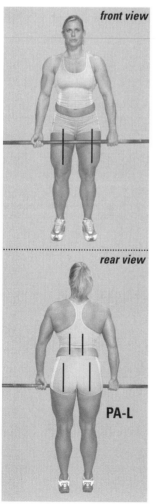

front view **Fig. 84.2: Mid-Phase**

rear view

PA-L

BENEFIT (Weight Training Truth #1):
This is a power-building exercise for the lower back; the primary target (PA-L) is the lower erector spinales muscles, while secondary targets include glutes and quads.

HOW:

• Stand with feet planted about twelve inches (thirty cm) apart, knees flexed ninety degrees and hips dropped down deeply.

• Grasp the bar with one palm facing forward and the other facing backward (for bar stability).

• Maintain a slight upward head tilt with a slight lower back arch throughout the entire exercise; this is the start/finish position (figure 84.1).

• Following the plane of action (PA-D), pull the bar straight up using your buttocks, legs and back — pause briefly in the upright stance; this is the mid-phase position (figure 84.2).

• Smoothly return the bar to the start/finish position.

• Optimal execution requires the upward path of the bar to be as close as possible to your shins, vertically, which is best accomplished by an initial leg "drive" from the bottom position, *not* by flexing the torso forward.

RISK (Weight Training Truth #2):

R/B	Injury Site
5	Spine/Back (Zone I — Lower)
6	Spine/Back (Zone II — Upper)
4	Knees
4	Elbow (of Palm-Up Side; Zone III — Front)
3	Elbows (Zone I — Inside)

VARIATIONS OF EXECUTION: Please see variations 50.h, 62.a, 62.b and 128.

Exercise 40: BENT-LEG DEADLIFT (DUMBBELLS)

Myths #6 & #7

Fig. 85.1: Start/Finish

PA-D

front view

Fig. 85.2: Mid-Phase

PA-L

rear view

PA-L

BENEFIT (Weight Training Truth #1):
This is a power-building exercise for the lower back; the primary target (PA-L) is the lower erector spinales muscles, while secondary targets include the gluteals and quads.

HOW:

- Begin with feet planted about ten inches (twenty-five cm) apart, knees flexed ninety degrees, and hips dropped down deeply enough to grasp two dumbbells (with your palms facing inward) on the floor; this is the start/finish position (fig. 85.1).

- Maintain a slight upward head tilt and a slight lower back arch throughout the entire exercise.

- Following the plane of action (PA-D) with the dumbbells, stand straight up using your legs and back — pause briefly in the upright stance; this is the mid-phase position (fig. 85.2).

- Smoothly return the dumbbells to the start/finish position.

- Optimal execution requires the path of the dumbbells to be vertical through your legs, which is best accomplished by an initial leg "drive" from the bottom position, *not* by flexing the torso.

RISK (Weight Training Truth #2):

R/B	Injury Site
6	Spine/Back (Zone I — Lower)
3	Spine/Back (Zone II — Upper)
4	Knees
3	Elbows (Zone I — Inside)

VARIATIONS OF EXECUTION: Please see variations 50.h and 62.a.

Exercise 41: "GOOD MORNINGS"

Myth #6

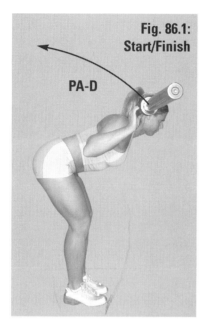

Fig. 86.1: Start/Finish

PA-D

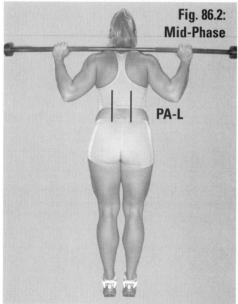

Fig. 86.2: Mid-Phase

PA-L

BENEFIT (Weight Training Truth #1):
This is a thickening and strengthening exercise for the lower back; the primary targets (PA-L) are the lower erector spinales muscles.

HOW:

- Stand with your feet planted about six inches (fifteen cm) apart, knees flexed about fifteen degrees, and a barbell rested across the top of the shoulders but not touching the spinal vertebrae.

- Bend your torso forward ninety degrees; this is the start/finish position (fig. 86.1).

- Keep your lower back slightly but firmly arched throughout.

- Following the plane of action (PA-D), smoothly raise your torso to the vertical position — pause briefly; this is the mid-phase position (fig. 86.2).

- Smoothly return the bar to the start/finish position.

RISK (Weight Training Truth #2):

R/B	Injury Site
6	Spine/Back (Zone I — Lower)

VARIATIONS OF EXECUTION: Please see variations 50.g and 50.i.

Exercise 42: LOWER BACK EXTENSIONS ("HYPER")

Myth # 15

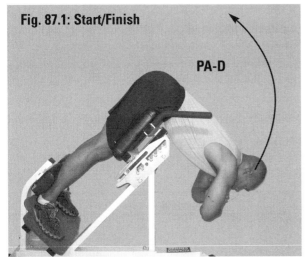

Fig. 87.1: Start/Finish

PA-D

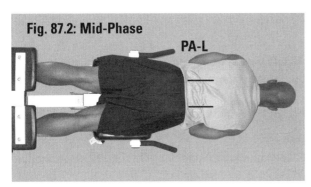

Fig. 87.2: Mid-Phase

PA-L

BENEFIT (Weight Training Truth #1):
This is a thickening and strengthening exercise for the lower back; the primary targets (PA-L) are the lower erector spinales muscles.

HOW:

- Begin with your legs positioned on the apparatus such that your hips are supported fully but your torso can still flex and extend fully at the waist.

- Cross your arms in front of you, grasping your elbows across your chest.

- Allow your upper body to flex down toward the floor as far as possible; this is the start/finish position (figure 87.1).

- Following the plane of action (PA-D), smoothly raise your torso as high as possible — pause briefly; this is the mid-phase position (figure 87.2).

- Smoothly return to the start/finish position.

RISK (Weight Training Truth #2):

R/B	Injury Site
7	Spine/Back (Zone I — Lower)
6	Hamstrings

VARIATIONS OF EXECUTION: See variations 43.a, 43.b.

LOWER BACK EXTENSION Execution Variations

**Fig. 88
Half Range**

Variation 43.a — Half Range
The risk of injuring the lower back can be reduced by only elevating your torso to the horizontal position — not higher.

RISK (Weight Training Truth #2):

R/B	Injury Site
(–) 2	Spine/Back (Zone I — Lower)

The other R/B value remains unchanged from exercise 42.

LOWER BACK EXTENSION Execution Variations cont'd

Fig. 89: On the Floor

Fig. 90.1: Start/Finish

Machine Resistance

Fig. 90.2: Mid-Phase

Variation 43.b — On the Floor

The risk of injuring the lower back can be further reduced, and the risk of injuring the hamstrings can be eliminated (relative to exercise 42), by lying prone on the floor and smoothly lifting just your head and shoulders off the floor. In this case, elbows are flared outward and the fingers are interlocked behind the head (figure 89).

RISK (Weight Training Truth #2):

R/B	Injury Site
(–) 4	Spine/Back (Zone I — Lower)
(–) 6	Hamstrings

Variation 43.c — Machine Resistance
BENEFIT (Weight Training Truth #1):

The use of a variable resistance machine (figs. 90.1, 90.2) allows for the development of power within the lower back erector spinales muscles (PA-L). This benefit is accompanied by a much reduced risk of lower back injury and the elimination of any risk of hamstring injury (relative to exercise 42).

RISK (Weight Training Truth #2):

R/B	Injury Site
(–) 3	Spine/Back (Zone I — Lower)
(–) 6	Hamstrings

Exercise 44: BENT-OVER ROWING (BARBELL)

Myth #6

**Fig. 91.1:
Start/Finish**

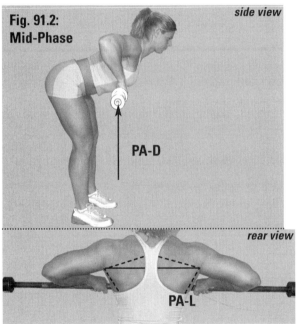

**Fig. 91.2:
Mid-Phase**

side view

PA-D

rear view

PA-L

BENEFIT (Weight Training Truth #1):

- This is a strengthening and thickening exercise for the mid-back; the primary targets (PA-L) are the rhomboid, upper trapezius, and latissimus dorsi muscles.

- There is also a considerable amount of bicep and brachioradialis muscle activity.

HOW:

- With feet placed shoulder-width apart, knees slightly bent, and torso flexed forward ninety degrees, grasp a barbell — palms down — with your hands placed just wider than shoulder width; this is the start/finish position (figure 91.1).

- Maintain a slight arch in your lower back throughout the exercise.

- Following the plane of action (PA-D), smoothly raise the bar until it touches your upper abdomen (at the bottom of your ribcage) — pause briefly; this is the mid-phase position (figure 91.2).

- Do not jerk the bar up.

- Do not alter your torso position throughout the exercise.

- Smoothly return the bar to the start/finish position.

RISK (Weight Training Truth #2):

R/B	Injury Site
6	Spine/Back (Zone I — Lower)
5	Spine/Back (Zone II — Upper)
5	Shoulders (Zone I — Front)
4	Elbows (Zone III — Front)
3	Elbows (Zone I — Inside)
7	Elbows (Zone II — Outside)

VARIATIONS OF EXECUTION: Please see variations 45.a, 45.b, 50.a, 50.b, 50.e, 50.f, 50.h, 50.i, 62.a and 62.b.

BENT-OVER ROWING (BARBELL) Execution Variations

**Fig. 92
T-Bar**

**Fig. 93
Supported
T-Bar**

Variation 45.a — T-Bar
Instead of the barbell, grasp a T-bar in a palms-down grip, hands spaced about eighteen inches (46 cm) apart, while standing on the platform provided (as shown in fig. 92). The exercise execution is otherwise the same as exercise 44.

RISK (Weight Training Truth #2):

R/B	Injury Site
(+) 1	Spine/Back (Zone II — Upper)
(+) 1	Shoulders (Zone I — Front)
(−) 1	Elbows (Zone II — Outside)
All other R/B values remain as in exercise 44.	

VARIATIONS OF EXECUTION: Please see variations 45.b, 50.a, 50.b, 50.c, 50.e, 50.f, 50.h, 50.i, 62.a and 62.b.

Variation 45.b — Supported T-Bar
The purpose of the chest-supported T-Bar rowing apparatus (as shown in fig. 93) is to remove the risk of lower back injury. The benefit and execution of the exercise are otherwise the same as exercise 44.

RISK (Weight Training Truth #2):

R/B	Injury Site
(−) 6	Spine/Back (Zone I — Lower)
(−) 1	Spine/Back (Zone II — Upper)
(−) 1	Elbows (Zone II — Outside)
All other R/B values remain as in exercise 44.	

VARIATIONS OF EXECUTION: Please see variations 50.a, 50.b, 50.e, 62.a, and 62.b.

Exercise 46: SEATED CABLE ROWING (STRAIGHT BAR/WIDE GRIP)

Myth #10

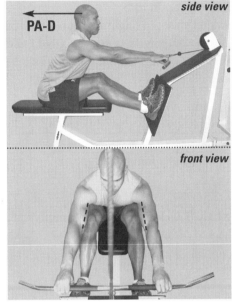

side view **Fig. 94.1:**
PA-D **Start/Finish**

front view

side view **Fig. 94.2:**
PA-D **Mid-Phase**

rear view

PA-L

BENEFIT (Weight Training Truth #1):

- This is a thickening and strengthening exercise for the mid-back; the primary target (PA-L) is the rhomboid muscle, and the secondary target is the latissimus dorsi muscle.
- There is also a considerable amount of bicep, brachioradialis and erector spinales muscle activity.

HOW:

- Brace your feet firmly and flex your knees moderately as you sit on the apparatus.
- Lean forward to grasp the bar with your palms down and about sixteen inches (forty cm) apart.
- Slightly arch your lower back and hold it firmly throughout; this is the start/finish position (figs. 94.1).
- Following the plane of action (PA-D), pull the bar toward your lower chest as you elevate your torso, lean backward slightly and squeeze your shoulder blades together.
- Keeping your elbows tight to your sides, pull the bar toward yourself until it touches your lower chest — pause briefly; this is the mid-phase position (figs. 94.2).
- Smoothly return the bar to the start/finish position.

RISK (Weight Training Truth #2):

R/B	Injury Site
6	Spine/Back (Zone I -Lower)
6	Spine/Back (Zone II — Upper)
4	Shoulders (Zone I — Front)
4	Elbows (Zone III — Front)
3	Elbows (Zone I — Inside)
7	Elbows (Zone II — Outside)

VARIATIONS OF EXECUTION: Please see variations 50.a, 50.b, 50.c, 50.d, 50.e, 50.h, 50.i, 62.a and 62.b.

* Seated individual arm pull instead

SEATED CABLE ROWING: Execution Variation 47 — "V" Grip

Myth #10

Fig. 95: "V" Grip

BENEFIT (Weight Training Truth #1):

The use of a "V" grip, rather than a straight bar during seated cable rowing adds a stretch component to the rhomboid and mid-latissimus muscles (PA-L). The exercise is otherwise performed as in exercise 46.

RISK (Weight Training Truth #2):

R/B	Injury Site
(–) 1	Shoulders (Zone I — Front)
(–) 1	Elbows (Zone II — Outside)

All other R/B values remain as in exercise 46.

VARIATIONS OF EXECUTION: Please see variations 50.b, 50.d, 50.e, 50.h, 50.i, 62.a and 62.b.

Exercise 48: DUMBBELL ROWING

Myths #6 & #7

Fig. 96.1: Start/Finish

PA-L

BENEFIT (Weight Training Truth #1):

- This is primarily a thickening exercise for the outer back region, but it also strengthens the mid-scapular region.

- The primary target (PA-L) is the latissimus dorsi muscle, and the secondary targets are the rhomboids, biceps and brachioradialis muscles.

HOW:

- Begin with your torso flexed forward ninety degrees with one hand and knee supported on a bench.

- Keep your lower back slightly arched throughout.

- Hold the dumbbell with your palm turned inward and your elbow fully extended; this is the start/finish position (figure 96.1).

- Following the plane of action (PA-D) while keeping your elbow close to your body, pull the dumbbell up until it is at waist level — pause briefly; this is the mid-phase position (figure 96.2).

- Do not jerk the dumbbell up.

- Smoothly return the dumbbell to the start/finish position. Repeat with the other arm.

(continues on next page)

(continued from previous page)

Fig. 96.2: Mid-Phase

side view

PA-D

rear view

PA-L

RISK (Weight Training Truth #2):

R/B	Injury Site
4	Spine/Back (Zone I — Lower)
4	Spine/Back (Zone II — Upper)
3	Shoulders (Zone I — Front)
4	Elbows (Zone III — Front)
3	Elbows (Zone I — Inside)
4	Elbows (Zone II — Outside)

VARIATIONS OF EXECUTION: Please see variations 49, 50.e, 50.h, 50.i, 62,a and 62.b.

DUMBBELL ROWING Execution Variation 49 — Elbow Flared Outward

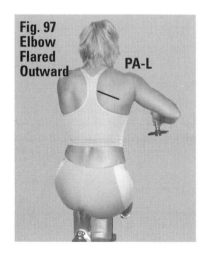

Fig. 97 Elbow Flared Outward

PA-L

BENEFIT (Weight Training Truth #1):
Rather than keeping your elbow close to your body, flare it out and away from your body as the weight is smoothly pulled as high as possible, adding a mid-scapular "squeeze" at the top. This primarily targets the rhomboid muscles (PA-L) for strengthening and thickening, with only moderate latissimus dorsi muscle participation. There is, with this change of execution, increased risk of injury to zone I of the shoulder.

RISK (Weight Training Truth #2):

R/B	Injury Site
(+) 2	Shoulders (Zone I — Front)
All other R/B values remain as in exercise 48.	

NOTE: Please see exercises/variations 50.h, 50.i, 62.a and 62.b.

ALL BENT-OVER & STRAIGHT-BAR SEATED ROW Execution Variations

Fig. 98
Narrow
Grip

Variation 50.a — Narrow Grip
BENEFIT (Weight Training Truth #1):
The performance of seated (straight-bar) rowing and bent-over rowing (barbell, T-Bar, and supported T-Bar varieties) with your hands placed close together (eight to twelve inches (twenty to thirty cm) apart) adds a stretch component for the rhomboid and the latissimus muscles (PA-L), while also altering the risks of injury.

RISK (Weight Training Truth #2):

R/B	Injury Site
(+) 1	Spine/Back (Zone II — Upper)
(+) 2	Shoulders (Zone I — Front)
(–) 2	Elbows (Zone II — Outside)
All other R/B values remain unchanged for that exercise.	

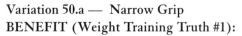

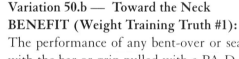

Variation 50.b — Toward the Neck
BENEFIT (Weight Training Truth #1):
The performance of any bent-over or seated rowing exercise, with the bar or grip pulled with a PA-D that approaches your chin, targets the rhomboid and mid-trapezius muscles (PA-L) for both stretch and strength components, while increasing the risk of injury in zone I of the shoulder.

RISK (Weight Training Truth #2):

R/B	Injury Site
(+) 2	Shoulders (Zone I -Front)
All other R/B values remain unchanged for that exercise.	

Fig. 99:
Toward
the Neck

NOTE: When performing a bent-over or seated rowing exercise with both the narrow grip (var. 50.a) and the toward-the-neck (var. 50.b) execution variations, the R/B value regarding zone I of the shoulders is altered by (+) 4.

WIDE T-BAR & SEATED ROWING Execution Variation 50.c — Palms-Facing Grip

Fig. 100:
Palms
Facing

BENEFIT (Weight Training Truth #1):
Performing a wide-grip T-Bar or a wide-grip seated rowing exercise with palms facing each other (see fig. 100) reduces the risks of injury while still maintaining the same muscle benefits.

RISK (Weight Training Truth #2):

R/B	Injury Site
(–) 3	Shoulders (Zone I — Front)
(–) 2	Elbows (Zone II — Outside)
All other R/B values remain unchanged for that exercise.	

ALL SEATED ROWING EXERCISES: Variation 50.d — Upright Torso

Fig. 101: Upright Torso

BENEFIT (Weight Training Truth #1):
Maintaining an upright and immobile torso during seated cable rowing exercises (i.e., not leaning forward or backward — see fig. 101) greatly diminishes the risk of injury to the lower and upper back, while diminishing the stretch benefit to the rhomboid and mid-latissimus muscles.

RISK (Weight Training Truth #2):

R/B	Injury Site
(–) 4	Spine/Back (Zone I — Lower)
(–) 2	Spine/Back (Zone II — Upper)
All other R/B values remain unchanged for that exercise.	

ALL ROWING EXERCISES: Execution Variation 50.e — Target-Specific Modification

PA-D

Fig. 102.1: Start/Finish

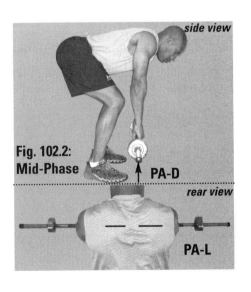

side view

Fig. 102.2: Mid-Phase   PA-D

rear view

PA-L

BENEFIT (Weight Training Truth #1):
All rowing exercises (44–48) use a considerable amount of bicep activity. The strength of the biceps, relative to the strength of the rhomboid, mid-trapezius and mid-latissimus muscles makes them the weak link between the grip and the target-muscle zone. By deliberately drawing the shoulder blades together (as shown) without using the biceps to flex the elbows, you can more directly, and more intensely, work the rhomboid muscle region (PA-L), while simultaneously reducing the risks of injury.

RISK (Weight Training Truth #2):

R/B	Injury Site
(–) 5	Shoulders (Zone I — Front)
(–) 7	Elbows (Zone II — Outside)

NOTES:

- The target-specific modification of seated rowing can only occur concurrent with the upright torso variation (var. 50.d), which makes the following R/B changes: spine/back (zone I) becomes 2, and back/spine (zone II) becomes 4.

- All other R/B values remain unchanged for bent-over and dumbbell rowing exercises when using this target-specific variation.

BARBELL AND T-BAR ROWING: Execution Variation 50.f — "Cheating"

Fig. 103.1

PA-D

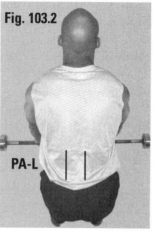

Fig. 103.2

PA-L

BENEFIT (Weight Training Truth #1):

"Cheating" during barbell or T-Bar bent-over rowing entails initiating movement of the bar with a jerk by the erector spinales muscles (PA-L). This adds more risk of injury to the lower back. Also see the discussion on cheating in Chapter 2.

RISK (Weight Training Truth #2):

R/B	Injury Site
(+) 2	Spine/Back (Zone I — Lower)

All other R/B values remain unchanged for that exercise.

"GOOD MORNINGS" & STANDING STIFF-ARM PULLDOWNS: Variation 50.g — Lower Back Round-Out

Myth #6

Fig. 104:
Lower Back Round-Out

BENEFIT (Weight Training Truth #1):

When performing "good mornings" or standing stiff-arm pulldowns, it is very important not to allow your lower back to curve backward (as shown). This is called "round-out." This body alignment unnecessarily increases the risk of injury in the lower back.

RISK (Weight Training Truth #2):

R/B	Injury Site
(+) 4	Spine/Back (Zone I — Lower)

All other R/B values remain unchanged for that exercise.

NOTE: Virtually all exercises that are performed standing or sitting present the opportunity for Lower Back Round-Out to occur. This makes zone I (lower) spine/back pain an extremely common (and unnecessary) weight-training injury.

DEADLIFTS & ALL ROWING EXERCISES: Execution Variation 50.h — Full Spine Round-Out

**Fig. 105.1:
Dead-Lift
(bar)**

When performing bent-leg dead-lifts, any variety of bent-over rowing, seated cable rowing, or dumbbell rowing, it is of critical importance not to allow your entire spine to "round out" (as shown). This body alignment puts you at high risk of injury, not only to the lower back, but also to the upper back region.

RISK (Weight Training Truth #2):

R/B	Injury Site
(+) 4	Spine/Back (Zone I — Lower)
(+) 3	Spine/Back (Zone II — Upper)

All other R/B values remain unchanged for that exercise.

**Fig. 105.2:
Bent-Over Rowing**

**Fig. 105.3:
Dead-lift
(Dumbbells)**

LOWER BACK ROUND-OUT IS THE SINGLE "DEADLY SIN" OF WEIGHT TRAINING

**Fig. 105.4:
Seated Rowing**

DEADLIFTS, "GOOD MORNINGS" & ALL ROWING EXERCISES:
Execution Variation 50.i — Locked Knees

**Fig. 106:
Locked Knees**

When performing deadlifts, "good mornings" or any style of rowing, if your knees are allowed to lock (as shown), considerable risk of injury to the hamstrings is added to the exercise.

RISK (Weight Training Truth #2):

R/B	Injury Site
(+) 8	Hamstrings
All other R/B values remain unchanged for that exercise.	

NOTE: When performing "good mornings" or any of the rowing exercises, if Lower Back Round-Out (var. 50.g or 50.h) is combined with locked knees (var. 50.i), the R/B value for the hamstrings becomes 10, and the R/B value for the lower back region becomes 10+.

This is the only exception to the R/B summation rule for the combining of execution variations. Lower Back Round-Out does not, in itself, create hamstring injury risk, just as locked knees in itself, does not create lower-back injury risk, but when combined they have a synergistic effect on both risk areas.

Exercise 51: BEHIND-HEAD CHIN-UPS

Myth #4

Fig. 107.1: Start/Finish

PA-D

PA-L

Fig. 107.2: Mid-Phase

rear view

top view

PA-L

BENEFIT (Weight Training Truth #1):

- This is a widening and strengthening exercise for the primary target, the latissimus dorsi muscles (PA-L).

- There is a moderate amount of bicep activity involved.

HOW:

- Begin by hanging by the arms from a chin-up station, placing your hands thirty inches (75 cm) apart, with the palms facing forward.

- Slightly flex your head forward.

- For balance, flex your knees and cross your lower legs behind you; this is the start/finish position (figure 107.1).

- Following the plane of action (PA-D), smoothly pull your body upward until the back of your head lightly touches the bar — pause briefly; this is the mid-phase position (figure 107.2).

- Smoothly lower yourself back to the start/finish position.

RISK (Weight Training Truth #2):

R/B	Injury Site
6	Shoulders (Zone II — Top)
6	Spine/Back (Zone II — Upper)
3	Elbows (Zone I — Inside)
4	Elbows (Zone III — Front)
7	Elbows (Zone II — Outside)
5	Shoulders (Zone III — at Chest)

VARIATIONS OF EXECUTION: Please see variations 57.a, 62.a, 62.b and 62.c(ii).

Exercise 52: FRONT CHIN-UPS

**Fig. 108.1:
Start/Finish**

side view

PA-D

PA-L

top view

PA-L

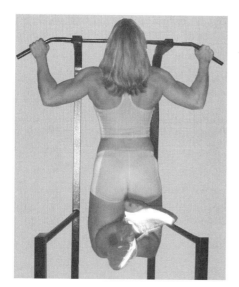

**Fig. 108.2:
Mid-Phase**

BENEFIT (Weight Training Truth #1):

- This is a widening and strengthening exercise for the latissimus dorsi muscles (PA-L).

- There is a moderate amount of bicep activity involved.

HOW:

- Begin by hanging by the arms at a chin-up station, placing your hands thirty inches (75 cm) apart, with the palms facing forward.

- Slightly retract your head.

- For balance, bend your knees and cross your lower legs behind you; this is the start/finish position (figure 108.1).

- Following the plane of action (PA-D), smoothly pull your body upward until your chin is just above the bar — pause briefly; this is the mid-phase position (figure 108.2).

- Smoothly lower yourself back to the start/finish position.

RISK (Weight Training Truth #2):

R/B	Injury Site
3	Shoulders (Zone II — Top)
3	Elbows (Zone I — Inside)
4	Elbows (Zone III — Front)
7	Elbows (Zone II — Outside)
3	Shoulders (Zone III — at Chest)

VARIATIONS OF EXECUTION: Please see variations 57.b, 62.a, 62.b and 62.c(i).

Exercise 53: REVERSE-GRIP CHIN-UPS

Fig. 109.1: Start/Finish

Fig. 109.2: Mid-Phase

BENEFIT (Weight Training Truth #1):

- This is a strengthening exercise for the biceps and wide back muscles; the primary targets (PA-L) are first, the biceps, and second, the latissimus dorsi muscles.

- There is good stretch of the lower bicep region, as well as a moderate latissimus stretch.

HOW:

- Begin by hanging by the arms at a chin-up station with your palms facing you, shoulder-width apart.

- Slightly retract your head.

- For balance, bend your knees and cross your lower legs behind you; this is the start/finish position (figure 109.1).

- Following the plane of action (PA-D), smoothly pull your body upward until you are at eye level with the bar — pause briefly; this is the mid-phase position (figure 109.2).

- Smoothly lower yourself back to the start/finish position.

RISK (Weight Training Truth #2):

R/B	Injury Site
5	Shoulders (Zone II — Top)
6	Elbows (Zone I — Inside)
6	Elbows (Zone III — Front)

VARIATIONS OF EXECUTION: Please see variations 57.c, 62.a, and 62.b.

Exercise 54: BEHIND-HEAD PULLDOWNS

Myth #4

Fig. 110.1: Start/Finish

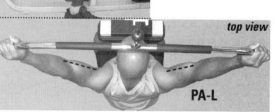

BENEFIT (Weight Training Truth #1):

- This is a widening and strengthening exercise for the wide back muscles; the primary target (PA-L) is the latissimus dorsi muscle.

- There is a moderate amount of bicep activity involved.

HOW:

- Extend your arms upward to grasp the bar with your hands thirty inches (seventy-five cm) apart and your palms facing forward.

- Adjust the seat elevation such that your knees are firmly braced under the supports.

- Slightly flex your head forward; this is the start/finish position (figure 110.1).

- Following the plane of action (PA-D), smoothly pull the bar down until it lightly touches the base of your neck — pause briefly; this is the mid-phase position (figure 110.2).

- Smoothly return the bar to the start/finish position.

RISK (Weight Training Truth #2):

R/B	Injury Site
6	Shoulders (Zone II — Top)
6	Spine/Back (Zone II — Upper)
3	Elbow (Zone I — Inside)
4	Elbows (Zone III — Front)
7	Elbows (Zone II — Outside)
5	Shoulders (Zone III — at Chest)

VARIATIONS OF EXECUTION: Please see variations 57.a, 62.a, 62.b and 62.c(ii).

Fig. 110.2: Mid-Phase

Exercise 55: FRONT PULLDOWNS

Myth #12

**Fig. 111.1:
Start/Finish**

PA-L

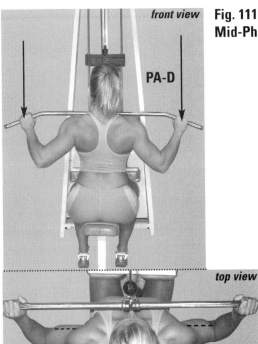

front view

PA-D

**Fig. 111.2:
Mid-Phase**

top view

PA-L

BENEFIT (Weight Training Truth #1):

- This is a stretching and strengthening exercise for the wide back muscles; the primary target (PA-L) is the latissimus dorsi muscle.

- There is a moderate amount of bicep activity involved, secondarily.

HOW:

- Extend your arms upward to grasp the bar with your hands thirty inches (seventy-five cm) apart and your palms facing forward.

- Adjust the seat elevation such that your knees are firmly braced under the supports.

- Slightly retract your head; this is the start/finish position (figure 111.1).

- Following the plane of action (PA-D), smoothly pull the bar down until the bar is two to three inches (five to eight cm) below your chin — pause briefly; this is the mid-phase position (figure 111.2).

- Do not lean backward (i.e., maintain an upright torso throughout).

- Smoothly return the bar to the start/finish position.

RISK (Weight Training Truth #2):

R/B	Injury Site
3	Shoulders (Zone II — Top)
3	Elbows (Zone I — Inside)
4	Elbows (Zone III — Front)
7	Shoulders (Zone II — Outside)
3	Shoulders (Zone III — at Chest)

VARIATIONS OF EXECUTION: Please see variations 57.b, 62.a, 62.b, 62.c(i) and 62.d.

Exercise 56: REVERSE-GRIP PULLDOWNS

Myth # 12

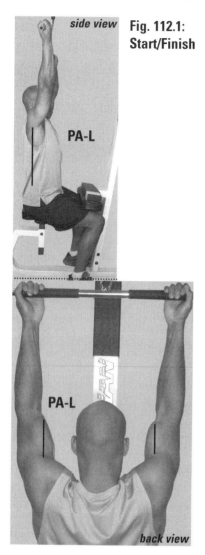

Fig. 112.1: Start/Finish

side view

PA-L

PA-L

back view

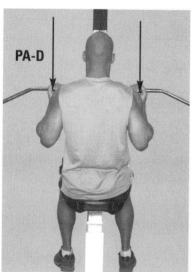

Fig. 112.2: Mid-Phase

PA-D

BENEFIT (Weight Training Truth #1):

- This is a strengthening exercise for the biceps and wide back muscles.
- The primary targets (PA-L) are the biceps and latissimus dorsi muscles.
- There is good stretch of the lower bicep region, as well as a moderate latissimus stretch.

HOW:

- Extend your arms up to grasp the bar shoulder-width apart, with your palms facing you.
- Adjust the seat elevation such that your knees are firmly braced under the supports.
- Slightly retract your head; this is the start/finish position (figure 112.1).
- Following the plane of action (PA-D), smoothly pull the bar down to two to three inches (five to eight cm) below your chin — pause briefly; this is the mid-phase position (figure 112.2).
- Do not lean backward (i.e., maintain an upright torso throughout).
- Smoothly return the bar to the start/finish position.

RISK (Weight Training Truth #2):

R/B	Injury Site
5	Shoulders (Zone II — Top)
6	Elbows (Zone I — Inside)
6	Elbows (Zone III — Front)

VARIATIONS OF EXECUTION: Please see variations 57.c, 62.a, 62.b and 62.d.

BEHIND HEAD, PALMS-FORWARD CHIN-UPS & PULLDOWNS:
Variation 57.a — Narrow Grip

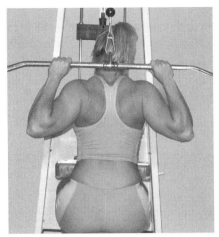

Fig. 113:
Narrow
Grip

BENEFIT (Weight Training Truth #1):
When performing palms-forward chin-ups and pulldowns (exercises 51 and 54), using a narrow grip on the bar (as shown) makes for both stretching and strengthening of the latissimus dorsi muscles, while also increasing the amount of bicep muscle activity. Several alterations of injury-risk accompany this variation of execution.

RISK (Weight Training Truth #2):

R/B	Injury Site
(+) 2	Shoulders (Zone II — Top)
(+) 1	Spine/Back (Zone II — Upper)
(–) 1	Elbows (Zone II — Outside)
(–) 5	Shoulders (Zone III — at Chest)

All other R/B values remain unchanged for that exercise.

FRONT, PALMS-FORWARD CHIN-UPS AND PULLDOWNS: Variation 57.b — Narrow Grip

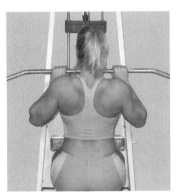

Fig. 114:
Narrow Grip

BENEFIT (Weight Training Truth #1):
In the performance of front, palms-forward chin-ups and pull-downs (exercises 52, 55), using a narrow grip on the bar (as shown) alters the purpose of the exercise to a combination of stretching and strengthening of the latissimus dorsi muscles, while decreasing the amount of bicep muscle activity. Several changes of injury-risk also accompany this variation.

RISK (Weight Training Truth #2):

R/B	Injury Site
(+) 2	Shoulders (Zone II — Top)
(–) 1	Elbows (Zone II — Outside)
(–) 3	Shoulders (Zone III — at Chest)

All other R/B values remain unchanged for that exercise.

REVERSE-GRIP CHIN-UPS AND PULLDOWNS: Variation 57.c — Narrow Grip

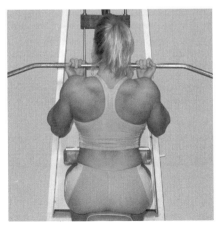

Fig. 115:
Narrow Grip

BENEFIT (Weight Training Truth #1):
Placing your hands six to eight inches apart (fifteen to twenty cm) as shown, reduces the risk of injury at zone II of the shoulder. Also, with this grip, the bicep muscles become the primary target, while the latissimus dorsi muscles are only slightly involved.

RISK (Weight Training Truth #2):

R/B	Injury Site
(–) 2	Shoulders (Zone II — Top)

All other R/B values remain unchanged for that exercise.

Exercise 58: STANDING STIFF-ARM PULLDOWNS

Fig. 116.1: Start/Finish

Fig. 116.2: Mid-Phase

BENEFIT (Weight Training Truth #1):

- This is a strengthening, and especially a thickening, exercise for the wide back muscles; the primary target (PA-L) is the latissimus dorsi muscle.

- Secondarily, there is considerable isometric activity of the abdominal and lower back muscles.

HOW:

- Stand facing a cable pulley system, about eighteen inches (45 cm) away.

- Grasp a bar, palms forward and shoulder-width apart, and hold the bar slightly above your head.

- Lean your torso forward about twenty to twenty-five degrees, and maintain this alignment throughout the exercise execution; this is the start/finish position (figure 116.1).

- While keeping a slight arch in your lower back and following the plane of action (PA-D), pull the bar down to approximately waist level, in front of your body — pause briefly; this is the mid-phase position (figure 116.2).

- Keep your elbows stiff, at a five- to ten-degree bend throughout.

- Smoothly return the bar to the start/finish position.

RISK (Weight Training Truth #2):

R/B	Injury Site
2	Shoulders (Zone II — Top)
5	Spine/Back (Zone I — Lower)
4	Elbows (Zone I — Inside)

VARIATIONS OF EXECUTION: Please see variations 59, 50.g and 62.a.

STANDING STIFF-ARM PULLDOWNS: Variation 59 — Narrow Grip

**Fig. 117.1
Narrow
Grip**

BENEFIT (Weight Training Truth #1):
The use of a narrow grip (less than ten inches/twenty-five cm apart — as shown) adds a latissimus dorsi muscle stretch to the exercise. However, this variation increases the risk of injury to zone II of the shoulders.

RISK (Weight Training Truth #2):

R/B	Injury Site
(+) 3	Shoulders (Zone II — Top)
All other R/B values remain unchanged for that exercise.	

Fig. 117.2

Exercise 60: SHRUGS (BARBELL)

Myths #6 & #7

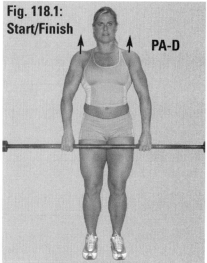

Fig. 118.1: Start/Finish

PA-D

side view **Fig. 118.2: Mid-Phase**

PA-D

top view

PA-L

BENEFIT (Weight Training Truth #1):
This is a strengthening and thickening exercise for the upper back and the base of the neck; the primary target (PA-L) is the upper region of the trapezius.

HOW:

• In an upright position, grasp the bar with your hands spaced just wider than your legs, palms-down.

• Look straight ahead and firmly hold a slight lower back arch throughout; this is the start/finish position (figure 118.1).

• Following the plane of action (PA-D), shrug your shoulders straight up toward your ears — pause briefly; this is the mid-phase position (figure 118.2).

• Keep your elbows straight throughout and do not roll your shoulders.

• Smoothly lower the bar to the start/finish position.

RISK (Weight Training Truth #2):

R/B	Injury Site
4	Back/Spine (Zone II — Upper)
3	Elbows (Zone I — Inside)

VARIATIONS OF EXECUTION: Please see variations 61.a, 61.b, 61.c, 61.e and 62.a.

SHRUGS Execution Variations

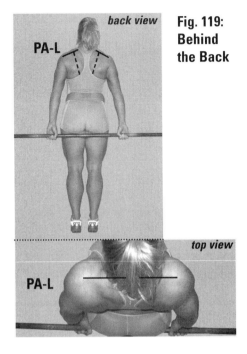

Fig. 119:
Behind
the Back

back view

PA-L

top view

PA-L

Variation 61.a — Behind the Back
BENEFIT (Weight Training Truth #1):
Performing barbell shrugs behind the back shortens the potential range of motion for scapular elevation and depression, which consequently demands more work by the lower region of the trapezius muscle (PA-L). Grasp the bar behind your back, with both palms facing backward, at shoulder width. This technique increases the risk of injury to zone I of the shoulders.

RISK (Weight Training Truth #2):

R/B	Injury Site
(+) 7	Shoulders (Zone I — Front)
All other R/B values remain as in exercise 60.	

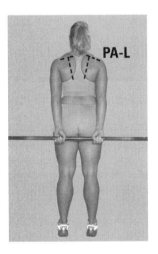

Fig. 120:
Behind the Back,
Narrow Grip

PA-L

Variation 61.b — Behind the Back, Narrow Grip
BENEFIT (Weight Training Truth #1)
In order to place more emphasis on the lower region of the trapezius muscle (PA-L), grasp the bar behind your back with your palms facing backward but spaced eight to ten inches (twenty to twenty-five cm) apart, as shown in figure 120. This technique does, however, add considerable risk of injury to zone I of the shoulders.

RISK (Weight Training Truth #2):

R/B	Injury Site
(+) 9	Shoulders (Zone I — Front)
All other R/B values remain as in exercise 60.	

Fig. 121:
One-Palm-Up,
One-Palm-Down Grip

Variation 61.c — One-Palm-Up and One-Palm-Down Grip
The use of the one-palm-up and one-palm-down grip (as shown) adds stability to the exercise, in that it prevents body or bar tilt or twist. This can be hard to control, especially as heavier weights are used with both hands palm-down.

RISK (Weight Training Truth #2):

R/B	Injury Site
(+) 4	Elbows (Zone III — Front; palm-up side only)
All other R/B values remain as in exercise 60.	

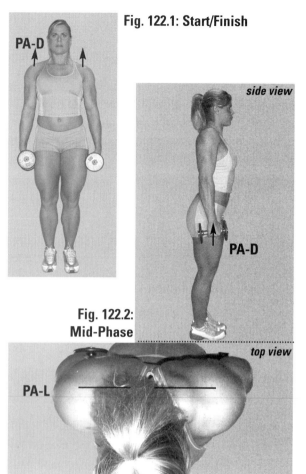

Fig. 122.1: Start/Finish

Fig. 122.2: Mid-Phase

side view

top view

PA-D

PA-L

Variation 61.d — Dumbbells
BENEFIT (Weight Training Truth #1):
This is a thickening exercise for the upper back and base of the neck; the primary target (PA-L) is the upper region of the trapezius muscles.

HOW:

* Standing with feet about six inches (fifteen cm) apart, grasp the dumbbells with palms facing each other.

* Rest the dumbbells against the front, outer part of your thighs.

* Look straight ahead and firmly hold a slight lower back arch throughout; this is the start/finish position (figure 122.1).

* Following the plane of action (PA-D), shrug both shoulders straight up toward your ears — pause briefly; this is the mid-phase position (figure 122.2).

* Keep your elbows straight throughout and do not roll your shoulders.

* Smoothly return the dumbbells to the start/finish position.

RISK (Weight Training Truth #2):
All R/B values remain as in exercise 60.

VARIATIONS OF EXECUTION: Please see variations 61.e and 62.a.

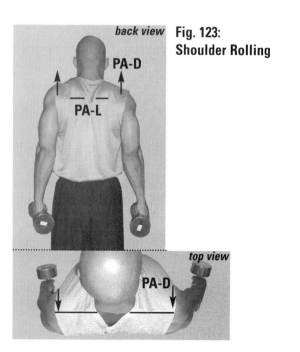

back view

Fig. 123: Shoulder Rolling

PA-D

PA-L

top view

PA-D

Variation 61.e — Shoulder Rolling   *Myths #5 & #6*
BENEFIT (Weight Training Truth #1):
If a backward shoulder-rolling motion (PA-D) is incorporated as the weight is being shrugged upward, the target muscles become the rhomboids as much as the lower portion of the trapezius (PA-L). Unfortunately, this creates a greater risk of injury in zone II of the spine/back. (Forward shoulder rolling, on the other hand, serves no real purpose.)

RISK (Weight Training Truth #2):

R/B	Injury Site
(+) 3	Spine/Back (Zone II — Upper)

All other R/B values remain unchanged for that exercise.

ALL DEADLIFT, ROWING, SHRUG, CHIN-UP & PULLDOWN Execution Variations

**Fig. 124.1:
Hook Grip**

**Fig. 124.2:
Wrist Strap**

**Fig. 125:
Elbow Flexion**

Variation. 62.a — Hook Grip or Wrist Straps

A frequent contributing factor toward injury of zone I of the elbow is the hard isometric contraction of the wrist flexor muscles while the back muscles execute the exercise. During such pulling exercises, wrist flexor muscle strain is common. To both prevent and to "train around" this pain, use one of two solutions — finger "hook" grip, or wrist straps.

The finger "hook" grip requires practice, in that only the hand muscles grasp tightly in a hook-like configuration, while deliberately relaxing the forearm muscles throughout the exercise (fig. 124.1).

Wrist straps are designed to loop your wrist and wrap the bar, thus eliminating hard forearm muscle contractions (fig. 124.2).

RISK (Weight Training Truth #2):

R/B	Injury Site
(–) 3	Elbows (Zone I — Inside)
All other R/B values remain unchanged for that exercise.	

Variation. 62.b — Elbow Flexion

For exercises that begin with the elbows fully extended, there is a moderate risk of straining zone III of the elbows. This risk is greatly diminished by ensuring that full elbow extension does not occur at the start/finish position. Always hold a five to ten degree angle of flexion at your elbows (as shown).

RISK (Weight Training Truth #2):

R/B	Injury Site
(–) 4	Elbows (Zone III — Front)
All other R/B values remain unchanged for that exercise.	

FRONT PALMS-FORWARD CHIN-UPS & PULLDOWNS
Variation 62.c(i) — Target-Specific (Partial Range)

Myth #12

Fig. 126.1;
Mid-Phase

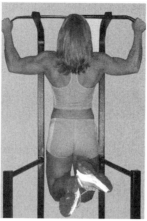

Fig. 126.2;
Mid-Phase

The palms-forward front pulldown and chin-up exercises described in exercises 52 and 55 use a considerable amount of bicep activity. The strength of the biceps, relative to the latissimus dorsi muscles, makes them the "weak link" between the grip and the target muscles. Pulling down with your elbows — not your hands — keeps your biceps relatively inactive. This will result in a shorter range of motion (as shown in figures 126.1 and 126.2) and will more directly, and more intensely, work the latissimus muscles while reducing the risks of injury.

RISK (Weight Training Truth #2):

R/B	Injury Site
(–) 2	Shoulders (Zone II — Top)
(–) 3	Elbows (Zone II — Outside)

All other R/B values remain unchanged for that exercise.

BEHIND-THE-HEAD, PALMS-FORWARD CHIN-UPS AND PULLDOWNS
Variation 62.c(ii) — Target-Specific (Partial Range)

Myth #12

Fig. 127.1;
Mid-Phase

Fig. 127.2:
Mid-Phase

BENEFIT (Weight Training Truth #1):
The palms-forward, behind-the-head pulldown and chin-up exercises described in exercises 51 and 54 use a considerable amount of bicep activity. The strength of the biceps, relative to the latissimus dorsi muscles, makes them the "weak link" between the grip and the target muscles. Pulling down with your elbows — not your hands — keeps your biceps relatively inactive. This results in a shorter range of motion (as shown) and will more directly, and more intensely, work the latissimus dorsi muscles while reducing the risks of injury.

RISK (Weight Training Truth #2):

R/B	Injury Site
(–) 2	Shoulders (Zone II — Top)
(–) 2	Spine/Back (Zone II — Upper)
(–) 3	Elbows (Zone II — Outside)

All other R/B values remain unchanged for that exercise.

FRONT PULLDOWNS (PALMS-FORWARD AND REVERSE GRIP)
Variation. 62.d — "Cheating"

Myth #17

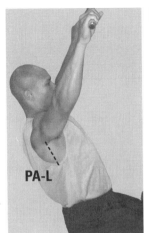

**Fig. 128.1:
Cheating**

**Fig. 128.2:
Cheating**

BENEFIT (Weight Training Truth #1):

"Cheating" on front pulldowns (palms-forward and reverse grip — exercises 55 and 56) entails an initiation of the bar movement by a forceful pull or lean backward by the lower back erector muscles. Not only does this put the lower back region at risk of injury, but it considerably alters the plane of action. This changes the target muscles (PA-L) for the palms-forward pulldown from the lats to the mid scapular and erector spinales, and for the reverse-grip pulldowns from the biceps to the mid-scapular and erector spinales muscles. (Also, see the discussion of cheating under weight-training shortcuts in Chapter 2.)

RISK (Weight Training Truth #2):

R/B	Injury Site
(+) 7	Spine/Back (Zone I — Lower)

All other R/B values remain unchanged for that exercise.

Figure 129
The Abdominals

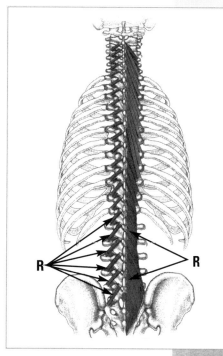

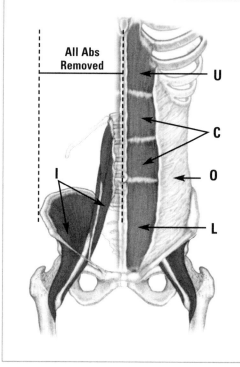

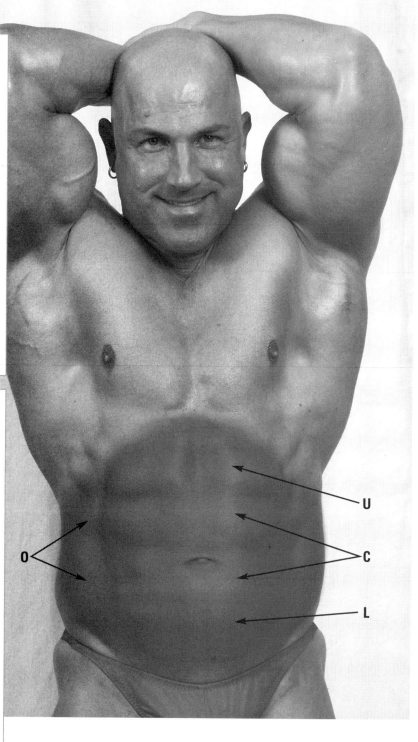

KEY:

U = Upper Abdominals   C = Central Abdominals   L = Lower Abdominals

O = Oblique Abdominals   R = Lumbar Rotators   I = Iliopsoas

Table 4 — ABDOMINAL EXERCISES

Name of Exercise/Variation		Benefit (WT#1)	R/B Values (WT #2)	No.	Pg.
Supine Straight Leg-Lifts		I-S + L-D	7	63	118
Hanging Straight Leg-Lifts		I-S + L-D	7	64	119
Supine Bent-Knee Leg-Lifts		I-S + L-D	7	65	120
Hanging Bent-Knee Leg-Lifts		I-S + L-D	7	66	121
Supine Bent-Knee Sit-Ups		I, C-D, S	6	67	122
Inclined Bent-Knee Sit-Ups		I, C-D, S	6	68	123
Supine Bent-Knee "V" Crunches		L, C, U-D, S	5	69	124
Execution Variation: Seated		L, C, U-D, S	(–) 2	70	125
Torso Twists	— Standing	O, R-D, S	6	71	126
Execution Variation: Seated		O, R-D, S	(–) 1	72	127
Crunches	— Supine/On Floor	C, U-D, S	2	73	128
Execution Variation: Mechanically Assisted		C, U-D, S	(–) 1	74	128
Cable Crunches		C, U-D, S	4	75	129
Reverse Crunches		L-D, S	2	76	130
Standing Oblique Crunches		O-D, S	2	77	131
Execution Variations: Situps	— Torso Twist	O-D, S	(–) 3	78.a	132
Crunches	— Torso Twist	O-D, S		78.b	132
Sit-Ups and Supine Crunches	— Neck Flexion		(+) 9	78.c	133
Torso Twists	— Head Rotation		(+) 5	78.d	133
	— Forward Lean (seated)	O-D, S	(+) 2	78.e	134
	— Forward Lean (standing)	O-D, S	(+) 2, (+) 2	78.e	134
Standing Torso Twists	— Locked Knees		(+) 4	78.f	134
Torso Twists and Standing Oblique Crunches	— Lower Back Round-Out		(+) 3	78.g	135
All Leg Lifts	— Pelvic "Crunch"	L-D, S		78.h	136

KEY:

U = Upper Abdominals   C = Central Abdominals   L = Lower Abdominals
O = Oblique Abdominals   I = Iliopsoas   R = Lumbar Rotators
D = Definition   S = Strength

Exercise 63: SUPINE STRAIGHT-LEG LIFTS

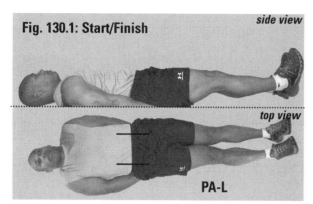

Fig. 130.1: Start/Finish *side view*

top view

PA-L

Fig. 130.2: Mid-Phase

PA-D

BENEFIT (Weight Training Truth #1):

- This is a hip flexor muscle exercise; the primary target (PA-L) is the iliopsoas muscle.

- There is only secondary isometric activity of the lower abdominal muscles, providing some definition benefit.

HOW:

- Lie on your back with your hands palm-down beneath your buttocks.

- Keep knees straight, head on the floor, ankles together, and heels about two inches (five cm) above the floor; this is the start/finish position (figure 130.1).

- Following the plane of action (PA-D), raise your heels off the floor — pause briefly; this is the mid-phase position (figure 130.2).

- Keep your knees locked throughout the exercise.

- Smoothly return your feet to the start/finish position.

RISK (Weight Training Truth #2):

R/B	Injury Site
7	Spine/Back (Zone I — Lower)

Exercise 64: HANGING STRAIGHT-LEG LIFTS

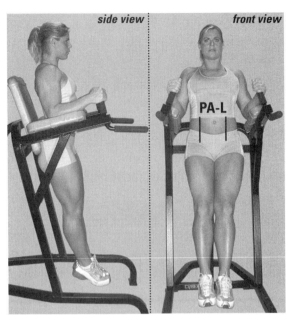

Fig. 131.1: Start/Finish

Fig. 131.2: Mid-Phase

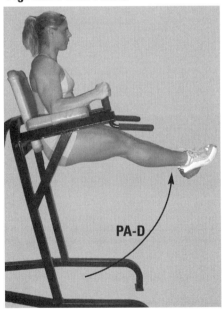

BENEFIT (Weight Training Truth #1):

- This is a hip flexor muscle exercise; the primary target (PA-L) is the iliopsoas muscle.

- There is only secondary isometric activity of the lower abdominal muscles, which provides some definition benefit.

HOW:

- Position yourself on a dip station with your buttocks placed firmly against the cushion and a slight arch in your lower back.

- Keep your knees straight and your ankles together; this is the start/finish position (figure 131.1).

- Following the plane of action (PA-D) raise your legs until they are horizontal —pause briefly; this is the mid-phase position (figure 131.2).

- Keep your knees locked throughout the exercise.

- Smoothly return your legs to the start/finish position.

RISK (Weight Training Truth #2):

R/B	Injury Site
7	Spine/Back (Zone I — Lower)

No!

Exercise 65: SUPINE BENT-KNEE LIFTS

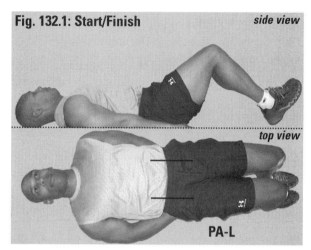

Fig. 132.1: Start/Finish   *side view*

top view

PA-L

Fig. 132.2: Mid-Phase

PA-D

BENEFIT (Weight Training Truth #1):

- This is a hip flexor muscle exercise; the primary target (PA-L) is the iliopsoas muscle.

- There is only secondary isometric activity of the lower abdominal muscles that provides some definition benefit.

HOW:

- Lie on your back with your hands palm-down beneath your buttocks and your heels resting on the floor.

- Keep your knees bent at ninety degrees and your ankles together; this is the start/finish position (figure 132.1).

- Following the plane of action (PA-D), raise your thighs upward until they are vertical — pause briefly; this is the mid-phase position (figure 132.2).

- Smoothly return your legs to the start/finish position.

RISK (Weight Training Truth #2):

R/B	Injury Site
7	Spine/Back (Zone I — Lower)

Exercise 66: HANGING BENT-KNEE LEG-LIFTS

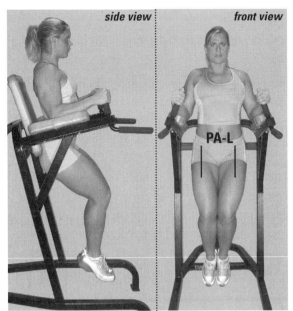

side view   *front view*

PA-L

Fig. 133.1: Start/Finish

BENEFIT (Weight Training Truth #1):

- This is a hip flexor muscle exercise.
- The primary target (PA-L) is the iliopsoas muscle.
- There is only secondary isometric activity of the lower abdominal muscles that provides some definition benefit.

HOW:

- Position yourself on a dip station with your buttocks placed firmly against the cushion and a slight arch in your lower back.
- Keep your knees bent to ninety degrees and your ankles together; this is the start/finish position (figure 133.1).
- Following the plane of action (PA-D), raise your thighs upward until they are horizontal — pause briefly; this is the mid-phase position (figure 133.2).
- Smoothly return your legs to the start/finish position.

RISK (Weight Training Truth #2):

R/B	Injury Site
7	Spine/Back (Zone I — Lower)

Fig. 133.2: Mid-Phase

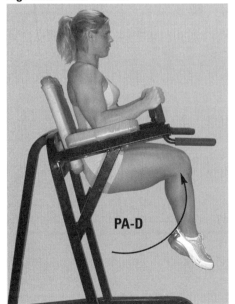

PA-D

Exercise 67: SUPINE BENT-KNEE SIT-UPS

Myth #3

Fig. 134.1: Start/Finish *side view*

top view

PA-L

Fig. 134.2: Mid-Phase

PA-D

BENEFIT (Weight Training Truth #1):

- This exercise strengthens both the hip flexors and the lower spine flexors.
- The primary targets (PA-L) are the iliopsoas and the central abdominal muscles.

HOW:

- Lie on your back, knees bent to ninety degrees and feet flat on the floor.
- Your feet can be held down or left free.
- Clench your hands and wedge them between your chin and chest with your elbows pointed toward your hips; this is the start/finish position (figure 134.1).
- Following the plane of action (PA-D), smoothly curl your body into an upright position; this is the mid-phase position (figure 134.2).
- Do not jerk up or flop back down; smoothly return to the start/finish position.

RISK (Weight Training Truth #2):

R/B	Injury Site
6	Spine/Back (Zone I — Lower)

VARIATIONS OF EXECUTION: Please see variations 78.a and 78.c.

Exercise 68: INCLINED BENT-KNEE SIT-UPS

Myth #3

Fig. 135.1: Start/Finish

side view

top view

PA-L

BENEFIT (Weight Training Truth #1):

- This exercise strengthens both the hip flexors and the lower spine flexors.
- The primary targets (PA-L) are the iliopsoas and the central abdominal muscles.

HOW:

- Lie on your back on an inclined abdominal board (elevation is variable — the steeper the incline, the more difficult the exercise).
- Flex your knees ninety degrees and secure your feet.
- Clench your hands and wedge them between your chin and chest, with your elbows pointed toward your hips; this is the start/finish position (figure 135.1).
- Following the plane of action (PA-D), smoothly curl your body into an upright position; this is the mid-phase position (figure 135.2).
- Do not jerk up or flop back down; smoothly return to the start/finish position.

RISK (Weight Training Truth #2):

R/B	Injury Site
6	Spine/Back (Zone I — Lower)

VARIATIONS OF EXECUTION: Please see variations 78.a and 78.c.

Fig. 135.2: Mid-Phase

PA-D

Exercise 69: SUPINE BENT-KNEE "V" CRUNCHES

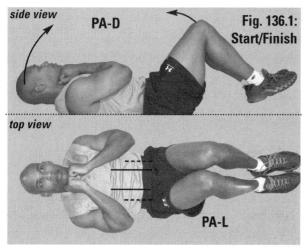

side view — PA-D — **Fig. 136.1: Start/Finish**

top view — PA-L

Fig. 136.2: Mid-Phase

BENEFIT (Weight Training Truth #1):

- This exercise strengthens all the abdominal regions.

- The primary targets (PA-L) are the lower, central and upper abdominal muscles; only slight hip flexor muscle (iliopsoas) activity is involved.

HOW:

- Lie on your back on the floor, knees slightly flexed and feet two to three inches (five to eight cm) above the floor.

- Clench your hands and wedge them between your chin and chest, with your elbows pointed downward; this is the start/finish position (figure 136.1).

- Following the plane of action (PA-D), simultaneously bring your knees up toward your chest and curl your torso upright — pause briefly; this is the mid-phase position (figure 136.2).

- Do not jerk up or flop back down; smoothly roll back, and partially straighten your knees into the start/finish position.

RISK (Weight Training Truth #2):

R/B	Injury Site
5	Spine/Back (Zone I — Lower)

VARIATIONS OF EXECUTION: Please see variation 70.

BENT-KNEE "V" CRUNCHES Execution Variation 70 — **Seated**

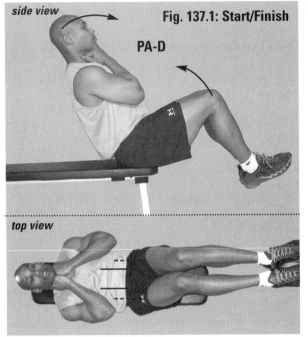

side view

Fig. 137.1: Start/Finish

PA-D

top view

HOW:

- Balance yourself on the end of a bench, with your hips and knees flexed and your torso leaning backwards, slightly (as shown).

- Clench your hands and wedge them between your chest and chin.

- Keep your feet together and your knees at a ninety-degree angle throughout; this is the start/finish position (figure 137.1).

- Following the plane of action (PA-D), simultaneously lift your thighs and curl your torso forward (smoothly enough to maintain your balance) — pause briefly; this is the mid-phase position (figure 137.2).

- Smoothly return to the start/finish position.

RISK (Weight Training Truth #2):

R/B	Injury Site
(–) 2	Spine/Back (Zone I — Lower)

Fig. 137.2: Mid-Phase

No

Exercise 71: STANDING TORSO TWISTS

Myth #14

Fig. 138.1: Start/Finish

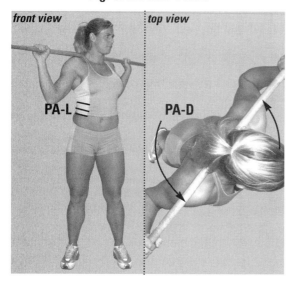

Fig. 138.2: Mid-Phase

front view   top view

PA-L   PA-D

BENEFIT (Weight Training Truth #1):
This exercise strengthens and defines the torso rotation muscles; the primary targets (PA-L) are the oblique abdominal muscles and the deep lumbar rotator muscles.

HOW:

- Standing with your feet eighteen inches (45 cm) apart, hold a broom handle across the top of your shoulders; slightly bend your knees.

- Maintain a slight lower back arch with an otherwise upright torso; this is the start/finish position (figure 138.1).

- Following the plane of action (PA-D), gently turn your torso to one side as far as possible — pause briefly; this is the mid-phase position (figure 138.2).

- Keep the broom handle motion on the horizontal plane.

- Do not over twist and do not use a forced or jerky motion.

- Smoothly return to the start/finish position and repeat in the opposite direction.

RISK (Weight Training Truth #2):

R/B	Injury Site
6	Spine/Back (Zone I — Lower)

VARIATIONS OF EXECUTION: Please see variations 72, 78.d, 78.e, 78.f, and 78.g.

TORSO TWISTS Execution Variation 72 — Seated

Myth #14

Fig. 139.1: Start/Finish

Fig. 139.2: Mid-Phase

front view

PA-L

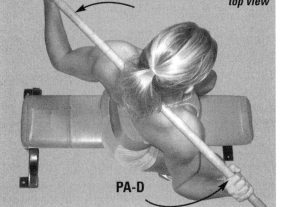

top view

PA-D

HOW:

• In a seated upright-torso position (preferably straddling a bench, which immobilizes your hips), hold a broom handle across the top of your shoulders; this is the start/finish position (figure 139.1).

• Following the plane of action (PA-D), gently turn your torso to one side as far as possible — pause briefly, this is the mid-phase position (figure 139.2).

• Keep the broom handle motion on the horizontal plane and maintain a slight lower back arch throughout.

• Do not over twist or use a forced or jerky motion.

• Smoothly return the broom handle to the start/finish position and then repeat in the opposite direction.

RISK (Weight Training Truth #2):

R/B	Injury Site
(–) 1	Spine/Back (Zone I — Lower)

VARIATIONS OF EXECUTION: Please see variations 78.d, 78.e, and 78.g.

Exercise 73: CRUNCHES (SUPINE/ON FLOOR)

Fig. 140.1: Start/Finish

side view
top view

PA-L

BENEFIT (Weight Training Truth #1):

• This exercise strengthens and defines the upper two-thirds of the abdominal region; the target muscles (PA-D) are the central and upper abdominal muscles.

• Hip flexor muscle (iliopsoas) activity is negligible during this exercise.

HOW:

• Lie on your back on the floor with your knees and hips flexed to ninety degrees.

• Your lower legs can either be rested on a bench or held in the air (crossed, for balance).

• Clench your hands and wedge them between your chest and chin, with your elbows pointed toward your hips; this is the start/finish position (figure 140.1).

• Following the plane of action (PA-D), slowly curl your torso upward as high as possible — pause briefly; this is the mid-phase position (figure 140.2).

• Keep your hips and legs motionless throughout.

• Do not jerk up or flop back down; smoothly return to the start/finish position.

Fig. 140.2: Mid-Phase

PA-D

RISK (Weight Training Truth #2):

R/B	Injury Site
2	Spine/Back (Zone I — Lower)

VARIATIONS OF EXECUTION: Please see variations 74, 78.b and 78.c.

CRUNCHES Execution Variation 74 — Mechanically Assisted

Fig. 142

The use of a mechanical device for abdominal strengthening (as shown) simplifies the execution of the crunch by using upper torso muscles. There is a resulting slight decrease in the risk of lower back injury.

RISK (Weight Training Truth #2):

R/B	Injury Site
(–) 1	Spine/Back (Zone I — Lower)

Exercise 75: CABLE CRUNCHES

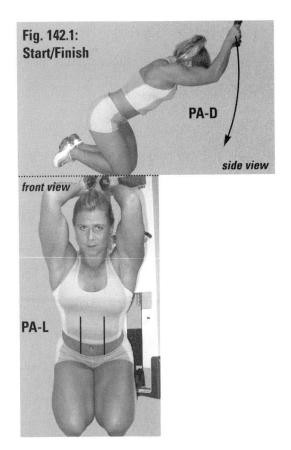

Fig. 142.1:
Start/Finish

PA-D

side view

front view

PA-L

Fig. 142.2: Mid-Phase

BENEFIT (Weight Training Truth #1):

- This exercise strengthens and defines the upper two-thirds of the abdominal region; the primary targets (PA-D) are the central and upper abdominal muscles.
- Hip flexor muscle (iliopsoas) activity is negligible.

HOW:

- Kneel on the floor in front of a cable pulldown machine.
- Hold a rope grip anywhere from above your head to just below your chin, with your elbows and shoulders locked; this is the start/finish position (figure 142.1).
- Following the plane of action (PA-D), smoothly curl your torso forward and downward — pause briefly; this is the mid-phase position (figure 142.2).
- Keep your knees bent to ninety degrees throughout.
- Do not jerk your torso downward; smoothly return to the start/finish position.

RISK (Weight Training Truth #2):

R/B	Injury Site
4	Spine/Back (Zone I — Lower)

VARIATIONS OF EXECUTION: Please see variaion 78.b.

Exercise 76: REVERSE CRUNCHES

Fig. 143.1: Start/Finish

PA-D

side view

top view

PA-L

Fig. 143.2: Mid-Phase

PA-D

BENEFIT (Weight Training Truth #1):

- This exercise strengthens and defines the lower third of the abdominal region; the primary target (PA-L) is the lower abdominal muscle region.

- Hip flexor (iliopsoas) muscle activity is negligible.

HOW:

- Lie on your back on the floor with your knees and hips flexed to ninety degrees.

- Your lower legs are held in the air, preferably crossed below the knees for stability.

- Place your palms down on the floor, partially under your buttocks; this is the start/finish position (figure 143.1).

- Following the plane of action (PA-D), lift your hips up off the floor about three to four inches (eight to ten cm) and squeeze your thighs into your abdomen — pause briefly; this is the mid-phase position (figure 143.2).

- Do not curl your torso or head upward.

- Keep your knee angle constant throughout the exercise.

- Smoothly return to the start/finish position.

RISK (Weight Training Truth #2):

R/B	Injury Site
2	Spine/Back (Zone I — Lower)

Exercise 77: STANDING OBLIQUE CRUNCHES

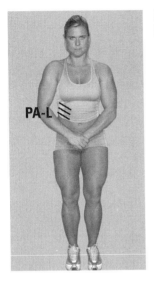

Fig. 144.1:
Start/Finish

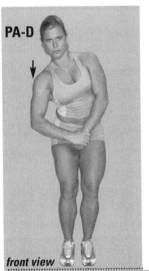

Fig. 144.2:
Mid-Phase

front view

top view

BENEFIT (Weight Training Truth #1):
This exercise strengthens and defines the outer and side abdominal regions; the primary targets (PA-L) are the oblique abdominal muscles.

HOW:

• Stand with your feet apart and flex your torso forward about twenty degrees.

• Clasp your hands together about three inches (eight cm) in front of your abdomen.

• Lock your arms and hands firmly in place; this is the start/finish position (figure 144.1).

• Following the plane of action (PA-D), slowly but firmly bend your torso sideways and slightly forward, squeezing your rib cage toward your pelvis as firmly as possible — pause briefly; this is the mid-phase position (figure 144.2).

• Smoothly return to the start/finish position; repeat in the opposite direction.

RISK (Weight Training Truth #2):

R/B	Injury Site
2	Spine/Back (Zone I — Lower)

VARIATIONS OF EXECUTION: Please see variation 78.g.

SIT-UPS Execution Variation 78.a — Torso Twist

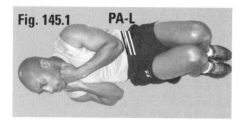

Fig. 145.1   PA-L

Fig. 145.2

PA-D

BENEFIT (Weight Training Truth #1):
This execution variation strengthens and defines the outer and side abdominal regions; the primary targets (PA-L) are the oblique abdominal muscles.

HOW:
This is performed essentially as in exercises 67 and 68, but your torso is twisted about forty-five degrees at the start of the motion, then twisted forty-five degrees in the opposite direction for the next repetition.

RISK (Weight Training Truth #2):

R/B	Injury Site
(–) 3	Spine/Back (Zone I — Lower)

CRUNCHES Execution Variation 78.b — Torso Twist

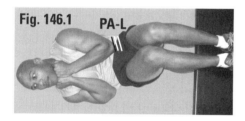

Fig. 146.1   PA-L

Fig. 146.2

PA-D

BENEFIT (Weight Training Truth #1):
This execution variation strengthens and defines the outer and side abdominal regions; the primary targets (PA-L) are the oblique abdominal muscles.

HOW:
This is performed essentially as in exercises 73 and 69, but your torso is twisted about forty-five degrees at the start of the motion, then twisted forty-five degrees in the opposite direction for the next repetition.

RISK (Weight Training Truth #2):

R/B	Injury Site
(–) 3	Spine/Back (Zone I — Lower)

SIT-UPS AND SUPINE CRUNCHES ExecutionVariation. 78.c — Neck Flexion

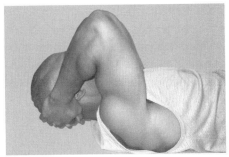

Fig. 147.1: Correct form for holding hands behind head.

Fig. 147.2: Do not force neck into flexion.

When performing any of exercises 67, 68, 69, 70, and 73, if you opt to clasp your hands behind your head, then your neck must not be held or forced into a position of flexion (as shown in 147.2). If such pressure is applied, a considerable risk of injury is added to the exercise. Neck motion is not part of abdominal muscle contractions.

RISK (Weight Training Truth #2)

R/B	Injury Site
(+) 9	Spine/Back (Zone II — Upper)

TORSO TWISTS Execution Variation 78.d — Head Rotation

Fig. 148: Do not forcefully rotate head during standing/seated torso twists.

When performing standing or seated torso twists (exercises 71, 72), if your head forcefully rotates (as shown in figure 148) during each repetition, there is an unnecessary risk of injury added to the exercise.

RISK (Weight Training Truth #2):

R/B	Injury Site
(+) 5	Spine/Back (Zone II — Upper)

TORSO TWISTS Execution Variation 78.e — Forward Lean

**Fig. 149.1:
Start/Finish**

PA-L

BENEFIT (Weight Training Truth #1):
When performing standing or seated torso twists (exercises 71 and 72), if your torso is flexed forward twenty-five to thirty degrees (as shown in figures 149.1, 149.2), the target muscles become strictly the oblique abdominals (PA-L). However, there is an accompanying increased risk of injury.

SEATED RISK (Weight Training Truth #2):

R/B	Injury Site
(+) 2	Spine/Back (Zone I — Lower)

STANDING RISK (Weight Training Truth #2):

R/B	Injury Site
(+) 2	Spine/Back (Zone I — Lower)
(+) 2	Hamstrings

**Fig. 149.2:
Mid-Phase**

NOTES:

• If standing torso twists are performed with both lower back round-out (var. 78.g) and a forward lean (var. 78.e), the R/B value for the lower back is increased by (+) 5.

• If standing torso twists are performed with both locked knees (var. 78.f) and a forward lean (var. 78.e), the R/B value for the hamstrings is altered by (+) 6.

STANDING TORSO TWISTS Execution Variation 78.f — Locked Knees

**Fig. 150:
Locked
Knees**

If standing torso twists are performed with locked knees, an unnecessary risk of injury is added to the exercise.

RISK (Weight Training Truth #2):

R/B	Injury Site
(+) 4	Hamstrings
The other R/B values remain unchanged for the exercise	

NOTE: If standing torso twists are performed with both the forward lean (var. 78.e) and locked knees (var. 78.f), the R/B value for the hamstrings is altered by (+) 6.

ALL TORSO TWISTS & STANDING OBLIQUE CRUNCHES
Execution Variation 78.g — Lower Back Round-Out

Fig. 151:
Lower Back Round-Out

If torso twists (seated or standing) or standing oblique crunches are performed with the lower back round-out (see variation 50.g) a notable increase of risk of injury occurs.

RISK (Weight Training Truth #2):

R/B	Injury Site
(+) 3	Spine/Back (Zone I — Lower)

NOTE: If standing torso twists are performed with both a forward lean (var. 78.e) and a Lower Back Round-Out (var. 78.g), the R/B value for the lower back is altered by (+) 5.

ALL LEG LIFTS Execution Variation 78.h — Pelvic "Crunch"

Fig. 152.1: Start/Finish

PA-D

side view

top view

PA-L

BENEFIT (Weight Training Truth #1):
When performing any of the leg-lift exercises (63 to 66), in order to target the lower abdominal muscles (PA-L), continue to lift your legs until they are ninety degrees to your torso, and then add a "crunch" (i.e., upward curl of your pelvis) to the exercise.

RISK (Weight Training Truth #2):
The R/B value remains unchanged for the exercise.

Fig. 152.2:
Mid-Phase

PA-D

Figure 153

The Biceps

Upper Biceps (U)

Outer Biceps Region (O)

Brachioradialis (B)

General/Middle Biceps (G)

Latissimus Dorsi (Ld)

Inner Biceps Region (I)

Lower Biceps (L)

Table 5 — BICEP EXERCISES

Name of Exercise		Benefit (WT #1)	R/B Values (WT #2)	No.	Pg.
Standing Barbell Curls		G-P	4, 6	79	138
Standing E-Z Bar Curls		G-P	2, 3, 2	80	139
Standing Straight-Bar Cable Curls		G-P	4, 6	81	140
Standing Alt. Dumbbell Curls		G-D	3, 4, 2	82	141
Standing One-Arm Cable Curls		G-D	3, 4, 2	83	142
"Preacher" Barbell Curls		L-P, S	4, 10, 10	84	143
"Preacher" E-Z Bar Curls		L-P, S	3, 6, 8, 3	85	144
"Preacher" Straight Bar Cable Curls		L-P, S	4, 10, 10	86	145
"Preacher" Dumbbell Curls		L-D	3, 6, 8, 4	87	146
Seated Alternating Dumbbell Curls		G-D	3, 4, 2	88	147
Seated "Concentration" Curls		G-D	3, 4, 2	89	148
Seated Inclined Alternating Curls		L, G-D, S	3, 2, 2, 4	90	149
Execution Variations:					
Straight Bar Curls	— Wide Grip	0	(+) 2	91.a	150
	— Narrow Grip	I	(+) 4	91.b	150
Palm-Up Curls	— Elbow Extension (Full)		(+) 2, (+) 6	91.c(i)	150
Locked Elbow Curls	— Elbow Extension (Part)		(−) 4, (−) 8	91.c(ii)	151
All Curls — Wrist Flexion			(+) 5	91.d	151
All Standing and Seated Dumbbell Curls	— "Cheating"		(+) 5	91.e	151
All Dumbbell and One-Handed Cable Curls	— Palm Up	L-S	(−) 4, (+) 4, (+) 2	91.f	152
All Dumbbell and Straight Bar Curls	— Wrist Extension		(−) 4	91.g	152
Reverse-Grip Chinups (Narrow)		L, Ld-S, P	3, 6, 6	53/57.c	
103/7					
Reverse-Grip Pulldowns (Narrow)		L, Ld-S, P	3, 6, 6	56/57.c	
103/7					
"Reverse" Curls		B-P	5, 4	92	153
Execution Variations:					
Narrow Grip		B-P	(+) 3	93.a	154
E-Z Bar		B-P	(−) 4, (−) 2	93.b	154
"Preacher" Bench		B-P	(+) 2	93.c	154
"Hammer" Curls		B-P	2	94	155
Standing Peak Cable Curls		G-D	4, 3, 8, 6	95	156

KEY:

G = General Bicep
B = Brachioradialis
Ld = Latissimus Dorsi *(see Table 3)*
S = Stretch

L = Lower Bicep
O = Outer Bicep Region
P = Power

U = Upper Bicep
I = Inner Bicep Region
D = Definition

Exercise 79: STANDING BARBELL CURLS

Myth #6

Fig. 154.1: Start/Finish

PA-L

Fig. 154.2: Mid-Phase

PA-D

BENEFIT (Weight Training Truth #1):
This exercise builds size and strength in its primary target, the biceps (PA-L), incorporating both a good stretch and a full range of contraction.

HOW:

- Standing, plant your feet twelve inches (thirty cm) apart and flex your knees slightly.

- Grasp a straight bar with a palms-up, shoulder-width grip.

- Keep your elbows flexed five to ten degrees and completely immobilized at your sides.

- Keep your torso upright and immobile; maintain a slight arch in your lower back throughout; this is the start/finish position (fig. 154.1).

- Ensure that your wrists stay in line with your forearms throughout the exercise (i.e., do not curl your wrists upward).

- Following the plane of action (PA-D), curl the bar up as high as possible — pause briefly; this is the mid-phase position (fig. 154.2).

- Smoothly return the bar to the start/finish position.

RISK (Weight Training Truth #2):

R/B	Injury Site
4	Elbows (Zone I — Inside)
6	Elbows (Zone III — Front)

VARIATIONS OF EXECUTION: Please see variations 91.a, 91.b, 91.c(i), 91.d, 91.e and 91.g.

Exercise 80: STANDING E-Z BAR CURLS

Fig. 155.1: Start/Finish

PA-L

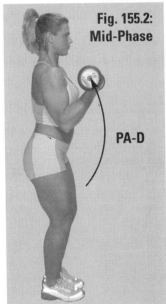

Fig. 155.2: Mid-Phase

PA-D

BENEFIT (Weight Training Truth #1):

This exercise builds size and strength in its primary target, the biceps (PA-L), but incorporates less stretch than a straight-bar curl.

HOW:

- Standing, plant your feet twelve inches (thirty cm) apart and flex your knees, slightly.
- Grasp the angled portions of the E-Z bar.
- Maintain a slight arch in your lower back and keep both elbows completely immobilized at your sides; this is the start/finish position (figure 155.1).
- Keep your torso upright and immobile throughout.
- Ensure that your wrists stay in line with your forearms throughout the exercise (i.e., do not curl your wrists upward).
- Following the plane of action (PA-D), curl the bar up as high as possible — pause briefly; this is the mid-phase position (figure 155.2).
- Smoothly return the bar to the start/finish position.

RISK (Weight Training Truth #2):

R/B	Injury Site
2	Elbows (Zone I — Inside)
3	Elbows (Zone II — Outside)
2	Elbows (Zone III — Front)

VARIATIONS OF EXECUTION: Please see variations 91.d and 91.e.

watch posture!

Exercise 81: STANDING STRAIGHT-BAR CABLE CURLS

Myth #6

**Fig. 156.1:
Start/Finish**

PA-L

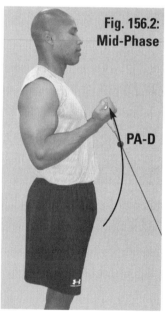

**Fig. 156.2:
Mid-Phase**

PA-D

BENEFIT (Weight Training Truth #1):

This exercise builds size and strength in its primary target, the biceps (PA-L), incorporating a full stretch and a full range of contraction.

HOW:

- Standing, plant your feet twelve inches (thirty cm) apart and flex your knees slightly.

- Grasp the bar with a palm-up, shoulder-width grip.

- Maintain a slight arch in your lower back throughout and ensure that your wrists stay in line with your forearms throughout the exercise (i.e., do not curl your wrists upward).

- Keep your elbows at five to ten degrees of flexion and completely immobile at your sides; this is the start/finish position (figure 156.1).

- Following the plane of action (PA-D), curl the bar up as high as possible — pause briefly; this is the mid-phase position (figure 156.2).

- Keep your torso upright and immobile throughout.

- Smoothly return the bar to the start/finish position.

RISK (Weight Training Truth #2):

R/B	Injury Site
4	Elbows (Zone I — Inside)
6	Elbows (Zone III — Front)

VARIATIONS OF EXECUTION: Please see variations 91.a, 91.b, 91.c(i), 91.d, 91.e and 91.g.

Exercise 82: STANDING ALTERNATING DUMBBELL CURLS

Myth #6

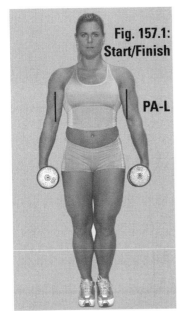

**Fig. 157.1:
Start/Finish**

PA-L

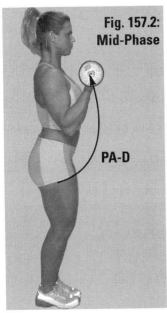

**Fig. 157.2:
Mid-Phase**

PA-D

BENEFIT (Weight Training Truth #1):

This exercise develops both strength and definition in its primary target, the biceps (PA-L).

HOW:

- Stand with your knees slightly flexed, and hold the dumbbells beside your legs, palms facing inward.

- Maintain a slight arch in your lower back throughout; this is the start/finish position (figure 157.1).

- Following the plane of action (PA-D), curl one hand up in front of your body, keeping your elbow completely immobilized at your side; gradually turn the hand until your palm is facing up at the end point of the movement for the "peak" contraction — pause briefly; this is the mid-phase position (figure 157.2).

- Ensure that your wrists stay in line with your forearms throughout the exercise (i.e., do not curl your wrists upward).

- Smoothly return the dumbbell to the start/finish position and repeat the process with the other arm.

RISK (Weight Training Truth #2):

R/B	Injury Site
3	Elbows (Zone I — Inside)
4	Elbows (Zone II — Outside)
2	Elbows (Zone III — Front)

VARIATIONS OF EXECUTION: Please see variations 91.d, 91.e, 91.f, 91.g and 91.c(i) with 91.f.

Exercise 83: STANDING ONE-ARM CABLE CURLS

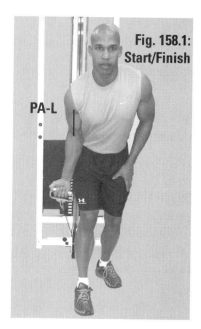

Fig. 158.1: Start/Finish

PA-L

Fig. 158.2: Mid-Phase

PA-D

BENEFIT (Weight Training Truth #1):
This exercise develops both strength and definition in its primary target, the biceps (PA-L).

HOW:

- Standing with one foot twelve inches (thirty cm) ahead of the other, flex your knees slightly and your torso forward about thirty degrees.

- Grasp the cable grip, palm up, with the arm on the same side as your forward leg and hold that elbow just in front of your hip.

- Maintain a slight lower back arch, throughout; this is the start/finish position (figure 158.1).

- Ensure that your wrist stays in line with your forearm throughout the exercise; do not curl your wrist upward.

- Following the plane of action (PA-D), curl the grip up toward your shoulder — pause briefly; this is the mid-phase position (figure 158.2).

- Briefly squeeze your biceps hard at the end point of the movement for the "peak" contraction.

- Keep your torso immobile throughout.

- Smoothly return the dumbbell to the start/finish position.

RISK (Weight Training Truth #2):

R/B	Injury Site
3	Elbows (Zone I — Inside)
4	Elbows (Zone II — Outside)
2	Elbows (Zone III — Front)

VARIATIONS OF EXECUTION: Please see variations 91.d, 91.e, 91.f, 91.g and 91.c(i) with 91.f.

Exercise 84: "PREACHER" BARBELL CURLS

Fig. 159.1: Start/Finish

PA-L

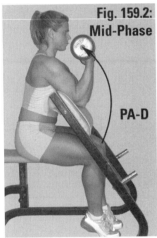

Fig. 159.2: Mid-Phase

PA-D

BENEFIT (Weight Training Truth #1):
This exercise stretches and strengthens its primary target, the biceps (PA-L); the arm position on the bench creates considerable lower biceps stretch.

HOW:

- Rest your upper arms flat on a preacher bench and grasp a straight bar at shoulder width, palms up and your arms fully extended; this is the start/finish position (figure 159.1).

- Ensure that your wrists stay in line with your forearms throughout the exercise (i.e., do not curl your wrists upward).

- Following the plane of action (PA-D), smoothly curl the bar up to three-quarters of maximum (at which point there is virtually no resistance remaining) — pause briefly; this is the mid-phase position (figure 159.2).

- Smoothly return the bar to the start/finish position.

RISK (Weight Training Truth #2):

R/B	Injury Site
4	Elbows (Zone I — Inside)
10	Elbows (Zone III — Front)
10	Elbows (Zone IV — Rear)

VARIATIONS OF EXECUTION: Please see variations 91.a, 91.b, 91.c(ii), 91.d and for 91.g.

Exercise 85: "PREACHER" E-Z BAR CURLS

Fig. 160.1:
Start/Finish

PA-L

Fig. 160.2:
Mid-Phase

PA-D

BENEFIT (Weight Training Truth #1):
This exercise stretches and strengthens its primary target, the biceps (PA-L), incorporating a good stretch of the lower biceps region.

HOW:

- Rest your upper arms flat on a preacher bench, grasping the angled portion of an E-Z bar with your arms fully extended; this is the start/finish position (figure 160.1).
- Ensure that your wrists stay in line with your forearms throughout the exercise (i.e., do not curl your wrists upward).
- Following the plane of action (PA-D), curl the bar up to three-quarters of maximum (at which point there is virtually no resistance remaining) — pause briefly; this is the mid-phase position (figure 160.2).
- Smoothly return the bar to the start/finish position.

RISK (Weight Training Truth #2):

R/B	Injury Site
3	Elbows (Zone I — Inside)
6	Elbows (Zone III — Front)
8	Elbows (Zone IV — Rear)
3	Elbows (Zone II — Outside)

VARIATIONS OF EXECUTION: Please see variations 91.c(ii) and 91.d.

Exercise 86: "PREACHER" STRAIGHT-BAR CABLE CURLS

Fig. 161.1: Start/Finish

PA-L

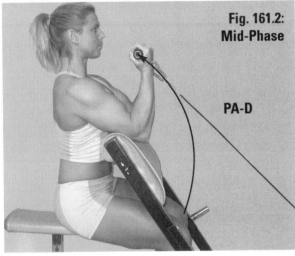

Fig. 161.2: Mid-Phase

PA-D

BENEFIT (Weight Training Truth #1):
This exercise stretches and strengthens its primary target, the biceps (PA-L), incorporating a full stretch and a full range of contraction.

HOW:

- Rest your upper arms flat on a preacher bench and grasp a straight bar at shoulder-width, palms up and arms fully extended; this is the start/finish position (figure 161.1).

- Ensure that your wrists stay in line with your forearms throughout the exercise (i.e., do not curl your wrists upward).

- Following the plane of action (PA-D), smoothly curl the bar up to three-quarters of maximum (at which point there is virtually no resistance remaining) — pause briefly; this is the mid-phase position (figure 161.2).

- Smoothly return the bar to the start/finish position.

RISK (Weight Training Truth #2):

R/B	Injury Site
4	Elbows (Zone I — Inside)
10	Elbows (Zone III — Front)
10	Elbows (Zone IV — Rear)

VARIATIONS OF EXECUTION: Please see variations 91.a, 91.b, 91.c(ii), 91.d and 91.g.

Exercise 87: "PREACHER" DUMBBELL CURLS

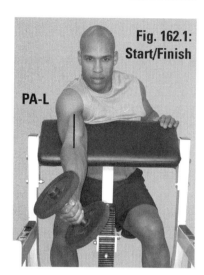

Fig. 162.1:
Start/Finish

PA-L

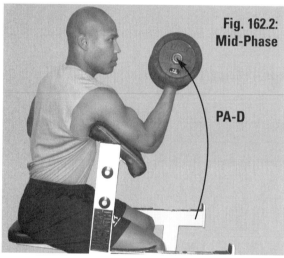

Fig. 162.2:
Mid-Phase

PA-D

BENEFIT (Weight Training Truth #1):
This exercise stretches and strengthens its primary target, the biceps (PA-L) and adds depth to the biceps using "peak" contractions.

HOW:

• Resting the upper portion of one arm flat on a preacher bench, grasp a dumbbell with your hand halfway between the palm-up and the thumb-up position, with your elbow fully extended; this is the start/finish position (figure 162.1).

• Ensure that your wrist stays in line with your forearm throughout the exercise; do not curl your wrist upward.

• Following the plane of action (PA-D), smoothly curl the dumbbell upward, gradually turning your palm fully up — pause briefly; this is the mid-phase position (figure 162.2).

• Briefly squeeze your bicep hard at the end point of the movement, for the "peak" contraction.

• Smoothly return the dumbbell to the start/finish position.

RISK (Weight Training Truth #2):

R/B	Injury Site
3	Elbows (Zone I — Inside)
6	Elbows (Zone III — Front)
8	Elbows (Zone IV — Rear)
4	Elbows (Zone II — Outside)

VARIATIONS OF EXECUTION: Please see variations 91.c(ii), 91.d, 91.f and 91.g.

Exercise 88: SEATED ALTERNATING DUMBBELL CURLS

Fig. 163.1:
Start/Finish

PA-L

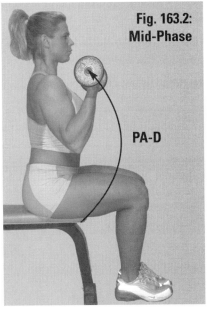

Fig. 163.2:
Mid-Phase

PA-D

BENEFIT (Weight Training Truth #1):
This exercise develops both strength and definition in its primary target, the bicep muscles (PA-L).

HOW:

- Seated with your torso erect and feet flat on the floor, hold the dumbbells at your sides with your palms facing inward; this is the start/finish position (figure 163.1).
- Ensure that your wrists stay in line with your forearms throughout the exercise (i.e., do not curl your wrists upward).
- Following the plane of action (PA-D), curl one dumbbell up in front of your body, keeping your elbow completely immobile at your side; turn the dumbbell, steadily, until your palm is facing you vertically — pause briefly; this is the mid-phase position (figure 163.2).
- Briefly squeeze the bicep hard at the top of the movement for the "peak" contraction.
- Keep a slight arch in your lower back throughout.
- Smoothly return the dumbbell to the start/finish position and repeat the process with the other arm.

RISK (Weight Training Truth #2):

R/B	Injury Site
3	Elbows (Zone I — Inside)
4	Elbows (Zone II — Outside)
2	Elbows (Zone III — Front)

VARIATIONS OF EXECUTION: Please see variations 91.d, 91.e, 91.f, 91.g and 91.c(i) with 91.f.

Exercise 89: SEATED "CONCENTRATION" CURLS

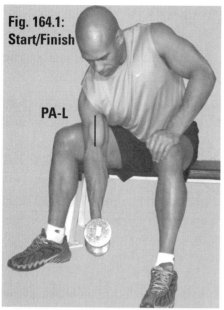

Fig. 164.1: Start/Finish

PA-L

Fig. 164.2: Mid-Phase

PA-D

BENEFIT (Weight Training Truth #1):
This exercise develops both strength and definition in its primary target, the biceps muscle (PA-L).

HOW:

- Sitting with your torso forward and knees apart, grasp a dumbbell such that your palm faces the opposite leg; brace your elbow against your knee and fully extend your arm.

- Your opposite hand should be braced against the leg for stability; this is the start/finish position (figure 164.1).

- Ensure that your wrist stays in line with your forearm throughout the exercise (i.e., do not curl your wrist upward).

- Following the plane of action (PA-D), curl the dumbbell up toward your shoulder, gradually turning your hand into the palm-up position — pause briefly; this is the mid-phase position (figure 164.2).

- Briefly squeeze your bicep hard at the top of the movement for the "peak" contraction.

- Keep your torso and upper arm completely immobilized and a slight arch in your lower back throughout the exercise.

- Smoothly return to the start/finish position.

RISK (Weight Training Truth #2):

R/B	Injury Site
3	Elbows (Zone I — Inside)
4	Elbows (Zone II — Outside)
2	Elbows (Zone III — Front)

VARIATIONS OF EXECUTION: Please see variations 91.d, 91.e, 91.f, 91.g and 91.c(i) with 91.f.

Exercise 90: SEATED, INCLINED ALTERNATING DUMBBELL CURLS

Fig. 165.1: Start/Finish

PA-L

Fig. 165.2: Mid-Phase

PA-D

BENEFIT (Weight Training Truth #1):
This exercise stretches and defines its primary target, the biceps muscle (PA-L) especially in the lower region.

HOW:

• Sit on a bench inclined back about thirty to forty degrees, with your shoulders and buttocks firmly against the bench.

• As you grasp the dumbbells with your palms facing inward, keep your arms parallel to your body, not hanging vertically toward the floor; this is the start/finish position (figure 165.1).

• Ensure that your wrists stay in line with your forearms throughout the exercise (i.e., do not curl your wrists upward).

• With your elbow immobile, follow the plane of action (PA-D), curling one hand up toward your shoulder, gradually bringing the hand to a full palm-up position — pause briefly; this is the mid-phase position (figure 165.2).

• Briefly squeeze your bicep hard at the top of the movement for the "peak" contraction.

• Smoothly return the dumbbell to the start/finish position and repeat the process with the other arm.

RISK (Weight Training Truth #2):

R/B	Injury Site
3	Elbows (Zone I — Inside)
2	Elbows (Zone III — Front)
2	Elbows (Zone IV — Rear)
4	Elbows (Zone II — Outside)

VARIATIONS OF EXECUTION: Please see variations 91.d, 91.e, 91.f, 91.g and 91.c(i) with 91.f.

STRAIGHT-BAR CURL Execution Variations

**Fig. 166:
Wide Grip**

PA-L

Variation 91.a — Wide Grip
BENEFIT (Weight Training Truth #1):

When performing any of the bicep straight-bar curls (exercises 79, 81, 84, and 86), taking a wide grip (as shown) targets the outer region of the biceps (PA-L). There is an additional risk of injury involved in this change.

RISK (Weight Training Truth #2):

R/B	Injury Site
(+) 2	Elbows (Zone I — Inside)

All other R/B values remain unchanged for that exercise.

**Fig. 167:
Narrow Grip**

PA-L

Variation 91.b — Narrow Grip
BENEFIT (Weight Training Truth #1):

When performing any of the bicep straight-bar curls (exercises 79, 81, 84, and 86), taking a narrow grip (as shown) targets the inner region of the biceps (PA-L). There is an additional risk of injury involved, at the wrists.

RISK (Weight Training Truth #2):

R/B	Injury Site
(+) 4	Wrists

All other R/B values remain unchanged for that exercise.

PALM-UP BICEP CURL Variation 91.c(i) — Elbow Extension (Full)

**Fig. 168:
Elbow
Extension**

For bicep curl exercises that inadvertently start with the elbows fully extended and the hands fully palms-up (exercises 79 and 81), there is considerable risk of injury added to zones III and IV of the elbow.

RISK (Weight Training Truth #2):

R/B	Injury Site
(+) 2	Elbows (Zone III — Front)
(+) 6	Elbows (Zone IV — Rear)

All other R/B values remain unchanged for that exercise.

NOTE: For dumbbell and cable curls that are executed with both the palm-up variation (91.f) and the full elbow extension variation (91.c(i)), the R/B value for zone III of the elbow is altered by (+) 6.

LOCKED ELBOW BICEP CURL Variation 91.c(ii) — Elbow Extension (Partial)

Fig. 169: Elbow Extension (Partial)

For bicep curl exercises that start with the elbows fully extended, (exercises 84 to 87 and 95), there is considerable risk of injury to zones III and IV of the elbow. These risks are greatly diminished by maintaining a five- to ten-degree flex of your elbows (as shown in figure 169).

RISK (Weight Training Truth #2):

R/B	Injury Site
(–) 4	Elbows (Zone III — Front)
(–) 8	Elbows (Zone IV — Rear)

All other R/B values remain unchanged for that exercise.

ALL BICEP CURLS Variation 91.d — Wrist Flexion

Fig. 170: Wrist Flexion

A frequent occurrence during the performance of any bicep curl exercise is hard isometric contraction of the wrist flexor muscles, thus inducing visible flexion of the wrists (as shown in figure 170), while the stronger bicep muscles work "through" them. This notably increases the risk of injury, in zone I of the elbow.

RISK (Weight Training Truth #2):

R/B	Injury Site
(+) 5	Elbows (Zone I — Inside)

All other R/B values remain unchanged for that exercise.

ALL STANDING AND SEATED DUMBBELL CURLS Variation 91.e — "Cheating" *Myths #7, #17*

Fig. 171: "Cheating"

It is both easy, and tempting, to use your torso for leverage on all standing bicep curls, and on seated dumbbell bicep curls. This, however, adds a great deal of unnecessary risk of lower back injury. (Also see the discussion of weight-training shortcuts in Chapter 2.)

RISK (Weight Training Truth #2):

R/B	Injury Site
(+) 5	Spine/Back (Zone I — Lower)

All other R/B values remain unchanged for that exercise.

ALL DUMBBELL AND ONE-HANDED CABLE CURLS
Execution Variation. 91.f — Palm-Up Position Throughout

Fig. 172: Palm-Up

I I PA-L

BENEFIT (Weight Training Truth #1):
Keeping palms up throughout a dumbbell or one-handed cable curl virtually eliminates any potential injury to zone II of the elbow, but increases the injury potential in zones III and IV of the elbow. With this variation the primary target of the exercise becomes the lower bicep region (PA-L), for stretch and definition.

RISK (Weight Training Truth #2):

R/B	Injury Site
(–) 4	Elbows (Zone II — Outside)
(+) 4	Elbows (Zone III — Front)
(+) 2	Elbows (Zone IV — Rear)

All other R/B values remain unchanged for that exercise.

NOTE: For dumbbell and cable curls (excluding those on a "preacher" bench) executed with palms up (var. 91.f) and elbows fully extended (var. 91.c(i)), the R/B value for zone III of the elbow is altered by (+) 6.

ALL DUMBBELL AND STRAIGHT-BAR CURLS Execution Variation 91.g — Wrist Extension

Fig. 173: Wrist Extension

The risk of straining your wrist flexor muscles (zone I of the elbows) during bicep curls can be virtually eliminated by dropping your wrist backward (as shown in fig. 173) throughout the entire exercise.

RISK (Weight Training Truth #2):

R/B	Injury Site
(–) 4	Elbows (Zone I — Inside)

All other R/B values remain unchanged for that exercise.

Exercise 92: "REVERSE" CURLS

Myth #6

Fig. 174.1:
Start/Finish

PA-L

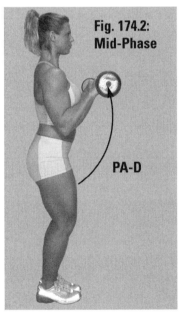

Fig. 174.2:
Mid-Phase

PA-D

BENEFIT (Weight Training Truth #1):

- This exercise develops size and strength in its primary target, the brachioradialis muscle (PA-L).

- The bicep activity in this exercise is negligible.

HOW:

- Standing with your knees slightly flexed, grasp a straight barbell with your palms down, at shoulder width.

- Keep a slight arch in your lower back and your elbows immobile at your sides throughout; this is the start/finish position (fig. 174.1).

- Following the plane of action (PA-D), smoothly curl the bar up as high as possible — pause briefly; this is the mid-phase position (fig. 174.2).

- Smoothly return the bar to the start/finish position.

RISK (Weight Training Truth #2):

R/B	Injury Site
5	Elbows (Zone II — Outside)
4	Wrists

All other R/B values remain unchanged for that exercise.

REVERSE CURL Execution Variations

Fig. 175: Narrow Grip

Variation 93.a — Narrow Grip

Performing "reverse" curls with a narrow grip (as shown in fig. 175) has no significant effect on the benefit of the exercise, but does increase the risk of wrist injury.

RISK (Weight Training Truth #2):

R/B	Injury Site
(+) 3	Wrists

All other R/B values remain unchanged for that exercise.

Fig. 176: E-Z Bar

Variation 93.b — E-Z Bar

Performing "reverse" curls with an E-Z bar and a standard grip width (as shown) eliminates the risk of wrist injury and decreases the risk of zone II elbow injury.

RISK (Weight Training Truth #2):

R/B	Injury Site
(–) 4	Wrists
(–) 2	Elbows (Zone II — Outside)

All other R/B values remain unchanged for that exercise.

Fig. 177: "Preacher" Bench

Variation 93.c — "Preacher" Bench

Performing "reverse" curls on a preacher bench (with a straight bar) adds a stretch component to the brachioradialis muscle that increases the risk of zone II elbow injury.

RISK (Weight Training Truth #2):

R/B	Injury Site
(+) 2	Elbows (Zone II — Outside)

All other R/B values remain unchanged for that exercise.

NOTE: If the E-Z bar variation (var. 93.b) is combined with the "preacher" bench variation (var 93.c) in a reverse-curl exercise, the R/B value for zone II of the elbow returns to 5.

Exercise 94: "HAMMER" CURLS

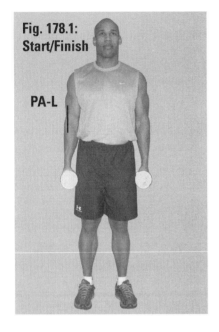

Fig. 178.1: Start/Finish

PA-L

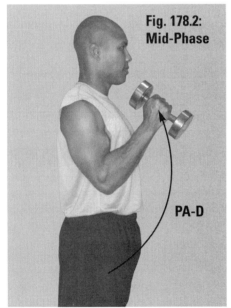

Fig. 178.2: Mid-Phase

PA-D

BENEFIT (Weight Training Truth #1):

- This exercise develops size and strength in its primary target, the brachioradialis muscle (PA-L).

- There is virtually no bicep activity involved in this exercise.

HOW:

- Standing with your feet planted twelve inches (thirty cm) apart and your knees slightly flexed, hold a pair of dumbbells at your sides, palms inward. This is the start/finish position (figure 178.1)

- Keep a slight arch in your lower back and your thumbs up.

- Following the plane of action (PA-D), curl one dumbbell up directly in front, keeping your elbow completely immobilized at your side — pause briefly; this is the mid-phase position (fig. 178.2).

- Keep your hand in the thumb-up position throughout the entire repetition.

- Smoothly return the dumbbell to the start/finish position and repeat the process with the other arm.

RISK (Weight Training Truth #2):

R/B	Injury Site
2	Elbows (Zone II — Outside)

Exercise 95: STANDING PEAK CABLE-CURLS

Myth #6

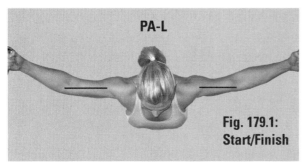

PA-L

Fig. 179.1: Start/Finish

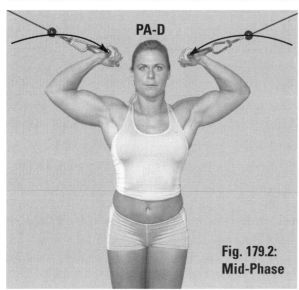

PA-D

Fig. 179.2: Mid-Phase

BENEFIT (Weight Training Truth #1):

This exercise develops definition in its primary target, the general biceps muscle (PA-L).

HOW:

- Standing, grasp the upper cable grips of a cable cross-over machine, palms up, with your upper arms parallel to the floor and elbows fully extended; this is the start/finish position (figure 179.1).

- Keep your torso immobile and your lower back slightly arched throughout the exercise.

- Following the plane of action (PA-D), curl both grips toward your head and briefly squeeze each bicep hard at the end point — pause briefly; this is the mid-phase position (figure 179.2).

- Keep your upper arms parallel to the floor throughout the exercise.

- Smoothly return the grips to the start/finish position.

RISK (Weight Training Truth #2):

R/B	Injury Site
4	Shoulders (Zone II — Top)
3	Elbows (Zone I — Inside)
8	Elbows (Zone IV — Rear)
6	Elbows (Zone III — Front)

VARIATIONS OF EXECUTION: Please see variations 91.c(ii), 91.d, 91.f and 91.g.

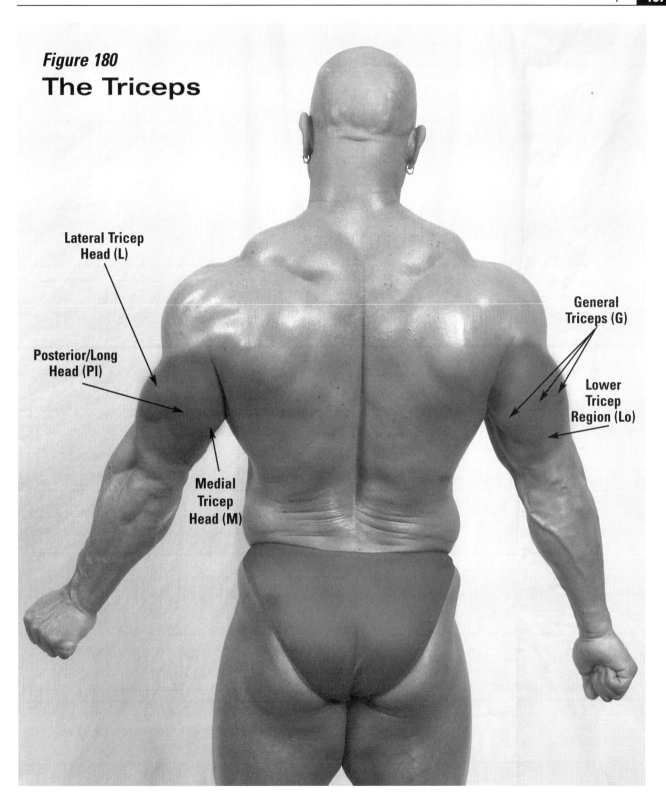

Figure 180
The Triceps

Lateral Tricep
Head (L)

Posterior/Long
Head (PI)

Medial
Tricep
Head (M)

General
Triceps (G)

Lower
Tricep
Region (Lo)

Table 6 — TRICEP EXERCISES

Name of Exercise/Variation	Benefit (WT #1)	R/B Values (WT #2)	No.	Pg.
Narrow-Grip Bench Press	G, Pm-P	8, 5, 4	96	160
Execution Variation:				
Toward the Neck	G, Pm-P	(+) 2, (+) 2	97	160
Barbell Extensions	M-P	6, 8	98	161
Execution Variations:				
E-Z Bar	M, Pl-P		99.a	162
Dumbbell	Pl-P		99.b	163
One-Arm Dumbbell Extensions				
Execution Variations:				
Palm-Backward Grip	L-D	6, 8, 4	100.a	164
Thumb-Downward Grip	G, Pl-P	(−) 4	100.b	165
Knuckles-Backward Grip	M-P	(−) 4	100.c	165
Body Dips				
Execution Variations:				
Parallel Bars	G, Pl-P	8, 8, 6	101.a	166
Between Benches	M-P	(+) 8	101.b	167
Elbows Flared	Pm, G-P, D	(+) 2, (+) 1	101.c	168
"French Presses" — E-Z Bar	M, Pl, Lo-P	5	102	169
Execution Variations:				
Straight Bar	M, Lo-P		103.a	170
Behind Head	M, Pl, Lo-S	(+) 4, (+) 6	103.b	170
Kneeling Cable Extensions				
Execution Variations:				
Knuckles-Backward Grip	M-D, S	7, 6	104.a	171
Thumbs-Backward Grip	G, Pl-D, S		104.b	172
Knuckles-Forward Grip	L-D, S	(+) 4	104.c	172
Inclined Cable Extensions	G-P	7, 6	105	173
Bent-Over Cable Pressdowns	G, Lo-P	3, 4	106	173
Execution Variations:				
High Hands Position	G, Lo-P, S	(+) 6, (+) 1, (+) 3	107	173
Upright Cable Pressdowns				
Execution Variations:				
Palms-Down Grip	M-P	4, 4	108.a	175
Thumbs-Up Grip	G, Pl-P		108.b	176
Palms-Up Grip	L-P	(+) 4	108.c	176
Dumbbell "Kickbacks"				
Execution Variations:				
Palm-Forward Grip	L-D	3, 4	109.a	177
Thumb-Forward Grip	G, Pl-D	(−) 4	109.b	178
Palm-Backward Grip	M-D	(+) 6, (−) 4	109.c	178
Cable "Isolation" Pressdowns				
Execution Variations:				
Palm-Up Grip	L-D	4, 4	110.a	179
Thumb-Up Grip	G, Pl-D	(−) 4	110.b	180
Palm-Down Grip	M-D	(−) 4	110.c	180
Execution Variations:				
All Tricep Exercises — Elbow Hyperextension		(+) 8	111.a	181
Straight Bar/Pronated Grip — Wrist Hyperextension		(+) 3	111.b	181
— Excess Narrow Grip		(+) 2	111.c	182
Pronated Tricep — Wrist Flexion		(+) 4	111.d	182
Supinated Tricep — Wrist Flexion		(−) 4	111.e	183

Name of Exercise/Variation		Benefit (WT #1)	R/B Values (WT #2)	No	Pg.
Standing and Sitting Tricep	— Lower Back Round-Out		(+) 4	111.f	183
Tricep Pressdowns	— "Cheating"		(+) 5	111.g	183

KEY:

G = General Tricep
Pl = Posterior/Long Head
P = Power

M = Medial Tricep Head
Lo = Lower Tricep Region
D = Definition

L = Lateral Tricep Head
Pm = Pectoralis Major *(see Table 1)*
S = Stretch

Exercise 96: NARROW-GRIP BENCH PRESS

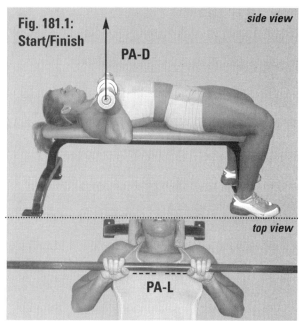

**Fig. 181.1:
Start/Finish**

side view

PA-D

top view

PA-L

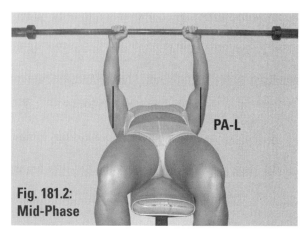

PA-L

**Fig. 181.2:
Mid-Phase**

BENEFIT (Weight Training Truth #1):

• This exercise strengthens the triceps, as the primary target (PA-L), and the chest, as the secondary target.

• It is especially good for power development of the tricep muscles.

HOW:

• Lying on your back on a flat bench, grasp a barbell with your hands about eight to ten inches (twenty to twenty-five cm) apart.

• Hold the bar above your sternum, with your wrists lightly touching your chest; this is the start/finish position (figure 181.1).

• Following the plane of action (PA-D), smoothly press the bar straight up until your elbows are fully extended — pause briefly; this is the mid-phase position (figure 181.2).

• Keep your wrists locked in line with your forearms (i.e., not bent backward) throughout.

• Smoothly return the bar to the start/finish position.

RISK (Weight Training Truth #2):

R/B	Injury Site
8	Shoulders (Zone I -Front)
5	Shoulders (Zone II — Top)
4	Wrists

VARIATIONS OF EXECUTION: Please see variations 97, 111.a, 111.b, 111.c, 3.b, 3.c, and 8.b.

NARROW-GRIP BENCH PRESS Variation 97 — Toward the Neck

**Fig. 182:
Toward
Neck**

PA-L

BENEFIT (Weight Training Truth #1):

Lowering the bar too close to your neck increases both the activity of the pectoralis muscle (making it the primary target — PA-L) and the risks of injury.

RISK (Weight Training Truth #2):

R/B	Injury Site
(+) 2	Shoulders (Zone I — Front)
(+) 2	Shoulders (Zone II — Top)

The other R/B value remains unchanged.

VARIATIONS OF EXECUTION: Please see variations 111.a–c and 8.b.

Exercise 98: STANDING BARBELL EXTENSIONS

Myth #6

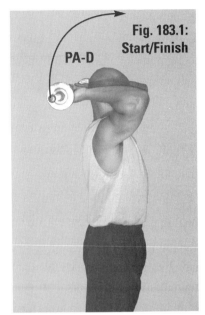

Fig. 183.1: Start/Finish

PA-D

PA-L

Fig. 183.2: Mid-Phase

BENEFIT (Weight Training Truth #1):
This exercise strengthens and develops the triceps region; the primary target is the medial head of the triceps muscle (PA-L).

HOW:

- Standing with your feet about twelve inches (thirty cm) apart, grasp a barbell with your hands ten to twelve inches (twenty-five to thirty cm) apart.

- Maintain a slight arch in your lower back throughout.

- Flex your elbows fully with the bar behind your head; this is the start/finish position (figure 183.1).

- Following the plane of action (PA-D), smoothly press the bar directly overhead until your elbows are fully extended — pause briefly; this is the mid-phase position (figure 183.2).

- Keep your wrists locked in line with your forearms (i.e., not bent backward) throughout

- Smoothly return the bar to the start/finish position.

RISK (Weight Training Truth #2):

R/B	Injury Site
6	Shoulders (Zone II — Top)
8	Elbows (Zone IV — Rear) (At Start/Finish)

NOTES:

- This exercise can also be performed while sitting, with no change to either the purpose or the risks of injury.

- Please see variations 111.a to 111.e.

STANDING BARBELL EXTENSIONS Execution Variations

Myth #6

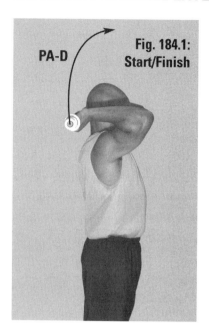

Fig. 184.1:
Start/Finish

PA-D

Fig. 184.2:
Mid-Phase

PA-L

Variation 99.a — E-Z Bar
BENEFIT (Weight Training Truth #1):
This exercise strengthens and develops the triceps region; the primary targets are the medial and posterior/long heads of the triceps muscle (PA-L).

HOW:

- Standing with your feet twelve inches (thirty cm) apart, grasp an E-Z bar.
- Maintain a slight arch in your lower back throughout.
- Flex your elbows fully with the bar behind your head; this is the start/finish position (figure 184.1).
- Following the plane of action (PA-D), smoothly press the bar directly overhead until your elbows are fully extended — pause briefly; this is the mid-phase position (figure 184.2).
- Keep your wrists locked and in line with your forearms (i.e., not bent backward) throughout.
- Smoothly return the bar to the start/finish position.

RISK (Weight Training Truth #2):
The R/B values remain as in exercise 98.

NOTES:

- This exercise can also be performed while sitting, with no change to either the purpose or the risks of injury.
- Please see variations 111.a and 111.d.

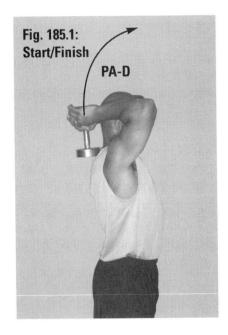

Fig. 185.1: Start/Finish

PA-D

Fig. 185.2: Mid-Phase

PA-L

Variation 99.b — Dumbbell
BENEFIT (Weight Training Truth #1):
This exercise strengthens and develops the triceps region; the primary target is the lateral head of the triceps muscle (PA-L).

HOW:

- Standing with your feet twelve inches (thirty cm) apart, grasp a single dumbbell with both hands, palms up.
- Maintain a slight arch in your lower back throughout.
- Flex your elbows fully with the dumbbell behind your head; this is the start/finish position (figure 185.1).
- Following the plane of action (PA-D), smoothly raise the dumbbell directly overhead until your elbows are fully extended — pause briefly; this is the mid-phase position (figure 185.2).
- Smoothly return the dumbbell to the start/finish position.

RISK (Weight Training Truth #2):
The R/B values remain as in exercise 98.

NOTES:
- This exercise can also be performed while sitting, with no change to either the purpose or the risks of injury.
- Please see variations 111.a and 111.d.

—Do seated with low back support.

ONE-ARM DUMBBELL EXTENSION Execution Variations

Myth #6

**Fig. 186.1:
Start/Finish**

PA-D

**Fig. 186.2:
Mid-Phase**

PA-L

Variation 100.a — Palm-Backward Grip
BENEFIT (Weight Training Truth #1):
This exercise strengthens the lateral head of the tricep, as the primary target (PA-L).

HOW:

- Standing with your feet twelve inches (thirty cm) apart, hold a dumbbell behind your head with one hand, palm facing backward and elbow fully bent.

- Place the other hand on your hip for balance and keep a slight arch in your lower back throughout; this is the start/finish position (figure 186.1).

- Following the plane of action (PA-D), smoothly raise the dumbbell directly overhead, keeping your wrist in line with your forearm, until your elbow is fully extended — pause briefly; this is the mid-phase position (figure 186.2).

- Keep your shoulder immobile throughout.

- Smoothly return the dumbbell to the start/finish position.

RISK (Weight Training Truth #2):

R/B	Injury Site
6	Shoulders (Zone II — Top)
8	Elbows (Zone IV — Rear) (At Start/Finish)
4	Elbows (Zone II — Outside)

NOTE:

- This exercise can also be performed while sitting, with no change to either the purpose or the risks of injury.

- Please see variations 100.b, 100.c, 111.a and 111.d.

Fig. 187: Thumb-Backward

PA-L

Variation 100.b — Thumb-Backward Grip
BENEFIT (Weight Training Truth #1):

Performed as in variation 100.a but maintaining the thumb backward position (as shown in figure 187) targets the posterior head of the tricep muscle primarily (PA-L).

RISK (Weight Training Truth #2):

R/B	Injury Site
(–) 4	Elbows (Zone II — Outside)

All other R/B values remain unchanged from variation 100.a.

VARIATIONS OF EXECUTION: Please see variations 111.a and 111.d.

Fig. 188: Knuckles Backward

PA-L

Variation 100.c — Knuckles-Backward Grip
BENEFIT (Weight Training Truth #1):

Performed as in variation 100.a, but maintaining the knuckles-backward position (as shown in figure 188) targets the medial head of the tricep muscle primarily (PA-L).

RISK (Weight Training Truth #2):

R/B	Injury Site
(–) 4	Elbows (Zone II — Outside)

All other R/B values remain unchanged from variaion 100.a.

VARIATIONS OF EXECUTION: Please see variations 111.a, 111.d and 111.e.

BODY DIP Execution Variations

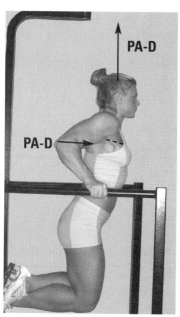

Fig. 189.1: Start/Finish

PA-D

PA-D

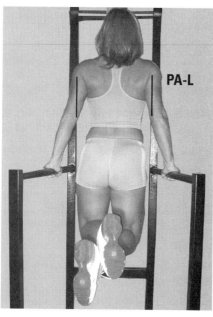

Fig. 189.2: Mid-Phase

PA-L

Variation 101.a — Parallel Bars

BENEFIT (Weight Training Truth #1):

- This exercise strengthens and develops the triceps region; the primary target is the posterior/long head of the triceps muscle (PA-L).

- There is pectoralis major muscle activity involved, secondarily.

HOW:

- Hold your wrists in line with your forearms (i.e., not bent backward) and grasp the bars while supporting your body weight on fully bent elbows.

- Point your elbows backward (not outward) throughout the exercise.

- Flex your knees and cross your ankles for balance; this is the start/finish position (figure 189.1).

- Following the plane of action (PA-D), smoothly press your body upward until your elbows are fully extended — pause briefly; this is the mid-phase position (figure 189.2).

- Smoothly return your body to the start/finish position.

RISK (Weight Training Truth #2):

R/B	Injury Site
8	Shoulders (Zone I — Front)
8	Shoulders (Zone II — Top)
6	Elbows (Zone IV — Rear) (At Start/Finish)

VARIATIONS OF EXECUTION: Please see variations 101.b, 101.c and 111.a.

Fig. 190.1: Start/Finish — PA-D — PA-D

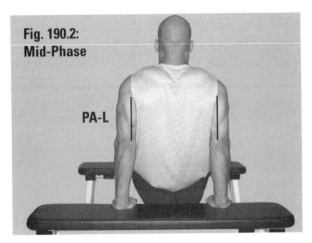

Fig. 190.2: Mid-Phase — PA-L

Variation 101.b — Between Benches

BENEFIT (Weight Training Truth #1):

- This exercise strengthens and develops the tricep region; the primary target is the medial head of the triceps muscle (PA-L).

- There is pectoralis major muscle activity involved, secondarily.

HOW:

- Rest both of your heels on one bench while your bodyweight is supported on a second bench, elbows fully bent.

- Place your palms on the front edge of the bench, wrapping your fingers around the edge and keeping your wrists as straight as possible; this is the start/finish position (figure 190.1).

- Keep your elbows pointed backward (not outward) throughout the exercise.

- Following the plane of action (PA-D), smoothly press your body upward until your elbows are fully straight — pause briefly; this is the mid-phase position (figure 190.2).

- Smoothly return your body to the start/finish position.

- Additional weight can be rested on your upper thighs, for power development.

RISK (Weight Training Truth #2):

R/B	Injury Site
(+) 8	Wrists

All other R/B values remain unchanged from variation 101.a.

VARIATIONS OF EXECUTION: Please see variation 111.a.

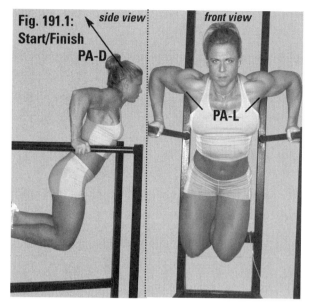

**Fig. 191.1:
Start/Finish**

side view   front view

PA-D

PA-L

Body Dip Variation 101.c — Elbows Flared Outward
BENEFIT (Weight Training Truth #1):

This exercise targets the lower region of the pectoralis major muscle (PA-L), and the entire tricep muscle (PA-L) for strength and definition.

HOW:

This exercise is performed as in variation 101.a, but modified such that your torso is lowered into a forward-leaning position about thirty degrees, with your elbows angled outward, not backward.

RISK (Weight Training Truth #2):

R/B	Injury Site
(+) 2	Shoulders (Zone I — Front)
(+) 1	Shoulders (Zone II — Top)

All other R/B values remain unchanged from variation 101.a.

VARIATIONS OF EXECUTION: Please see variation 111.a.

**Fig. 191.2:
Mid-Phase**

PA-L

Exercise 102: "FRENCH PRESSES" (E-Z BAR)

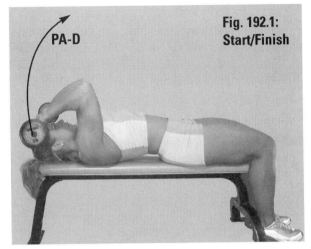

Fig. 192.1: Start/Finish

PA-D

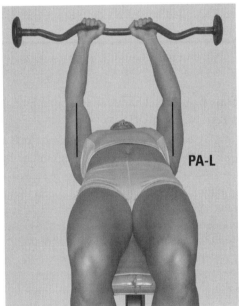

PA-L

Fig. 192.2: Mid-Phase

BENEFIT (Weight Training Truth #1):
This exercise strengthens and develops the tricep region; the primary targets are the medial and posterior/long heads of the triceps muscle (PA-L), especially the lower region.

HOW:

- Lying on your back on a bench, grasp an E-Z bar palms up, elbows fully bent, and the bar just above your forehead.

- Keep your wrists in line with your forearms (i.e., not bent forward or backward); this is the start/finish position (figure 192.1).

- Following the plane of action (PA-D), smoothly press the bar upward until your elbows are fully extended — pause briefly; this is the mid-phase position (figure 192.2).

- Keep your shoulders and upper arms immobile during the entire exercise.

- Smoothly return the bar to the start/finish position.

RISK (Weight Training Truth #2):

R/B	Injury Site
5	Elbows (Zone IV — Rear) (At Start/Finish)

VARIATIONS OF EXECUTION: Please see variations 103.a, 103.b and 111.a.

ページ

"FRENCH PRESS" Execution Variations

Fig. 193: Straight Bar Variation

Variation 103.a — Straight Bar
BENEFIT (Weight Training Truth #1):
The primary target of this exercise is the medial head of the triceps muscle (PA-L), especially the lower region, for power and size.

HOW:

- To be executed as described in exercise 102, but with your hands placed approximately ten to twelve inches (twenty-five to thirty cm) apart on a straight bar.

RISK (Weight Training Truth #2):
All R/B values remain unchanged from exercise 102.

VARIATIONS OF EXECUTION: Please see variations 103.b, 111.a, 111.b, 111.c and 111.e.

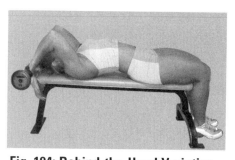

Fig. 194: Behind-the-Head Variation

Variation 103.b — Behind the Head
BENEFIT (Weight Training Truth #1):
A greater stretch for your triceps is created by lowering the bar behind your head. The greater the depth, the greater the stretch. During the active contraction of the exercise, your shoulders and upper arms must be held in a firm, immobile position. Unfortunately, with this shoulder position there is a greater risk of both shoulder and elbow injuries.

RISK (Weight Training Truth #2):

R/B	Injury Site
(+) 4	Elbows (Zone IV — Rear) (At Start/Finish)
(+) 6	Shoulders (Zone II — Top)

VARIATIONS OF EXECUTION: Please see variation 111.a.

KNEELING CABLE EXTENSIONS Execution Variations

**Fig. 195.1:
Start/Finish**

**Fig. 195.2:
Mid-Phase**

Variation 104.a — Knuckles-Backward Grip
BENEFIT (Weight Training Truth #1):
The exercise strengthens and develops the triceps region; the primary target is the medial head of the triceps muscle (PA-L).

HOW:

• Kneeling with your back to the apparatus and your torso flexed forward ten to twenty degrees, grasp a straight bar with your hands four to six inches (ten to fifteen cm) apart in a knuckles-backward grip.

• Maintain a slight arch in your lower back throughout.

• Fully bending your elbows, hold the bar behind your head; this is the start/finish position (figure 195.1).

• Keep your shoulders and elbows immobile throughout the exercise.

• Following the plane of action (PA-D), smoothly press the bar up and above your head, until your elbows are fully extended — pause briefly; this is the mid-phase position (figure 195.2).

• Smoothly return the bar to the start/finish position.

RISK (Weight Training Truth #2):

R/B	Injury Site
7	Elbows (Zone IV- Rear) (At Start/Finish)
6	Shoulders (Zone II — Top)

VARIATIONS OF EXECUTION: Please see variations 104.b, 104.c, 111.a to 111.c and 111.e.

Fig. 196: Thumbs-Backward Grip

Kneeling Cable Extensions Variation 104.b
— Thumbs-Backward Grip
BENEFIT (Weight Training Truth #1):

Performed as in variation 104.a but using a rope grip as shown in figure 196 partially supinates your hands, which will target the posterior/long head of the triceps muscle (PA-L).

RISK (Weight Training Truth #2):

All R/B values remain unchanged from variation 104.a.

VARIATIONS OF EXECUTION: Please see variations 104.c and 111.a.

Fig. 197: Knuckles-Forward Grip

Variation 104.c — Knuckles-Forward Grip
BENEFIT (Weight Training Truth #1):
Performed as in variation 104.a but using a straight-bar, knuckles-forward grip as shown in figure 197 almost fully supinates your hands, targeting the lateral head of the triceps muscle (PA-L).

RISK (Weight Training Truth #2):

R/B	Injury Site
(+) 4	Elbow (Zone II — Outside)

All other R/B values remain unchanged from variation 104.a.

VARIATIONS OF EXECUTION: Please see variation 111.a.

Exercise 105: INCLINED CABLE EXTENSIONS

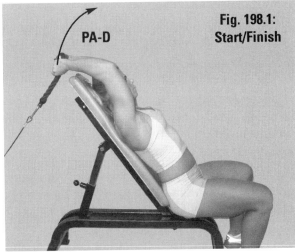

Fig. 198.1:
Start/Finish

PA-D

Fig. 198.2:
Mid-Phase

PA-L

BENEFIT (Weight Training Truth #1):
This exercise develops power and strength in the tricep region; the primary target is the entire general triceps muscle (PA-L).

HOW:

• Sitting on an incline bench with your back to the apparatus, grasp a rope grip behind your head, with fully bent elbows; this is the start/finish position (figure 198.1).

• Keep your shoulders and elbows immobile throughout the exercise.

• Following the plane of action (PA-D), smoothly press your hands up until your elbows are fully extended — pause briefly; this is the mid-phase position (figure 198.2).

• Keep your elbows pointed straight ahead and your upper arms immobile throughout.

• Smoothly return the bar to the start/finish position.

RISK (Weight Training Truth #2):

R/B	Injury Site
7	Elbows (Zone IV — Rear)
6	Shoulders (Zone II — Top)

VARIATIONS OF EXECUTION: Please see variation 111.a.

Exercise 106: BENT-OVER CABLE PRESSDOWNS

Myth #6

**Fig. 199.1:
Start/Finish**

PA-D

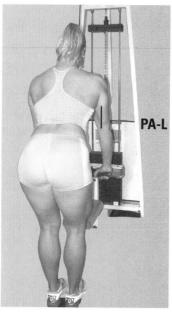

**Fig. 199.2:
Mid-Phase**

PA-L

BENEFIT (Weight Training Truth #1):
This exercise develops power and strength in the triceps region; the primary target is the lower portion of the entire general triceps muscle (PA-L).

HOW:

• Standing facing a cable pulldown station with your feet together and your knees slightly flexed, lean your torso forward about thirty degrees.

• Grasp a straight bar palms down, ten to twelve inches (twenty-five to thirty cm) apart and level with your chest; this is the start/finish position (figure 199.1).

• Maintain a slight arch in your back throughout.

• Following the plane of action (PA-D), smoothly press the bar vertically downward until your elbows are fully extended — pause briefly; this is the mid-phase position (figure 199.2).

• Keep your shoulders and elbows immobile throughout the exercise.

• Do not allow your wrists to bend backward — keep them firmly in line with your forearms.

• Smoothly return the bar to the start/finish position.

RISK (Weight Training Truth #2):

R/B	Injury Site
3	Elbows (Zone IV — Rear) (At Start/Finish)
4	Wrists

VARIATIONS OF EXECUTION: Please see variations 107 and 111.a–111.f.

BENT-OVER CABLE PRESSDOWN Variation 107 — High Hands Position

**Fig. 201:
High
Hands**

BENEFIT (Weight Training Truth #1):
A high-hand start position (as shown) adds a higher degree of stretch for the triceps, which increases the risk of injury.

RISK (Weight Training Truth #2):

R/B	Injury Site
(+) 6	Shoulders (Zone I — Front)
(+) 1	Wrists
(+) 3	Elbows (Zone IV — Rear) (At Start/Finish)

UPRIGHT CABLE PRESSDOWN Execution Variations

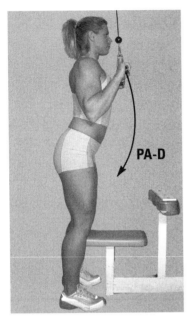

Fig. 201.1:
Start/Finish

PA-D

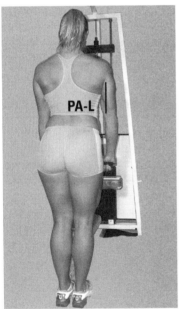

Fig. 201.2:
Mid-Phase

PA-L

Variation 108.a — Palms Down   *Myth #6*
BENEFIT (Weight Training Truth #1):
This exercise strengthens and develops the triceps region; the primary target is the medial head of the triceps muscle (PA-L).

HOW:

- Standing facing a cable pulldown station with knees slightly flexed, grasp a straight bar palms down with your hands ten to twelve inches (twenty-five to thirty cm) apart.

- Hold the bar at chest height with your elbows fully bent; this is the start/finish position (figure 201.1).

- Maintain a slight arch in your lower back throughout but keep your torso upright.

- Following the plane of action (PA-D), smoothly press the bar down until your elbows are fully extended — pause briefly; this is the mid-phase position (figure 201.2).

- Keep your shoulders and elbows immobile throughout the exercise.

- Do not allow your wrists to bend back — keep them firmly in line with your forearms.

- Smoothly return the bar to the start/finish position.

RISK (Weight Training Truth #2):

R/B	Injury Site
4	Elbows (Zone IV — Rear; at Start/Finish)
4	Wrists

VARIATIONS OF EXECUTION: Please see variations 108.b, 108.c and 111.a–.f.

UPRIGHT CABLE PRESSDOWN Execution Variations (cont'd)

Fig. 202.1: Start/Finish

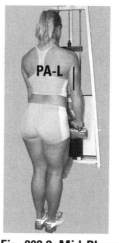

Fig. 202.2: Mid-Phase

Variation 108.b — Thumbs-Up Grip
BENEFIT (Weight Training Truth #1):

Performed as in variation 108.a but with a rope grip in place of a straight bar. Your palms should be facing each other throughout the exercise, thus targeting the posterior/long head of the tricep muscle (PA-L).

RISK (Weight Training Truth #2):

The R/B values remain as in var. 108.a.

VARIATIONS OF EXECUTION: Please see variations 108.c, 111.a, 111.d and 111.f.

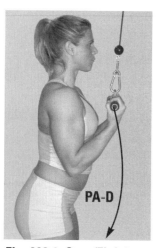

Fig. 203.1: Start/Finish

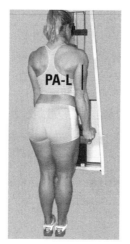

Fig. 203.2: Mid-Phase

Variation 108.c — Palms-Up Grip
BENEFIT (Weight Training Truth #1):
Performed as in variation 108.a, but with a palm-up grip, this exercise targets the lateral head of the tricep muscle (PA-L).

RISK (Weight Training Truth #2):

R/B	Injury Site
(+) 4	Elbow (Zone II — Outside)

The other R/B values remain unchanged from variation 108.a.

VARIATIONS OF EXECUTION: Please see variations 111.a, 111.d and 111.f.

DUMBBELL "KICKBACK" Execution Variations

Fig. 204.1: Start/Finish

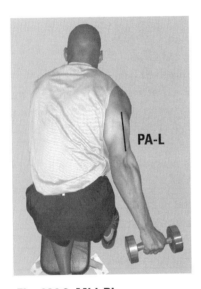

Fig. 204.2: Mid-Phase

Variation 109.a — Palm-Forward Grip   *Myth #6*
BENEFIT (Weight Training Truth #1):
This is a definition exercise for the triceps region; the primary target is the lateral head of the triceps muscle (PA-L).

HOW:

- Standing, place one knee and one hand on a flat bench.
- Maintaining a slight arch in your lower back but keeping your torso otherwise parallel to the floor, grasp a dumbbell with your free hand.
- Keep your elbow immobile against the side of your body and your palm facing forward; this is the start/finish position (figure 204.1).
- Following the plane of action (PA-D), press the dumbbell backward until your elbow is fully extended — pause briefly; this is the mid-phase position (figure 204.2).
- Smoothly return the dumbbell to the start/finish position.

RISK (Weight Training Truth #2):

R/B	Injury Site
3	Elbows (Zone IV — Rear) (At Start/Finish)
4	Elbow (Zone II — Outside)

VARIATIONS OF EXECUTION: Please see variations 109.b, 109.c, 111.a and 111.e.

DUMBBELL "KICKBACK" Execution Variations (cont'd)

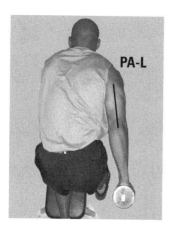

Fig. 205:
Thumb-Forward Grip

Variation 109.b — Thumb-Forward Grip
BENEFIT (Weight Training Truth #1):
Performed as in variation 109.a but with a thumb-forward grip (i.e., your palm facing your torso) throughout the exercise makes the exercise one of definition for the posterior/long head of the triceps muscle (PA-L).

RISK (Weight Training Truth #2):

R/B	Injury Site
(–) 4	Elbow (Zone II — Outside)

The other R/B value remains unchanged from variation 109.a.

VARIATIONS OF EXECUTION: Please see variations 109.c, 111.a and 111.d.

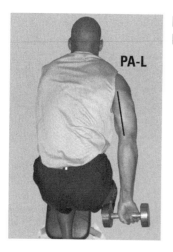

Fig. 206:
Palm-Backward Grip

Variation 109.c — Palm-Backward Grip
BENEFIT (Weight Training Truth #1):
Performed as in variation 109.a, but with your palm facing backward throughout the entire exercise makes the exercise one of definition for the medial head of the tricep muscle (PA-L). This alters the risk of injury.

RISK (Weight Training Truth #2):

R/B	Injury Site
(+) 6	Shoulders (Zone I — Front)
(–) 4	Elbow (Zone II — Outside)

The other R/B value remains unchanged from variation 109.a.

VARIATIONS OF EXECUTION: Please see variations 111.a, 111.d and 111.e.

CABLE "ISOLATION" PRESSDOWN Execution Variations

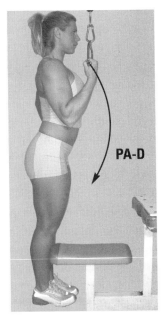

**Fig. 207.1:
Start/Finish**

PA-D

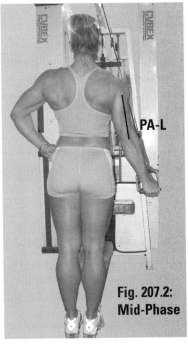

PA-L

**Fig. 207.2:
Mid-Phase**

Variation 110.a — Palm-Up Grip   *Myth #6*

BENEFIT (Weight Training Truth #1):

This is a definition exercise for the triceps region; the primary target is the lateral head of the triceps muscle (PA-L).

HOW:

- Standing facing an upright cable machine, grasp the grip with one hand, palm-up, and with that elbow immobile against the side of your body.

- Hold your opposite hand against your hip for balance and maintain a slight arch of your lower back throughout; this is the start/finish position (figure 207.1).

- Following the plane of action (PA-D), smoothly press the grip downward until your elbow is fully extended — pause briefly; this is the mid-phase position (figure 207.2).

- Keep your thumb pointed away from your body throughout the exercise.

- Smoothly return the grip to the start/finish position and repeat the process on the other side.

RISK (Weight Training Truth #2):

R/B	Injury Site
4	Elbows (Zone IV — Rear) (At Start/Finish)
4	Elbow (Zone II — Outside)

VARIATIONS OF EXECUTION: Please see variations 110.b, 110.c, 111.a and 111.e.

CABLE "ISOLATION" PRESSDOWN Execution Variations (cont'd)

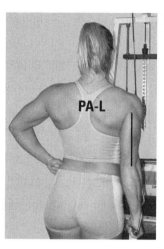

Fig. 208:
Thumb-Up Grip

Variation 110.b — Thumb-Up Grip
BENEFIT (Weight Training Truth #1):
Performed as in variation 110.a but with a thumb-up grip (i.e., your palm facing inward) throughout the entire exercise makes the exercise one of definition for the posterior/long head of the tricep muscle (PA-L).

RISK (Weight Training Truth #2):

R/B	Injury Site
(−) 4	Elbow (Zone II — Outside)

The other R/B value remains unchanged from variation 110.a.

VARIATIONS OF EXECUTION: Please see variations 110.c, 111.a and 111.e.

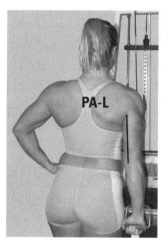

Fig. 209:
Palm-Down Grip

Variation 110.c — Palm-Down Grip
BENEFIT (Weight Training Truth #1):
Performed as in variation 110.a but with your palm facing downward throughout the entire exercise makes the exercise one of definition for the medial head of the tricep muscle (PA-L).

RISK (Weight Training Truth #2):

R/B	Injury Site
(−) 4	Elbow (Zone II — Outside)

The other R/B value remains unchanged from variation 110.a.

VARIATIONS OF EXECUTION: Please see variations 111.a, 111.d and 111.e.

ALL TRICEP EXERCISES AND CHEST OR SHOULDER PRESSES
Execution Variation 111.a — Elbow Hyperextension

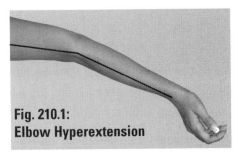

Fig. 210.1:
Elbow Hyperextension

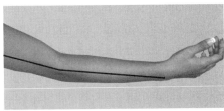

Fig. 210.2: Correct Elbow Extension

If your elbow is capable of hyperextension (as shown in figure 210.1), it is very important not to do so when performing tricep exercises, chest presses or shoulder presses (extend only as far as shown in figure 210.2). If excess elbow extension does occur during these exercises, the risk of injury is increased considerably.

RISK (Weight Training Truth #2):

R/B	Injury Site
(+) 8	Elbows (Zone IV — Rear) (At Mid-phase)

All other R/B values remain unchanged for that exercise.

PRONATED GRIP Execution Variation 111.b — Wrist Hyperextension

Fig. 211
Wrist
Hyperextension

When performing straight-bar tricep exercises with a pronated grip (exercises/variations 96, 98, 100.c, 103.a, 104.a, 106, 107, 108.a, and 109.a) it is important to ensure that your wrists are not allowed to bend backward excessively (as shown in figure 211). This position creates a moderate but unnecessary risk of injuring your wrists.

RISK (Weight Training Truth #2):

R/B	Injury Site
(+) 3	Wrists

All other R/B values remain unchanged for that exercise.

STRAIGHT BAR/PRONATED GRIP Execution Variation 111.c — Excessively Narrow Grip

**Fig. 212:
Excessively
Narrow Grip**

When performing straight-bar tricep exercises with a pronated grip (exercises/variations 96, 98, 103.a, 104.a, 106, 107, and 108.a) it is important that you not grip the bar with your hands too closely together (i.e., less than eight inches or twenty cm). An excessively narrow grip (as shown in figure 212) creates an angled strain within the wrist, thus increasing the risk of injury.

RISK (Weight Training Truth #2):

R/B	Injury Site
(+) 2	Wrists

All other R/B values remain unchanged for that exercise.

VARIATIONS OF EXECUTION: If wrist hyperextension (variation 111.b) is combined with an excessively narrow grip (variation 111.c) on a straight-bar tricep exercise, the R/B value regarding the wrists is altered by (+) 5.

PRONATED TRICEP EXERCISES Execution Variation 111.d — Wrist Flexion

**Fig. 213.1:
Wrist Flexion**

When performing tricep exercises with hands in a pronated position (exercises/variations 98, 100.c, 103.a, 104.a, 106, 108.a, 109.c and 110.c), it is important to ensure that you do not forcibly bend your hands downward (as shown in figure 213.1). This action creates a moderate but unnecessary risk of injuring zone I of the elbow.

RISK (Weight Training Truth #2):

R/B	Injury Site
(+) 4	Elbow (Zone I — Inside)

All other R/B values remain unchanged for that exercise.

SUPINATED TRICEP EXERCISES Execution Variation 111.e — Wrist Flexion

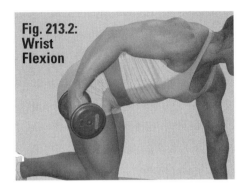

Fig. 213.2: Wrist Flexion

When performing a tricep exercise that has the hands in a supinated position (exercises/variations 100.a, 104.c, 108.c, 109.a and 110.a), the risk of injury to zone II of the elbows can be eliminated by holding a position of moderate wrist flexion (as shown in figure 213.2) throughout its execution.

RISK (Weight Training Truth #2):

R/B	Injury Site
(−) 4	Elbows (Zone II — Outside)

All other R/B values remain unchanged for that exercise.

STANDING OR SEATED TRICEP EXERCISES Variation 111.f — Lower Back Round-Out

Myth #6

Fig. 214: Lower Back Round-Out

When performing any tricep exercise while standing, seated or bent-over, caution must be taken to never round out the lower back. This creates an unnecessary risk of injury to the lower back. (Also see variation 50.g.)

RISK (Weight Training Truth #2):

R/B	Injury Site
(+) 4	Spine/Back (Zone I — Lower)

All other R/B values remain unchanged for that exercise.

TRICEP PRESSDOWNS Execution Variation 111.g — "Cheating"

Myths #16 & #17

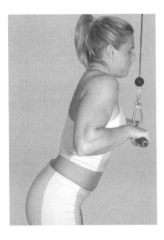

Fig. 215: "Cheating"

Cheating in tricep pressdowns is done with a forceful forward lean of your torso to start the bar moving downward from the start position. This creates momentum, thus giving the triceps a boost, but unfortunately puts the lower back at risk of injury. (See the discussion of weight-training shortcuts in Chapter 2.)

RISK (Weight Training Truth #2):

R/B	Injury Site
(+) 5	Spine/Back (Zone I — Lower)

All other R/B values remain unchanged for that exercise.

NOTE: If tricep pressdown exercises are performed with both lower back round-out (variation 111.f) and "cheating" (variation 111.g), then the R/B value for the lower back becomes 9.

Figure 216
The Forearms

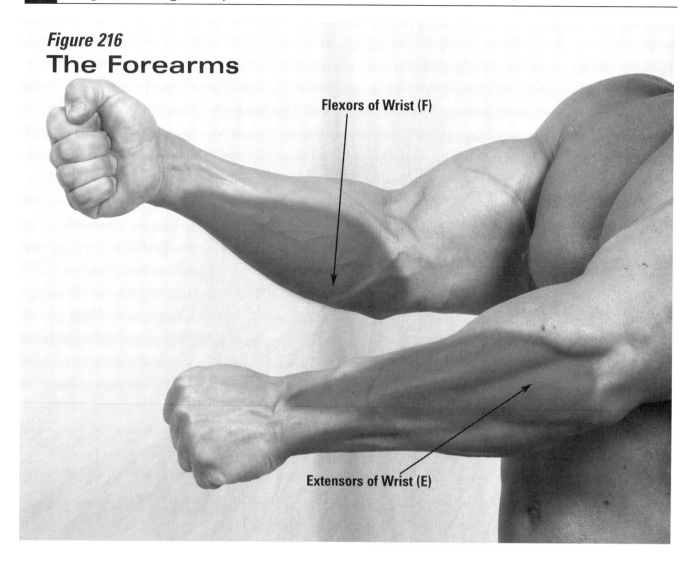

Flexors of Wrist (F)

Extensors of Wrist (E)

Table 7 — FOREARM EXERCISES

Name of Exercise/Variations		Benefit (WT #1)	R/B Values (WT #2)	No.	Pg.
Barbell Forearm Curls		F-S	4, 5	112	185
Dumbbell Forearm Curls		F-S, D	2, 5	113	186
Barbell Forearm Raises		E-S	6, 5	114	187
Dumbbell Forearm Raises		E-S, D	4, 5	115	188
Execution Variations:					
Barbell Forearm Curls & Raises	— Wide Grip		(−) 2	116.a	189
	— Narrow Grip		(+) 2	116.b	189
All Forearm Curls	— Partial Range		(−) 3, (−) 2	116.c	190
All Forearm Raises	— Partial Range		(−) 3, (−) 4	116.d	190
All Forearm Exercises	— Arms on Bench			116.e	190

KEY:

F = Flexors of Wrist   E = Extensors of Wrist   S = Size/Strength

D = Definition

Exercise 112: BARBELL FOREARM CURLS

Fig. 217.1: Start/Finish

PA-D

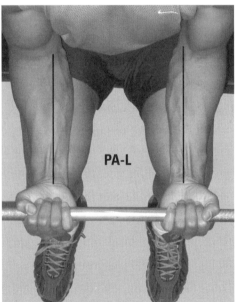

PA-L

Fig. 217.2: Mid-Phase

BENEFIT (Weight Training Truth #1):
This exercise develops the size and strength of the medial region of the forearm; the primary targets are the wrist and hand flexor muscles (PA-L).

HOW:

• Sitting on the end of a flat bench, grasp a straight barbell with your hands palms-up and eight inches (twenty cm) apart.

• Rest your forearms flat on your thighs (also eight in./twenty cm apart), so that your wrists and hands extend out beyond your knees.

• Hold the barbell in your curled fingers with your wrists bent backward fully; this is the start/finish position (figure 217.1).

• Following the plane of action (PA-D), slowly curl the bar upward, first using only your fingers, then the entire hand as the bar reaches your mid-palm, and then curl your wrist up as high as possible — pause briefly; this is the mid-phase position (figure 217.2).

• Smoothly return the bar to the start/finish position.

RISK (Weight Training Truth #2):

R/B	Injury Site
4	Wrists
5	Elbows (Zone I — Inside)

VARIATIONS OF EXECUTION: Please see variations 116.a, 116.b, 116.c and 116.e.

Exercise 113: DUMBBELL FOREARM CURLS

Fig. 218.1: Start/Finish

PA-D

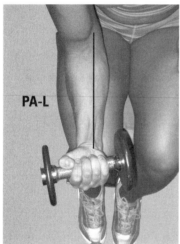

PA-L

Fig. 218.2: Mid-Phase

BENEFIT (Weight Training Truth #1):
This exercise develops the size and definition of the medial region of the forearm; the primary targets are the wrist and hand flexor muscles (PA-L).

HOW:

• Sitting on the end of a flat bench, grasp a dumbbell with a palm-up grip.

• Rest your forearm flat on your thigh such that your wrist extends out beyond your knee and it bends backward fully; this is the start/finish position (figure 218.1).

• Following the plane of action (PA-D), slowly curl the dumbbell upward as high as possible keeping your palm facing upward throughout — pause briefly; this is the mid-phase position (figure 218.2).

• Smoothly return the dumbbell to the start/finish position.

RISK (Weight Training Truth #2):

R/B	Injury Site
2	Wrists
5	Elbows (Zone I — Inside)

VARIATIONS OF EXECUTION: Please see variations 116.c and 116.e.

Exercise 114: BARBELL FOREARM RAISES

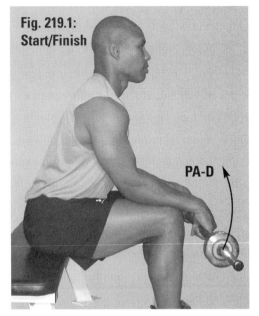

Fig. 219.1: Start/Finish

PA-D

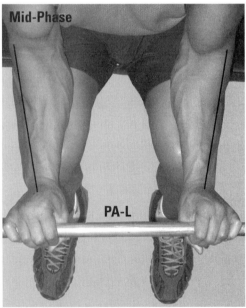

Mid-Phase

PA-L

Fig. 219.2: Mid-Phase

BENEFIT (Weight Training Truth #1):
This exercise develops the size and strength of the lateral region of the forearm; the primary target is the wrist/hand extensor muscles (PA-L).

HOW:

- Sitting on the end of a flat bench, grasp a straight barbell with your palms up and about ten inches (twenty-five cm) apart.

- Rest your forearms flat on your thighs (also ten inches (twenty-five cm) apart) such that your wrists and hands extend out beyond your knees and they flex downward fully; this is the start/finish position (figure 219.1).

- Following the plane of action (PA-D), smoothly raise your hands as high as possible — pause briefly; this is the mid-phase position (figure 219.2).

- Smoothly return to the start/finish position.

RISK (Weight Training Truth #2):

R/B	Injury Site
6	Wrist
5	Elbows (Zone II — Outside)

VARIATIONS OF EXECUTION: Please see variations 116.a, 116.b, 116.d and 116.e.

Exercise 115: DUMBBELL FOREARM RAISES

Fig. 220.1: Start/Finish

PA-D

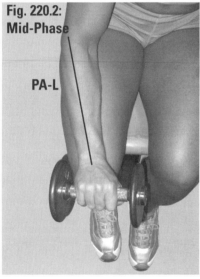

Fig. 220.2: Mid-Phase

PA-L

BENEFIT (Weight Training Truth #1):

This exercise develops the size and definition of the lateral region of the forearm; the primary targets are the wrist and hand extensor muscles (PA-L).

HOW:

- Sitting on the end of a flat bench, grasp a dumbbell with a palm-down grip.

- Rest your forearm flat on your thigh, such that your wrist and hand extends out beyond your knee and it flexes downward fully; this is the start/finish position (figure 220.1).

- Following the plane of action (PA-D), smoothly raise the back of your hand as high as possible, keeping the dumbbell parallel to the floor throughout — pause briefly; this is the mid-phase position (figure 220.2).

- Smoothly return to the start/finish position.

RISK (Weight Training Truth #2):

R/B	Injury Site
4	Wrist
5	Elbows (Zone II — Outside)

VARIATIONS OF EXECUTION: Please see variations 116.d and 116.e.

BARBELL FOREARM CURLS AND RAISES Execution Variations

Fig. 221.1: Wide Grip (curls)

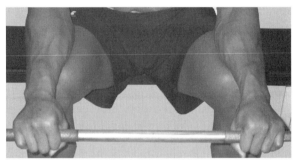

Fig. 221.2: Wide Grip (raises)

Variation 116.a — Wide Grip

Performing barbell forearm curls or raises (exercises 112 and 114) with your knees about fifteen inches (forty cm) apart maintains the same muscle benefit, but with a reduced risk of injury to the wrist.

RISK (Weight Training Truth #2):

R/B	Injury Site
(–) 2	Wrist

All other R/B values remain unchanged for that exercise.

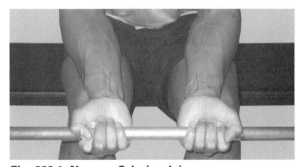

Fig. 222.1: Narrow Grip (curls)

Fig. 222.2: Narrow Grip (raises)

Variation 116.b — Narrow Grip

Performing barbell forearm curls or raises (exercises 112 and 114) with your knees about four inches (ten cm) apart maintains the same muscle benefit, but with an increased risk of injury to the wrist.

RISK (Weight Training Truth #2):

R/B	Injury Site
(+) 2	Wrist

All other R/B values remain unchanged for that exercise.

ALL FOREARM CURLS: Variation 116.c — Partial-Range

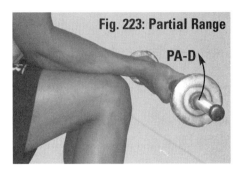

Fig. 223: Partial Range

PA-D

In the performance of either barbell or dumbbell forearm curls, the use of a shortened range of motion will significantly reduce the risks of injury. Rather than allow your wrists to fully extend downward (exercises 112 and 113), restrict the range of motion by approximately fifteen degrees (as shown in figure 223).

RISK (Weight Training Truth #2):

R/B	Injury Site
(–) 3	Elbows (Zone I -Inside)
(–) 2	Wrists

ALL FOREARM RAISES: Variation 116.d — Partial-Range

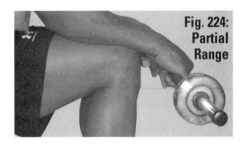

Fig. 224: Partial Range

In the performance of either barbell or dumbbell forearm raises, the use of a shortened range of motion will significantly reduce the risks of injury. Rather than allow your wrists to fully flex (exercises 114 and 115), restrict the range of motion by approximately fifteen degrees (as shown in figure 224).

RISK (Weight Training Truth #2):

R/B	Injury Site
(–) 3	Elbows (Zone II — Outside)
(–) 4	Wrists

ALL FOREARM EXERCISES: Variation 116.e — Arms on a Bench

Fig. 225.1: Arms on a Bench (curls)

An alternative method of performing any of the forearm exercises is to rest your arms on a bench (as shown in figures 225.1, 225.2) rather than upon your thighs. There is no change to either the benefit, or the risks, of the exercise, with this technique.

RISK (Weight Training Truth #2):

All other R/B values remain unchanged for that exercise.

Fig. 225.2: Arms on a Bench (raises)

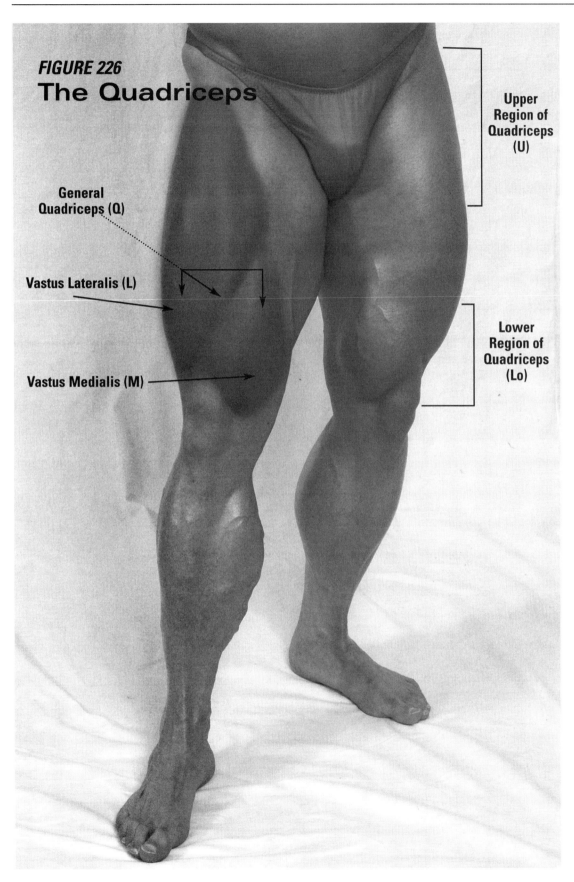

FIGURE 226
The Quadriceps

General
Quadriceps (Q)

Vastus Lateralis (L)

Lower
Region of
Quadriceps
(Lo)

Vastus Medialis (M)

Table 8 — QUADRICEP EXERCISES

Name of Exercise/Variation	Benefit (WT #1)	R/B Values (WT #2)	No.	Pg.
Barbell Squats				
Execution Variations:				
"Bodybuilding"	Q-S, D	3, 3, 4	117.a	193
"Powerlifting"	Q, G-S	(+) 1, (+) 4, (+) 3, (+) 6	117.b	194
Wide Hand Placement		(−) 2	117.c	195
Narrow Stance and Deep Hips		(+) 1, (+) 7, (+) 4	117.d	195
Dumbbell Squats	Q-S, D	(−) 3	117.e	196
Front Squats	Q-D, S	4, 6	118	197
"Hack" Squats	Q-S	9, 3	119	198
Execution Variations:				
Narrow Toed-In Stance	L-S	(+) 1	120.a	198
Wide Toed-Out Stance	M-S	(+) 1	120.b	199
Leg Press (Shallow)	Q-S	5, 5	121	199
Execution Variations:				
Narrow Toed-In Stance	L-S	(+) 2	122.a	200
Wide Toed-Out Stance	M-S	(+) 2	122.b	200
Lunges	Q, G-S, D	3, 5, 3, 3	123	201
Execution Variations:				
Dumbbells	Q, G-S, D	(−) 3	124.a	202
Shallow	Q-S, D	(−) 1, (−) 2, (−) 3	124.b	202
Deep	G-P, D	(+) 1, (+) 1, (+) 2	124.c	203
"Sissy" Squats	Q, U-D	3	125	204
Thigh Extensions	M-S/Lo-D	2	126	205
Execution Variation:				
One Leg at a Time	M-D		127	205

KEY:

Q = General Quadriceps   G = Gluteal Muscles *(see Table 10)*   U = Upper Region of Quadriceps

M = Vastus Medialis   Lo = Lower Region of Quadriceps   L = Vastus Lateralis

S = Size/Strength   D = Definition

BARBELL SQUAT Execution Variations

Fig. 227.1: Start/Finish

front view   *side view*

PA-D   PA-D

Fig. 227.2: Mid-Phase

PA-L

Fig. 227.3: Board under heels

Variation 117.a — "Bodybuilding"
BENEFIT (Weight Training Truth #1):
This exercise strengthens and defines the quadriceps muscle, as the primary target (PA-L).

HOW:

* Standing in front of a squat rack, feet ten to twelve inches (twenty-five to thirty cm) apart, place a barbell across your shoulders, at the base of your neck.

* Lower your hips by flexing your knees (not by leaning your torso forward), until your heels almost lift up off the floor; this is the start/finish position (figure 227.1).

* Your head should be held firmly in a forward gaze throughout the exercise.

* Following the plane of action (PA-D), smoothly stand upright by extending your knees — pause briefly; this is the mid-phase position (figure 227.2).

* Do not bounce out of the start position.

* Maintain a slight arch in your lower back and a fully erect torso throughout the exercise.

* Smoothly return to the start/finish position.

RISK (Weight Training Truth #2):

R/B	Injury Site
3	Shoulders (Zone II — Top)
3	Spine/Back (Zone I — Lower)
4	Knees

NOTES:

* To make your quadriceps work harder, you can place a one- to two-inch (three to five cm) thick board under your heels. This allows for a slightly deeper squat, with a slightly altered center of balance and more forward lean in the torso (as shown in figure 227.3). The R/B values are not altered by this technique, as long as all other execution parameters are maintained.

* Please see variations 117.b–e.

BARBELL SQUAT Execution Variations (cont'd)

Fig. 228.1: Start/Finish

front view

side view

PA-D

PA-D

PA-L

Fig. 228.2: Mid-Phase

front view

back view

PA-L

PA-L

Variation 117.b — "Powerlifting"
BENEFIT (Weight Training Truth #1):
This exercise strengthens and develops the entire thigh, buttocks, and lower torso; the primary targets are the quadriceps and gluteal muscles (PA-L).

HOW:

- Standing in front of a squat rack with your feet placed about twenty-eight inches (seventy cm) apart, slightly wider at the toes, place a barbell across your shoulders, about three to four inches (eight to ten cm) below the base of your neck.

- Lower your hips by flexing your knees, until the top surfaces of your thighs are parallel to the floor; be sure that your knees are in line with your feet; this is the start/finish position (figure 228.1).

- Maintain a forward gaze, a twenty-degree forward lean and a slightly arched lower back throughout the entire exercise.

- Following the plane of action (PA-D), smoothly stand upright by extending your knees and hips — pause briefly; this is the mid-phase position (figure 228.2).

- Do not bounce out of the start position.

- Smoothly return to the start/finish position.

RISK (Weight Training Truth #2):

R/B	Injury Site
(+) 1	Shoulders (Zone — II Top)
(+) 4	Spine/Back (Zone I — Lower)
(+) 3	Knees
(+) 6	Other (Zone IV — Groin)

NOTES:

(1) A stance wider than illustrated in figure 228.1 will increase the work done by the groin and buttock muscles, but too wide a stance will cause a decrease in the total power capacity for those muscles.

(2) To take some work away from the buttock muscles, and thus make the quadriceps work harder, a board one to two inches (three to five cm) thick can be placed under your heels.

(3) The R/B values are not altered by Notes 1 and 2, as long as all other execution parameters are maintained.

(4) Please see variations 117.c and 117.e for further variations of execution.

Fig. 229: Wide Hands

Variation 117.c — Wide Hand Placement

If your performance of any barbell squat creates pain in zone II of your shoulders, the use of a wider hand placement on the bar (as shown in figure 229) will reduce the pain considerably.

RISK (Weight Training Truth #2):

R/B	Injury Site
(–) 2	Shoulders (Zone II — Top)

All other R/B values remain unchanged for that exercise.

Fig. 230: Narrow Stance, Deep Hips   *side view*   *front view*

Variation 117.d — Narrow Stance and Deep Hips

The most common cause of lower back injuries in squatting occurs when the high bar-placement and narrow stance features of "bodybuilding" squats are combined with the deep-hip mid-phase position of "powerlifting" squats.

This combination causes a forceful backward arch of the lower back while the lumbar facet joints, discs, and deep spinal soft tissues are fully "loaded." Tremendous forces are thus applied to these tissues, and the risk of lower back strain/injury becomes very high as the lower back attempts to restore the inward (lordotic) curve of the lumbar spine for the upward phase of the exercise.

- The R/B changes, listed below, are relative to variation 117.a.

RISK (Weight Training Truth #2):

R/B	Injury Site
(+) 1	Shoulders (Zone II — Top)
(+) 7	Spine/Back (Zone I — Lower)
(+) 4	Knees

BARBELL SQUAT Execution Variations (cont'd)

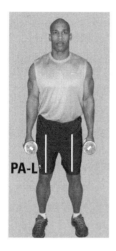

Fig. 231.1:
Start/Finish

Fig. 231.2:
Mid-Phase

Variation. 117.e — Dumbbell Squats   *Myths #6 & 7*
BENEFIT (Weight Training Truth #1):
In this exercise, dumbbells are held next to your outer thighs, which necessitates a narrow stance. Following the "Golden Rule of Squatting" (as presented in variation 117.d), once your stance is established as narrow, you must perform a "bodybuilding" variety of squat (i.e., upright torso, shallow depth, heels flat on the floor). Thus the purpose is quadricep strengthening and defining (PA-L). Maintain a slight arch in your lower back throughout.

RISK (Weight Training Truth #2):

R/B	Injury Site
(–) 3	Shoulders (Zone II — Top)

All other R/B values remain unchanged from variation 117.a.

• THE GOLDEN RULE OF SQUATTING •
*Do not combine the different components of
"bodybuilding" and "powerlifting" squats.*

"BODYBUILDING" SQUATS	DO NOT MIX	"POWERLIFTING" SQUATS
narrow stance		wide stance
upright torso		forward torso lean
high bar placement		low bar placement
shallow hip position		deep hip position

Exercise 118: FRONT SQUATS

Myths #6 and 7

Fig. 232.1: Start/Finish

PA-D

Fig. 232.2: Mid-Phase

PA-L

BENEFIT (Weight Training Truth #1):

- This exercise strengthens and defines the quadriceps muscles, as the primary target (PA-L).
- The upright torso alignment in this exercise protects the lower back, and precludes the proper execution of a deep "power-lifting" squat.

HOW:

- Standing in front of a squat rack with your feet twenty inches (fifty cm) apart, support a barbell across the front of your shoulders, with your arms crossed.
- Lower your hips by flexing your knees (not by leaning your torso forward), until your heels almost lift up off the floor; this is the start/finish position (figure 232.1).
- Your head should be held firmly in a forward gaze and your lower back slightly arched throughout the exercise.
- Following the plane of action (PA-D), smoothly stand upright by extending your knees — pause briefly; this is the mid-phase position (figure 232.2).
- Do not bounce out of the start position.
- Smoothly return to the start/finish position.

RISK (Weight Training Truth #2):

R/B	Injury Site
4	Spine/Back (Zone I — Lower)
6	Knees

Exercise 119: "HACK" SQUATS

Myth #7

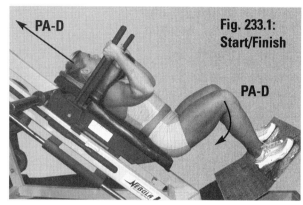

Fig. 233.1: Start/Finish

PA-D

PA-D

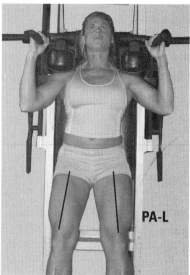

PA-L

Fig. 233.2: Mid-Phase

BENEFIT (Weight Training Truth #1):
This exercise strengthens and develops the quadriceps muscles, as the primary target (PA-L).

HOW:

• Standing under the shoulder padding of a hack squat machine, with your entire back and shoulders pressed firmly against the cushions and your feet parallel and ten inches (twenty-five cm) apart, lower your hips by flexing your knees, until your hip-torso angle is ninety degrees; this is the start/finish position (figure 233.1).

• Following the plane of action (PA-D), smoothly stand upright by extending your knees — pause briefly; this is the mid-phase position (figure 233.2).

• Do not bounce out of the start position.

• Smoothly return to the start/finish position.

RISK (Weight Training Truth #2):

R/B	Injury Site
9	Knees
3	Spine/Back (Zone I — Lower)

VARIATIONS OF EXECUTION: Please see exercises/variations 120.a, 120.b and 142.

"HACK" SQUAT Execution Variations

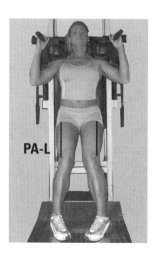

Fig. 234: Narrow Toed-In Stance

PA-L

Variation 120.a — Narrow Toed-In Stance
BENEFIT (Weight Training Truth #1):
A narrow stance (heels ten to twelve inches or twenty-five to thirty cm apart) and toes angled in (as shown in figure 234), will target the vastus lateralis region of the quadriceps (PA-L) muscle.

RISK (Weight Training Truth #2):

R/B	Injury Site
(+) 1	Knees

The other R/B value remains unchanged.

VARIATIONS OF EXECUTION: Please see exercises/variations 120.b and 142.

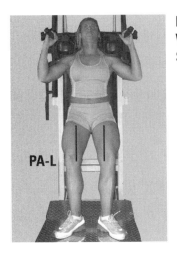

**Fig. 235:
Wide Toed-Out
Stance**

PA-L

Variation 120.b — Wide Toed-Out Stance
BENEFIT (Weight Training Truth #1):
A wide stance (toes at least fifteen inches/thirty-eight cm apart) and toes angled out (as shown in fig. 235), will target the vastus medialis region of the quadriceps (PA-L) muscle.

RISK (Weight Training Truth #2):

R/B	Injury Site
(+) 1	Knees
The other R/B value remains unchanged.	

VARIATIONS OF EXECUTION: Please refer to exercise 142.

Exercise 121: LEG PRESS (SHALLOW)

Myth #2 & #7

**Fig. 236.1:
Start/Finish**

PA-D

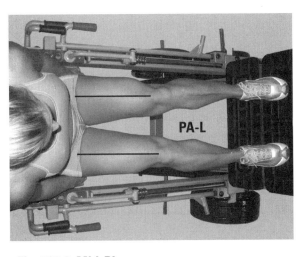

PA-L

Fig. 236.2: Mid-Phase

BENEFIT (Weight Training Truth #1):
This exercise strengthens and develops the quadriceps muscle as the primary target (PA-L).

HOW:

• Sitting or lying on the seat of a leg press machine with the back adjusted so that your torso-hip angle is about 120 degrees, place your feet about twelve inches (thirty cm) apart on the central region of the push-plate (see Note #1).

• Lower the push-plate by flexing your knees until your torso-hip angle is sixty degrees; this is the start/finish position (figure 236.1).

• Following the plane of action (PA-D), smoothly press the plate away from you by fully extending your knees — pause briefly; this is the mid-phase position (figure 236.2).

• Hold the "locked-out" knees position briefly.

• Do not shift your hips or your lower back to assist in the lift.

• Smoothly return the push-plate to the start/finish position.

RISK (Weight Training Truth #2):

R/B	Injury Site
5	Spine/Back (Zone I — Lower)
5	Knees

NOTES:

• Foot placement on the push-plate (i.e., higher or lower than indicated here) has little effect on this variation of leg press, but is quite significant when applied to deep leg presses (exercise 135).

• Please see exercises/variations 122.a, 122.b and 135.

LEG PRESS (SHALLOW) Execution Variations

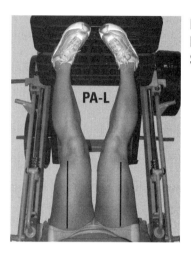

**Fig. 237:
Narrow Toed-In
Stance**

Variation 122.a — Narrow Toed-In Stance
BENEFIT (Weight Training Truth #1):
A narrow stance (the heels eight to ten inches/twenty to twenty-five cm apart), with your toes angled in (as shown in figure 237), will target the vastus lateralis region of the quadriceps (PA-L) muscle.

RISK (Weight Training Truth #2):

R/B	Injury Site
(+) 2	Knees

The other R/B value remains unchanged.

VARIATIONS OF EXECUTION: Please see exercises/variations 122.b and 135.

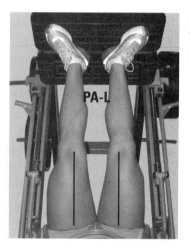

**Fig. 238:
Wide Toed-Out
Stance**

Variation 122.b — Wide Toed-Out Stance
BENEFIT (Weight Training Truth #1):
A wide stance (the toes twelve to fifteen inches/thirty to forty-five cm apart), with your toes angled out as shown in figure 238 will target the vastus medialis region of the quadriceps (PA-L) muscles.

RISK (Weight Training Truth #2):

R/B	Injury
(+) 2	Knees

The other R/B values remain unchanged.

VARIATIONS OF EXECUTION: Please see exercise 135.

Exercise 123: LUNGES (BARBELL)

Myths #6 & 7

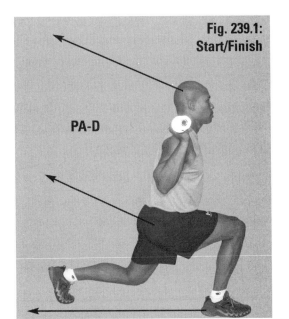

Fig. 239.1: Start/Finish

PA-D

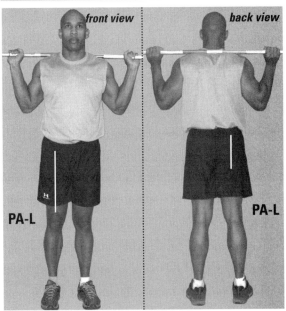

front view back view

PA-L PA-L

Fig. 239.2: Mid-Phase

BENEFIT (Weight Training Truth #1):
This exercise strengthens and develops the entire thigh and buttock; the primary targets are the quadriceps and gluteal muscles (PA-L).

HOW:

• Standing upright with your feet eight to ten inches (twenty to twenty-five cm) apart, place a barbell across your shoulders, at the base of your neck.

• Take a full stride forward, about thirty inches (76 cm), with one leg and plant that foot firmly on the floor.

• Lower the weight by flexing the front knee to ninety degrees; this is the start/finish position (figure 239.1).

• Following the plane of action (PA-D), smoothly drive your body upward, putting your legs together; this is the mid-phase position (figures 239.2a, 239.2b).

• Do not bounce out of the start position.

• Maintain a slight arch in your lower back throughout.

• Smoothly return to the start/finish position.

RISK (Weight Training Truth #2):

R/B	Injury Site
3	Spine/Back (Zone I — Lower)
5	Knees
3	Shoulders (Zone II — Top)
3	"Others" (Zone IV -Groin)

VARIATIONS OF EXECUTION: Please see exercises/variations 124.a, 124.b, 124.c and 141.

LUNGE Execution Variations

**Fig. 240:
Dumbbell
Lunge**

Variation 124.a — Dumbbells

The execution of a dumbbell lunge is identical to a barbell lunge, except that your arms hang down by your outer thighs holding the dumbbells. The benefits of this variation are:

(1) easier balance,

(2) no shoulder stress, and

(3) no change in purpose/benefit (Weight Training Truth #1).

RISK (Weight Training Truth #2):

R/B	Injury Site
(–) 3	Shoulders (Zone II — Top)

All other R/B values remain unchanged from exercise 123.

VARIATIONS OF EXECUTION: Please see exercises/variations 124.b, 124.c and 141.

**Fig. 241:
Shallow
Lunge**

PA-L

Variation 124.b — Barbell/Shallow

BENEFIT (Weight Training Truth #1):

Taking a shorter stride of about twenty-four inches (sixty cm) creates a noticeably shallower movement, which makes the quadriceps the single primary target muscle (PA-L) and reduces the risks of injury.

RISK (Weight Training Truth #2):

R/B	Injury Site
(–) 1	Spine/Back (Zone I — Lower)
(–) 2	Knees
(–) 3	"Other" (Zone IV — Groin)

The other R/B value remains unchanged from exercise 123.

VARIATIONS OF EXECUTION: Please see exercises/variations 124.c and 141.

top view

PA-L

back view

PA-L

Fig. 242:
Deep Lunge

Variation 124.c — Barbell/Deep
BENEFIT (Weight Training Truth #1):
Taking a longer stride of about thirty-eight inches (one meter) makes a noticeably deeper movement, which makes the gluteals the primary target muscle (PA-L) but increases the risks of injury.

RISK (Weight Training Truth #2):

R/B	Injury Site
(+) 1	Spine/Back (Zone I — Lower)
(+) 1	Knees
(+) 2	"Other" (Zone IV — Groin)

The other R/B value remains unchanged.

VARIATIONS OF EXECUTION: Please refer to exercise 141.

Exercise 125: "SISSY" SQUATS

Fig. 243.1: Start/Finish

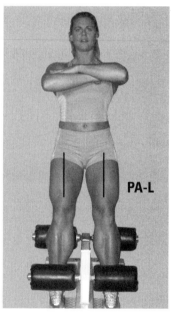

Fig. 243.2: Mid-Phase

BENEFIT (Weight Training Truth #1):
This exercise defines the quadriceps muscle; the primary targets are the central and upper quadricep regions (PA-L).

HOW:

- Cross your arms on your chest (with or without additional weight held against your chest) and place your feet and ankles in the "sissy" squat apparatus, with the leg support positioned just below the knee.

- Squat down until your buttocks are at or just below knee height; this is the start/finish position (figure 243.1).

- Following the plane of action (PA-D), smoothly contract your quadriceps until you are upright — pause briefly; this is the mid-phase position (figure 243.2).

- Maintain a slight arch in your lower back but an otherwise upright torso throughout the exercise.

- Smoothly return to the start/finish position.

RISK (Weight Training Truth #2):

R/B	Injury Site
3	Knees

Exercise 126: THIGH EXTENSIONS

Myth #9

Fig. 244.1: Start/Finish

PA-D

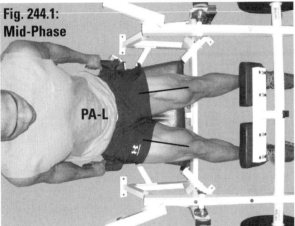

Fig. 244.1: Mid-Phase

PA-L

BENEFIT (Weight Training Truth #1):
This exercise develops strength and definition in the quadriceps muscles; the primary targets are the central and lower region — especially the vastus medialis (PA-L).

HOW:

- Sitting on a thigh extension machine, place your back firmly against the support-pad.
- Adjust the press-pads to fit just above your ankles.
- Keep your buttocks firmly in place throughout the exercise; this is the start/finish position (figure 244.1).
- Following the plane of action (PA-D), smoothly raise your feet until your knees are fully extended and hold the position very briefly; this is the mid-phase position (figure 244.2).
- Smoothly return the weight to the start/finish position.

RISK (Weight Training Truth #2):

R/B	Injury Site
2	Knees

VARIATIONS OF EXECUTION: Please see exercise 127.

THIGH EXTENSION Execution Variation 127 — One Leg at a Time

Fig. 245

PA-L

BENEFIT (Weight Training Truth #1):
Performed as in exercise 126 but use just one leg at a time. This strictly develops the vastus medialis muscle (PA-L) for both strength and definition.

RISK (Weight Training Truth #2):
The R/B value remains unchanged from exercise 126.

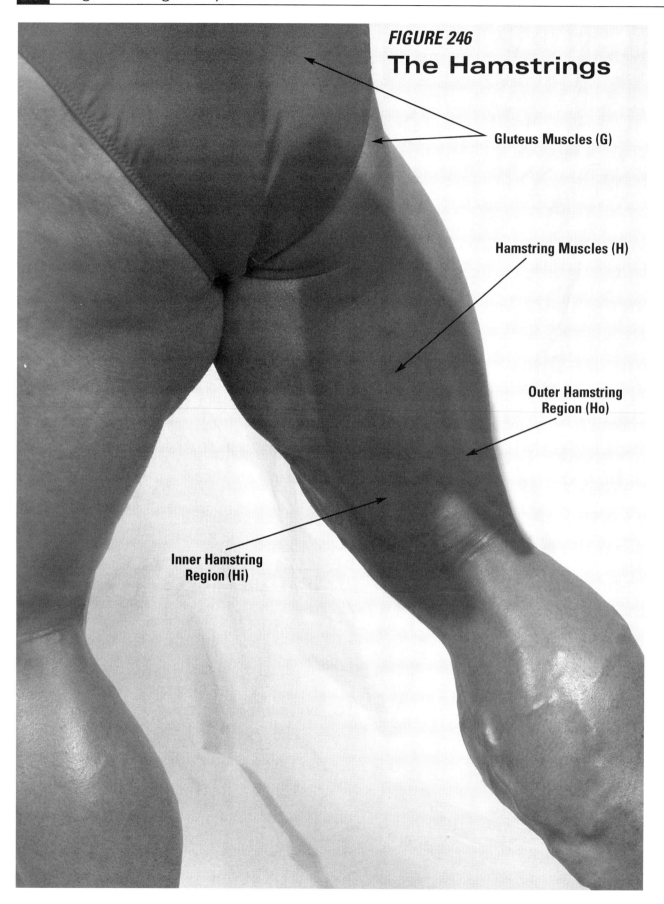

FIGURE 246
The Hamstrings

Gluteus Muscles (G)

Hamstring Muscles (H)

Outer Hamstring
Region (Ho)

Inner Hamstring
Region (Hi)

Table 9 — HAMSTRING EXERCISES

Name of Exercise/Variation	Benefit (WT #1)	R/B Values (WT #2)	No.	Pg.
Straight-Leg Deadlift	H-S/G, E-P	10, 10, 9, 3	128	208
Execution Variation:				
On a Platform	H, E-S/E-P	(+) 2, (+) 1	129	209
Standing One-Leg Ham Curls	H-D	5, 3	130	210
Execution Variations:				
Toed-In Leg Position	Hi-D		131.a	211
Toed-Out Leg Position	Ho-D		131.b	211
Prone Hamstring Curls	H-P	3, 3	132	212
Execution Variations:				
Toed-In Leg Position	Hi-P	(+) 5	133.a	212
Toed-Out Leg Position	Ho-P	(+) 5	133.b	213
One-Leg Variation	H-D	(−) 2	133.c	213
Toed-In Leg Position	Hi-D		133.d	213
Toed-Out Leg Position	Ho-D		133.e	214
Execution Variation For:				
All Hamstrings Curls — Knee Hyperext.		(+) 2	134	214

KEY:

H = Hamstring Muscles   E = Erector Spinal Muscles *(see Table 3)*   G = Gluteus Muscles *(see Table 10)*

Hi = Inner Hamstring Region   Ho = Outer Hamstring Region   P = Power/Size

S = Stretch   D = Definition

Exercise 128: STRAIGHT-LEG DEADLIFT

Myths #13 & #7

Fig. 247.1: Start/Finish

PA-D

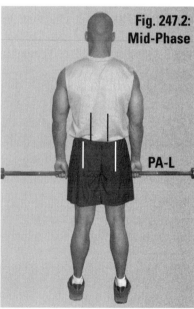

Fig. 247.2: Mid-Phase

PA-L

BENEFIT (Weight Training Truth #1):

• This exercise primarily develops power and thickness in the gluteal and erector spinales muscles (PA-L), while stretching the hamstring muscles secondarily.

• This exercise causes a demanding stretch in the hamstring, which makes it a poor exercise for strengthening that zone.

HOW:

• Standing with your feet about six inches (fifteen cm) apart, lock your knees in full extension, bend forward at your waist to grasp the bar (on the floor) with your palms facing down and shoulder-width apart; this is the start/finish position (figure 247.1).

• Following the plane of action (PA-D), smoothly stand upright using your lower back, buttock and hamstring muscles simultaneously; this is the mid-phase position (figure 247.2).

• Keep your knees and elbows fully extended throughout the entire exercise.

• Smoothly return the bar to the start/finish position.

RISK (Weight Training Truth #2):

R/B	Injury Site
10	Spine/Back (Zone I — Lower)
10	Hamstrings
9	Spine/Back (Zone II — Upper)
3	Elbows (Zone I — Inside)

VARIATIONS OF EXECUTION: Please see exercises/variations 129, 39, 40 and 62.a.

STRAIGHT-LEG DEADLIFT Execution Variation 129 — On a Platform

**Fig. 248:
Straight-Leg
Deadlift on a
Platform**

BENEFIT (Weight Training Truth #1):
The hamstring and erector spinales stretch benefit of straight-leg deadlifts is further enhanced by standing on a platform (as shown in figure 248).

The exercise should be performed as described in exercise 128, except that the weights are lifted from and returned to a position below your feet in each repetition. This, however, increases the degree of risk of injury to both the lower back and the hamstrings.

RISK (Weight Training Truth #2):

R/B	Injury Site
(+) 2	Spine/Back (Zone I — Lower)
(+) 1	Hamstrings

All other R/B values remain unchanged from exercise 128.

Exercise 130: STANDING ONE-LEG HAMSTRING CURLS

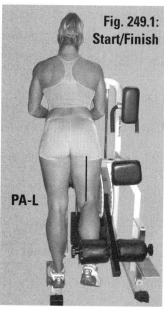

Fig. 249.1:
Start/Finish

PA-L

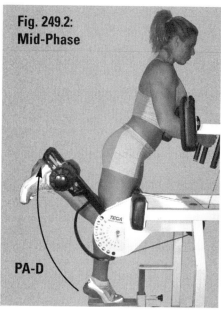

Fig. 249.2:
Mid-Phase

PA-D

BENEFIT (Weight Training Truth #1):
This exercise primarily creates definition in the hamstring muscles (PA-L) and strengthens them only moderately.

HOW:

- At a standing hamstring-curl machine, grasp the support bar and place one leg behind the press-pad.

- Flex your torso slightly forward; this is the start/finish position (figure 249.1).

- Maintain a slight arch in your lower back throughout.

- Following the plane of action (PA-D), smoothly bring your heel up toward your buttock — pause briefly; this is the mid-phase position (figure 249.2).

- Do not twist or excessively arch your lower back during exertion.

- Smoothly return to the start/finish position.

RISK (Weight Training Truth #2):

R/B	Injury Site
5	Spine/Back (Zone I — Lower)
3	Hamstrings

VARIATIONS OF EXECUTION: Please see variations 131.a, 131.b and 134.

STANDING ONE-LEG HAMSTRING CURL Execution Variations

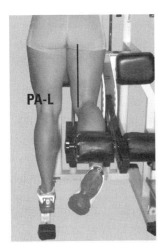

Fig. 250:
Toed-In
Leg Position

Variation 131.a — Toed-In Leg Position
BENEFIT (Weight Training Truth #1):
Standing one-legged hamstring curls performed with the entire leg slightly rotated internally (as shown) specifically targets the inner hamstrings muscle region (PA-L).

RISK (Weight Training Truth #2):
All R/B values remain unchanged from exercise 130.

VARIATIONS OF EXECUTION: Please see variations 131.b and 134.

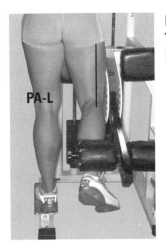

Fig. 251:
Toed-Out
Leg Position

Variation 131.b — Toed-Out Leg Position
BENEFIT (Weight Training Truth #1):
Standing one-legged hamstring curls performed with the entire leg rotated slightly externally (as shown) specifically targets the outer hamstring muscle region (PA-L).

RISK (Weight Training Truth #2):
All R/B values remain unchanged from exercise 130.

VARIATIONS OF EXECUTION: Please see variation 134.

Exercise 132: PRONE HAMSTRING CURLS

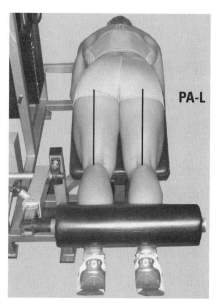

Fig. 252.1: Start/Finish

PA-L

BENEFIT (Weight Training Truth #1):
This exercise strengthens and develops the hamstring muscles as the primary target (PA-L).

HOW:

• Lie face down on a hamstring-curl bench with the press-pads adjusted to your Achilles tendon or heel region; this is the start/finish position (figure 252.1).

• Following the plane of action (PA-D), smoothly curl your heels up toward your buttocks without lifting your thighs from the bench or arching your lower back — pause briefly; this is the mid-phase position (figure 252.2).

• Do not jerk your heels up.

• Smoothly return to the start/finish position.

RISK (Weight Training Truth #2):

R/B	Injury Site
3	Spine/Back (Zone I — Lower)
3	Hamstrings

VARIATIONS OF EXECUTION: Please see exercises/variations 133.a–e, 134 and 137.

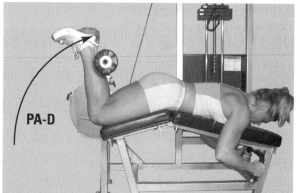

PA-D

Fig. 252.2: Mid-Phase

PRONE HAMSTRING CURL Execution Variations

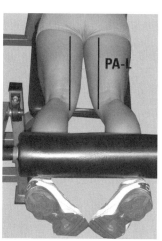

Fig. 253: Toed-In Leg Position

PA-L

Variation 133.a — Toed-In Leg Position
BENEFIT (Weight Training Truth #1):
Hamstring curls performed with both legs rotated slightly internally (as shown in figure 253) specifically target the inner hamstring muscle region (PA-L) but add a risk of injury at the knee.

RISK (Weight Training Truth #2):

R/B	Injury Site
(+) 5	Knees

All other R/B values remain unchanged from exercise 132.

VARIATIONS OF EXECUTION: Please see exercises/variations 133.c-133.e, 134 and 137.

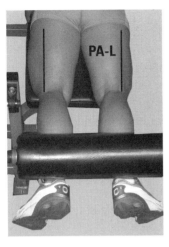

Fig. 254:
Toed-In
Leg Position

Variation 133.b — Toed-Out Leg Position
BENEFIT (Weight Training Truth #1):
Hamstring curls performed with both legs rotated slightly externally (as shown in figure 254) specifically target the outer hamstring muscle region (PA-L) but add a risk of injury at the knee.

RISK (Weight Training Truth #2):

R/B	Injury Site
(+) 5	Knees

All other R/B values remain unchanged from exercise 132.

VARIATIONS OF EXECUTION: Please see exercises/variations 133.c–e, 134 and 137.

Fig. 255:
One Leg

Variation 133.c — One Leg
BENEFIT (Weight Training Truth #1):
Performing prone hamstring curls one leg at a time diminishes the risk of injury to the lower back but makes the exercise more for hamstring (PA-L) definition than for strength.

RISK (Weight Training Truth #2):

R/B	Injury Site
(–) 2	Spine/Back (Zone I — Lower)

The other R/B value remains unchanged from exercise 132.

VARIATIONS OF EXECUTION: Please see exercises/variations 133.d, 133.e, 134 and 137.

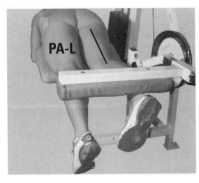

Fig. 256:
Toed-In Position
— One Leg

Variation 133.d — Toed-In Leg Position, One Leg
BENEFIT (Weight Training Truth #1):
One-leg hamstring curls performed with the entire leg rotated slightly internally (as shown in figure 256) specifically targets the inner region of the hamstring muscles (PA-L) without the knee strain that occurs when both legs are curled together (as in variations. 133.a and 133.b).

RISK (Weight Training Truth #2):
The R/B values remain unchanged from variation 133.c

VARIATIONS OF EXECUTION: Please see exercises/variations 133.e, 134 and 137.

PRONE HAMSTRING CURL Execution Variations (cont'd)

Fig. 257: Toed-Out Position — One Leg

Variation 133.e — Toed-Out Leg Position, One-Leg
BENEFIT (Weight Training Truth #1):
One-leg hamstring curls performed with the entire leg rotated slightly externally (as shown in figure 257) specifically targets the outer region of the hamstring muscles (PA-L) without the knee strain that occurs when both legs are curled together (as in variations 133.a and 133.b).

RISK (Weight Training Truth #2):
The R/B values remain unchanged from variation 133.c

VARIATIONS OF EXECUTION: Please see exercises/variations 134 and 137 for further variations of execution.

ALL HAMSTRING CURLS Execution Variation 134 — Knee Hyperextension

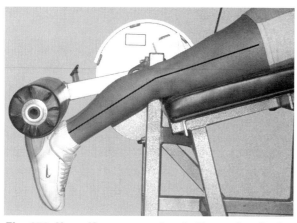

If your knees are capable of more than 180 degrees of extension, or the apparatus itself forces your knee(s) into excessive extension, there is an increased risk of hamstring injury.

RISK (Weight Training Truth #2):

R/B	Injury Site
(+) 2	Hamstrings

All other R/B values remain constant for that exercise.

Fig. 258: Knee Hyperextension in Hamstring Curl

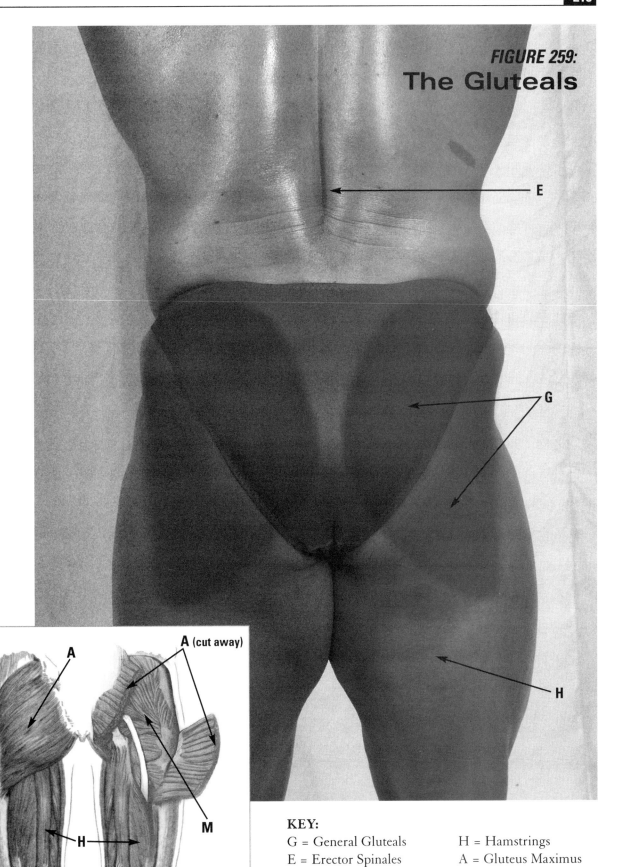

FIGURE 259:
The Gluteals

KEY:

G = General Gluteals

E = Erector Spinales

M = Gluteus Medius

H = Hamstrings

A = Gluteus Maximus

Table 10 — GLUTEAL EXERCISES

Name of Exercise/Variation	Benefit (WT #1)	R/B Values (WT #2)	No.	Pg.
Deep Leg Press	G, Q-P	10, 7	135	217
Execution Variations:				
High Foot Placement	G-P	(+) 1, (+) 5	136.a	218
Low Foot Placement	Q-P	(+) 2	136.b	219
"Modified" Hamstrings Curls	A, H-P, D	6	137	220
Execution Variation:				
One Leg at a Time		(−) 3	138	220
Cable Buttock Pulls — To the Rear	A-D	5	139	221
Execution Variation:				
To the Side	M-D	(−) 2	140	222
Deep Lunges	G-P, D	4, 6, 3, 5	124.c	203
"Platform" Lunges	G, Q-P	3, 7	141	223
Deep "Hack" Squats	G, Q-P	7, 10+	142	221
Straight-Leg Deadlift	G, E-P/H-S	10, 10, 9, 3	128	208

KEY:

G = General Gluteals   H = Hamstrings *(see Table 9)*   E = Erector Spinales *(see Table 3)*

A = Gluteus Maximus   M = Gluteus Medius   P = Power/Size

D = Definition   S = Stretch

Exercise 135: DEEP LEG PRESS

Myths #2 & #7

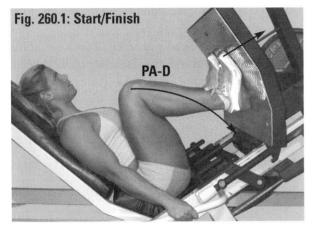

Fig. 260.1: Start/Finish

PA-D

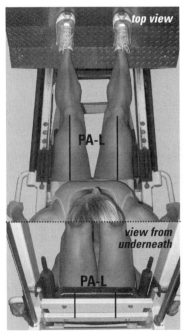

top view

Fig. 260.2: Mid-Phase

PA-L

view from underneath

PA-L

BENEFIT (Weight Training Truth #1):
This exercise strengthens and develops the buttocks and entire thigh muscles; the primary targets are the gluteals and quadriceps muscles (PA-L).

HOW:

- Sitting or lying in the seat of a leg press machine adjusted so your torso-hip ratio is about 120 degrees, place your feet eight to ten inches (twenty to twenty-five cm) apart and parallel to each other in the middle to lower area of the push-plate.

- Lower the push-plate toward you by flexing your knees until your thighs touch your chest; this is the start/finish position (figure 260.1).

- Following the plane of action (PA-D), smoothly press the plate upward until your knees are fully extended — pause briefly; this is the mid-phase position (figure 260.2).

- Smoothly return the push-plate to the start/finish position.

RISK (Weight Training Truth #2):

R/B	Injury Site
10	Spine/Back (Zone I — Lower)
7	Knees

VARIATIONS OF EXECUTION: Please see exercises/variations 136.a, 136.b and 121.

— lower weight
— ↓ angle (exception)

DEEP LEG PRESS Execution Variations

Fig. 261.1:
Start/Finish

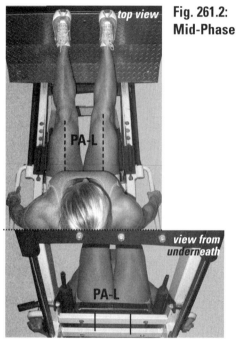

top view

PA-L

view from underneath

PA-L

Fig. 261.2:
Mid-Phase

Variation 136.a — High Foot Placement   *Myth #18*
BENEFIT (Weight Training Truth #1):
Placing your feet high on the push-plate (as shown in figure 261.1) makes the gluteal muscles the primary target (PA-L) but increases the risk of injury to the lower back. It also adds a risk of injury to the upper hamstrings without significant benefit to the hamstring muscles.

RISK (Weight Training Truth #2):

R/B	Injury Site
(+) 1	Spine/Back (Zone I — Lower)
(+) 5	Hamstrings

The other R/B value remains unchanged from exercise 135.

VARIATIONS OF EXECUTION: Please see exercises/variations 136.b and 121.

Fig. 262.1: Start/Finish

PA-L

Fig. 262.2: Mid-Phase

Variation 136.b — Low Foot Placement   *Myths #2 & #7*

BENEFIT (Weight Training Truth #1):

The placement of your feet low on the push-plate (as shown in figure 262.1) targets the quadriceps (PA-L) slightly more than the gluteals. Unfortunately, this increases the risk of injury to the knees.

RISK (Weight Training Truth #2):

R/B	Injury Site
(+) 2	Knees

The other R/B value remains unchanged from exercise 135.

VARIATIONS OF EXECUTION: Please refer to exercise 121.

Exercise 137: "MODIFIED" HAMSTRINGS CURLS

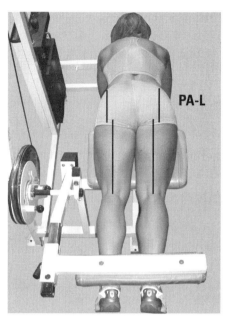

Fig. 263.1: Start/Finish

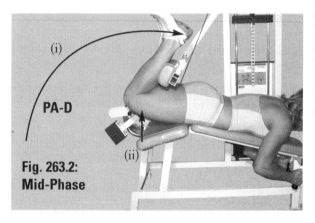

Fig. 263.2: Mid-Phase

BENEFIT (Weight Training Truth #1):
This exercise develops strength in both the gluteal and hamstring muscles, and as such is an excellent "tie-in" exercise for the hamstring and gluteal regions.

HOW:

- Lie face down on a hamstring curl bench with the press pads touching the lowest part of your Achilles tendon/heel region; this is the start/finish position (figure 263.1).
- Following the plane of action (PA-D),

  (i) smoothly curl your heels up toward your buttock until your knees are flexed to ninety degrees,

  (ii) then elevate your thighs off the bench with a non-jerking contraction of your gluteals. Pause briefly; this is the mid-phase position (figure 263.2).

- Smoothly lower your thighs, then your heels, returning to the start/finish position.

RISK (Weight Training Truth #2):

R/B	Injury Site
6	Spine/Back (Zone I — Lower)

VARIATIONS OF EXECUTION: Please see exercises/variations 138 and 132.

"MODIFIED" HAMSTRING CURL Execution Variation 138 — One Leg at a Time

Fig. 264

BENEFIT (Weight Training Truth #1):
In a modified hamstring curl (exercise 137), curling one leg at a time allows for a fuller contraction of the gluteal muscle while reducing the risk of injury in the lower back.

RISK (Weight Training Truth #2):

R/B	Injury Site
(–) 3	Spine/Back (Zone I — Lower)

VARIATIONS OF EXECUTION: Please refer to exercise 132.

Exercise 139: CABLE BUTTOCK PULLS — TO THE REAR

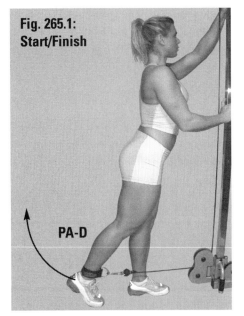

Fig. 265.1: Start/Finish

PA-D

Fig. 265.2: Mid-Phase

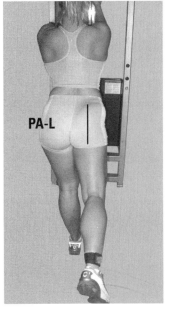

PA-L

BENEFIT (Weight Training Truth #1):
This is a definition exercise for the gluteal muscles; the primary target is the central region of the longitudinally oriented gluteus maximus muscle fibers (PA-L).

HOW:

- Standing facing a cable pulley machine, grasp the support bar with both hands, stand with one foot about twelve inches (thirty cm) in front of the other and loop a strap around the far ankle; this is the start/finish position (figure 265.1).

- Keep your knee fully extended throughout the exercise.

- Following the plane of action (PA-D), smoothly pull your ankle backward to the highest point possible — pause briefly; this is the mid-phase position (figure 265.2).

- Flex your torso slightly forward and maintain a slight arch in your lower back throughout.

- Smoothly return to the start/finish position.

RISK (Weight Training Truth #2):

R/B	Injury Site
5	Spine/Back (Zone I — Lower)

VARIATIONS OF EXECUTION: Please refer to exercise 140.

CABLE BUTTOCK PULL Execution Variation 140 — To the Side

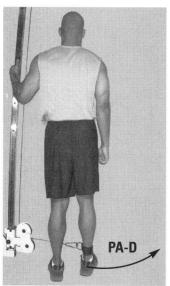

Fig. 266.1: Start/Finish

PA-D

back view **Fig. 266.2: Mid-Phase**

top view
PA-L

BENEFIT (Weight Training Truth #1):
This is a definition exercise for the gluteal muscles; the primary target is the outer region of horizontally-oriented gluteus medius muscle fibers (PA-L).

HOW:

- Standing beside a cable pulley machine, grasp the support bar with one hand and loop a strap around the outer ankle; this is the start/finish position (figure 266.1).
- Keep your knee fully extended throughout the exercise.
- Following the plane of action (PA-D), smoothly pull your ankle sideways to the highest point possible — pause briefly; this is the mid-phase position (figure 266.2).
- To protect your lower back, flex your torso slightly forward and arch your lower back slightly throughout.
- Smoothly return to the start/finish position.

RISK (Weight Training Truth #2):

R/B	Injury Site
(–) 2	Spine/Back (Zone I — Lower)

Exercise 141: "PLATFORM" LUNGES

Myths #6 & 7

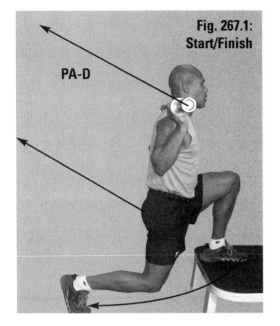

Fig. 267.1: Start/Finish

PA-D

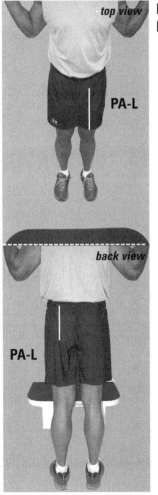

top view

Fig. 267.2: Mid-Phase

PA-L

back view

PA-L

BENEFIT (Weight Training Truth #1):

- This exercise strengthens and develops the thigh and buttock region; the primary targets are the gluteal and quadriceps muscles (PA-L).

- The higher the platform used, the greater the gluteal work and the lesser the quadriceps work.

HOW:

- Standing about three feet in front of a six- to twelve-inch (fifteen to thirty cm) high platform, place a barbell across your shoulders at the base of your neck.

- Step forward with one foot, placing it firmly on the platform, then shift your upright torso over that foot, allowing the knee to bend until your abdomen touches your thigh; this is the start/finish position (figure 267.1).

- Following the plane of action (PA-D), smoothly press out of the bent-knee position until you are fully upright, then step back onto the floor; this is the mid-phase position (figure 267.2).

- Maintain a slight arch in your lower back throughout.

- Smoothly return to the start/finish position.

RISK (Weight Training Truth #2):

R/B	Injury Site
3	Spine/Back (Zone I — Lower)
7	Knees

NOTES:

- This exercise can also be performed (with no change of purpose or risks) using dumbbells held suspended at your sides.

- Please refer to exercise 123 for the variation of execution.

Exercise 142: DEEP "HACK" SQUATS

Myth #7

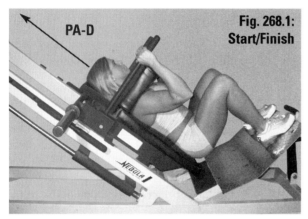

PA-D

Fig. 268.1: Start/Finish

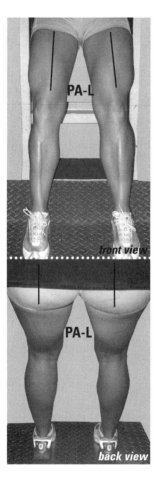

Fig. 268.2: Mid-Phase

PA-L

front view

PA-L

back view

BENEFIT (Weight Training Truth #1):
This exercise strengthens and develops the thigh and buttock regions; the primary targets are the gluteal and quadriceps muscles (PA-L).

HOW:

• Standing under the shoulder padding of a hack squat machine, press your buttocks and shoulders firmly into the back cushion.

• With your feet twelve inches (thirty cm) apart and pointing straight ahead, lower your hips until they are well below knee height; this is the start/finish position (figure 268.1).

• Following the plane of action (PA-D), smoothly press yourself up until your knees are fully extended — pause briefly; this is the mid-phase position (figure 268.2).

• Do not bounce out of the start position.

• Smoothly return to the start/finish position.

RISK (Weight Training Truth #2):

R/B	Injury Site
7	Spine/Back (Zone I — Lower)
10+	Knees

VARIATIONS OF EXECUTION: Please refer to exercise 119.

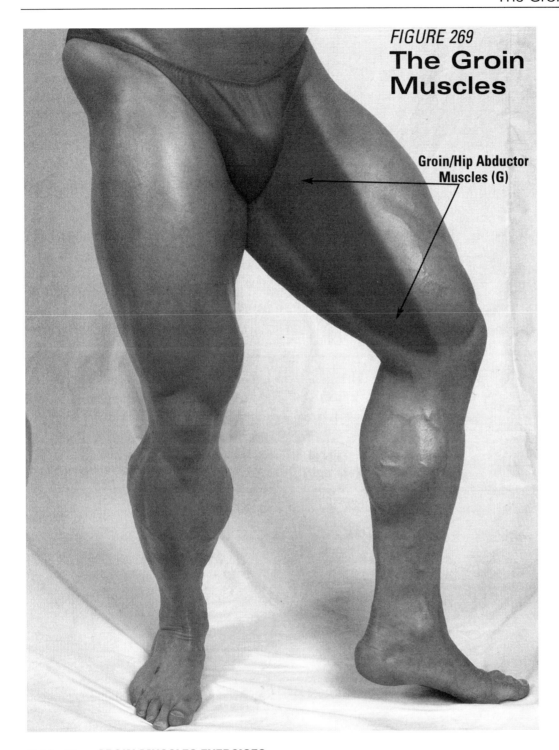

FIGURE 269
The Groin Muscles

Groin/Hip Abductor
Muscles (G)

Table 11 — GROIN MUSCLES EXERCISES

Name of Exercise/Variation	Benefit (WT #1)	R/B Values (WT #2)	No.	Pg.
Side Lunges	G-P, S	4, 7, 7	143	226
Front Cable Leg-Crossovers	G-D	2, 2	144	227

KEY:
G = Groin/Hip Adductor Muscles   P = Power/Size   S = Stretch
D = Definition

Exercise 143: SIDE LUNGES

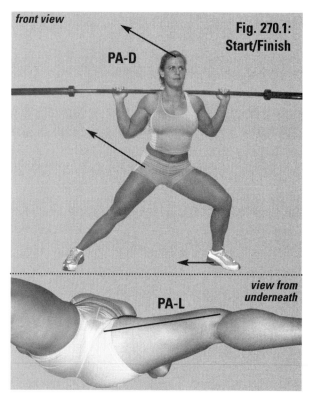

front view

Fig. 270.1: Start/Finish

PA-D

PA-L

view from underneath

Fig. 270.2: Mid-Phase

BENEFIT (Weight Training Truth #1):

• This exercise strengthens and stretches the groin region muscles; the primary targets are the hip adductor muscles (PA-L).

• There is considerable gluteal and quadricep muscle activity on the side with the bent knee.

HOW:

• Standing upright with your feet shoulder-width apart, place a barbell across the top of your shoulders (at the base of the neck) and step sideways three to four feet, keeping your feet parallel to each other.

• Shift your body to one side and bend that knee until a slight pressure is felt in the opposite groin; this is the start/finish position (figure 270.1).

• Following the plane of action (PA-D), using the groin muscles of the outstretched leg along with the glutes and quadriceps of the bent leg, smoothly shift your body into the upright position — pause briefly; this is the mid-phase position (figure 270.2).

• Do not lean your torso forward during exertion.

• Maintain a slight arch in your the lower back throughout.

• Smoothly return to the start/finish position.

RISK (Weight Training Truth #2):

R/B	Injury Site
4	Spine/Back (Zone I — Lower)
7	Knees
7	"Other" (Zone IV — Groin)

Exercise 144: FRONT CABLE LEG-CROSSOVERS

Fig. 271.1: Start/Finish

PA-L

Fig. 271.2: Mid-Phase

PA-D

BENEFIT (Weight Training Truth #1):
This is a definition exercise for the groin muscle region; the primary targets are the hip adductor muscles (PA-L).

HOW:

• Standing beside a cable pulley machine, loop the ankle of the leg closest to the cable machine with a strap; this is the start/finish position (figure 271.1).

• Keep your knee fully extended throughout the exercise.

• Following the plane of action (PA-D), smoothly pull your ankle across in front of your other leg as far as possible — pause briefly; this is the mid-phase position (figure 271.2).

• Keep the foot pointing straight ahead during the exertion.

• Do not lean your torso forward during exertion.

• Maintain a slight arch in your lower back throughout.

• Smoothly return to the start/finish position.

RISK (Weight Training Truth #2):

R/B	Injury Site
2	"Other" (Zone IV — Groin)
2	Spine/Back (Zone I — Lower)

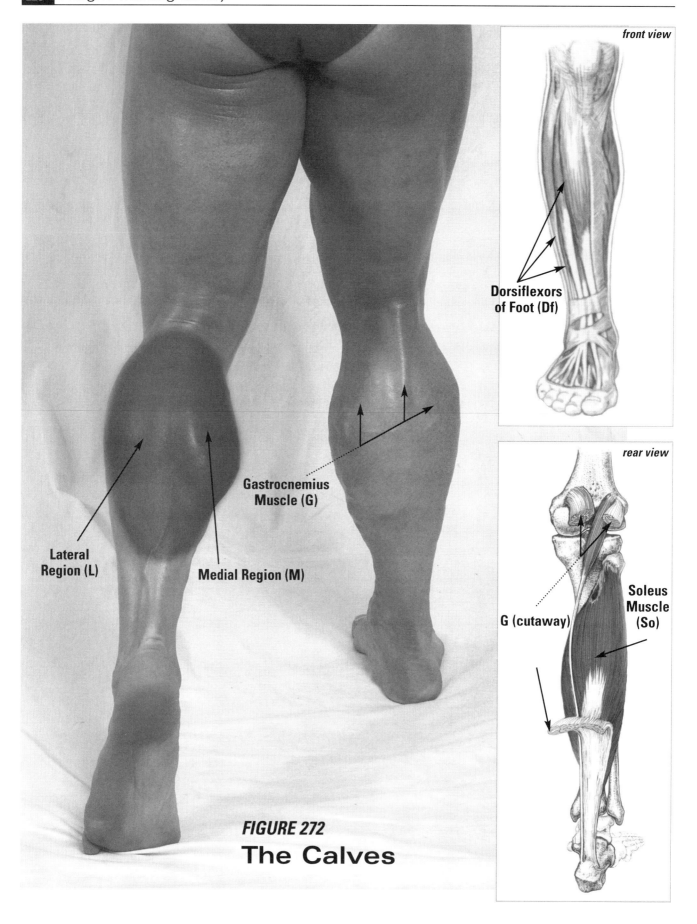

front view

Dorsiflexors of Foot (Df)

Gastrocnemius Muscle (G)

Lateral Region (L)

Medial Region (M)

rear view

G (cutaway)

Soleus Muscle (So)

FIGURE 272

The Calves

Table 12 — Calf Muscle Exercises

Name of Exercise/Variation		Benefit (WT #1)	R/B Values (WT #2)	No.	Pg.
Standing Calf Raises		G-P, S	2, 3, 2	145	230
"Donkey" Calf Raises		G-P, S	4, 6, 3	146	231
Leg-Press Calf Raises		G-P, S	4, 3, 6	147	232
"Hack" Calf Raises		G-P, S	4, 3, 2	148	233
Standing, One-Leg Calf Raises		G-D	3, 2	149	234
Seated Calf Raises		So-P	3	150	235
Execution Variations For:					
All Calf Exercises	— Toed-In	M-P		151.a	235
	— Toed-Out	L-P		151.b	236
All Standing Calf Exercises	— On Toes	G-S	(+) 7, (+) 3, (+) 3	151.c	236
Seated Calf Raises	— On Toes	So-S	(+) 7, (+) 3	151.d	236
Seated, Front-Foot-Raises		Df-P	3, 4	152	237
Cable, Front-Foot-Raises		Df-P	3	153	238

KEY:

G = Gastrocnemius Muscle   So = Soleus Muscle   M = Medial Region of Calf

L = Lateral Region Of Calf   Df = Dorsiflexors of foot   P = Power/Size

D = Definition   S = Stretch

Exercise 145: STANDING CALF RAISES

Myths #6 & #9

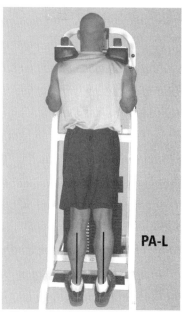

**Fig. 273.1:
Start/Finish**

PA-L

**Fig. 273.2:
Mid-Phase**

PA-D

BENEFIT (Weight Training Truth #1):
This exercise strengthens and stretches the calf muscles; the primary target is the gastrocnemius muscle (PA-L).

HOW:

- Standing at a calf raise machine with your shoulders under the support pads, place your feet on the support bar, parallel to each other.

- With the entire ball of each foot on the support bar, allow your heels to drop as low as possible; this is the start/finish position (figure 273.1).

- Following the plane of action (PA-D), smoothly raise your heels as high as possible — pause briefly; this is the mid-phase position (figure 273.2).

- Keep your knees fully (but not excessively) extended and your lower back slightly arched throughout.

- Smoothly return to the start/finish position.

RISK (Weight Training Truth #2):

R/B	Injury Site
2	Spine/Back (Zone I — Lower)
3	"Other" (Zone III — Achilles)
2	Hamstrings

VARIATIONS OF EXECUTION: Please see variations 151.a–151.c.

Exercise 146: "DONKEY" CALF RAISES

Myth #9

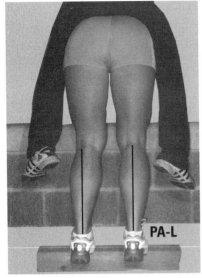

Fig. 274.1: Start/Finish

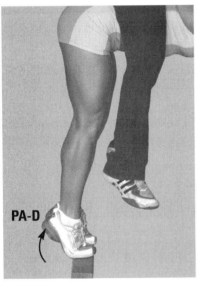

Fig. 274.2: Mid-Phase

BENEFIT (Weight Training Truth #1):
This exercise strengthens and stretches the calf muscles; the primary target is the gastrocnemius muscle (PA-L).

HOW:

- Standing, bend forward until your hands are solidly braced against a wall or other solid structure, so that your upper body is firmly supported in a horizontal position.

- Keeping them parallel to each other, place your feet on a block of wood about five inches (13 cm) high, with the entire ball of each foot on the block and your heels dropped down as low as possible; this is the start/finish position (figure 274.1).

- Have another person sit on your back, just above your hips.

- Following the plane of action (PA-D), smoothly raise your heels as high as possible — pause briefly; this is the mid-phase position (figure 274.2).

- Keep your knees fully (but not excessively) extended throughout.

- Smoothly return to the start/finish position.

RISK (Weight Training Truth #2):

R/B	Injury Site
4	Spine/Back (Zone I — Lower)
6	Hamstrings
3	"Other" (Zone III — Achilles)

NOTES:

- This exercise can also be performed with no change in benefit or risks on a "donkey" calf-raise machine.

- Please see variations 151.a to 151.c.

Exercise 147: LEG-PRESS CALF RAISES

Myth #9

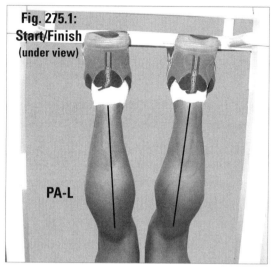

Fig. 275.1: Start/Finish (under view)

PA-L

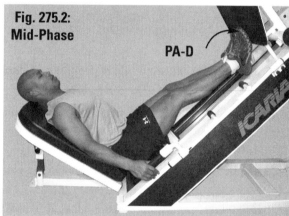

Fig. 275.2: Mid-Phase

PA-D

BENEFIT (Weight Training Truth #1):
This exercise strengthens and stretches the calf muscles; the primary target is the gastrocnemius muscle (PA-L).

HOW:

- Sitting in the seat of a leg press machine adjusted so your torso-hip angle is ninety degrees, place your feet firmly on the press plate, and push the weight up until your knees are fully extended.

- Re-position your feet at the bottom of the press plate, keeping your feet parallel and the entire ball of each foot in contact with the press-plate.

- Smoothly lower the press plate by allowing the balls of your feet to drop toward you; this is the start/finish position (figure 275.1).

- Following the plane of action (PA-D), smoothly press the balls of your feet upward as high as possible — pause briefly; this is the mid-phase position (figure 275.2).

- Keep your knees fully (but not excessively) extended, throughout.

- Smoothly return to the start/finish position.

RISK (Weight Training Truth #2):

R/B	Injury Site
4	Spine/Back (Zone I — Lower)
3	"Other" (Zone III — Achilles Tendon)
6	Hamstrings

VARIATIONS OF EXECUTION: Please see variations 151.a –151.c.

Exercise 148: "HACK" CALF RAISES

Myth #9

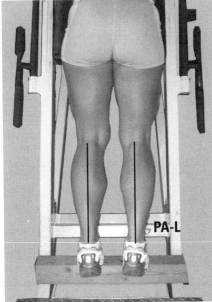

Fig. 276.1: Start/Finish

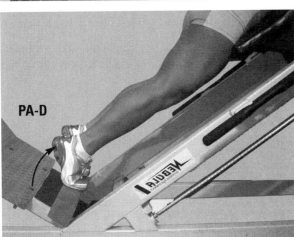

Fig. 276.2: Mid-Phase

BENEFIT (Weight Training Truth #1):

This exercise strengthens and stretches the calf muscles; the primary target is the gastrocnemius muscle (PA-L).

HOW:

- Standing facing a hack squat machine, place a block of wood about five inches (13 cm) high and four inches (10 cm) wide across the mid-region of the platform and place your shoulders under the support pads.

- Stand up with the weight, then position your feet on the wood so they are parallel to each other and the entire ball of each foot is on the wood.

- Allow your heels to drop down as low as possible; this is the start/finish position (figure 276.1).

- Following the plane of action (PA-D), smoothly raise your heels as high as possible — pause briefly; this is the mid-phase position (figure 276.2).

- Keep your knees fully (but not excessively) extended and maintain a slight arch in your lower back throughout.

- Smoothly return to the start/finish position.

RISK (Weight Training Truth #2):

R/B	Injury Site
4	Spine/Back (Zone I — Lower)
3	"Other" (Zone III — Achilles)
2	Hamstrings

VARIATIONS OF EXECUTION: See variations 151.a–151.c.

Exercise 149: STANDING, ONE-LEG CALF RAISES

Myth #9

**Fig. 277.1:
Start/Finish**

**Fig. 277.2:
Mid-Phase**

BENEFIT (Weight Training Truth #1):
This is a definition exercise for the calf muscles; the primary target is the gastrocnemius muscle (PA-L).

HOW:

• Standing on the spotter's platform of any chest- or shoulder-press bench (so that the uprights can be used for balance and support), place the ball of one foot on the edge of the platform.

• Lift your other foot completely off the support by bending that knee to ninety degrees, then shift your entire body weight onto the ball of your support foot, dropping the heel down as low as possible; this is the start/finish position (figure 277.1).

• Hold a dumbbell in your hand on the support leg side and grasp the upright support with your free hand.

• Following the plane of action (PA-D), smoothly raise your heel as high as possible — pause briefly; this is the mid-phase position (figure 277.2).

• Keep your weight-bearing knee fully (but not excessively) extended throughout the exercise.

• Smoothly return to the start/finish position.

RISK (Weight Training Truth #2):

R/B	Injury Site
3	"Other" (Zone III — Achilles)
2	Hamstrings

VARIATIONS OF EXECUTION: See variations 151.a–c.

Exercise 150: SEATED CALF RAISES

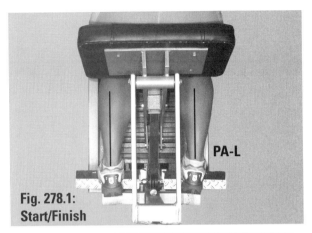

Fig. 278.1: Start/Finish

PA-L

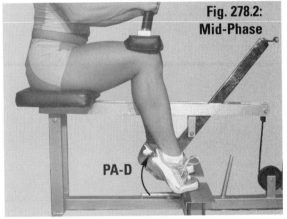

Fig. 278.2: Mid-Phase

PA-D

BENEFIT (Weight Training Truth #1):
This exercise strengthens the calf muscles; the primary target is the soleus muscle (PA-L).

HOW:

- Sit at a calf-raise machine adjusted so that the press-pads touch the tops of your legs while your feet are flat on the foot-support bar.
- Place your knees under the pads and the balls of both feet on the support bar, parallel to each other.
- Release the safety bar and allow your heels to drop as low as possible; this is the start/finish position (figure 278.1).
- Following the plane of action (PA-D), smoothly raise your heels as high as possible — pause briefly; this is the mid-phase position (figure 278.2).
- Smoothly return to the start/finish position.

RISK (Weight Training Truth #2):

R/B	Injury Site
3	"Other" (Zone III — Achilles)

VARIATIONS OF EXECUTION: Please see variations 151.a, 151.b, and 151.d.

ALL CALF EXERCISES Execution Variations

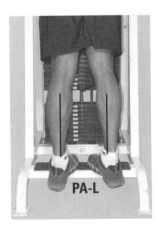

PA-L

Fig. 279 Toed-In Foot Position for Calf Exercises

Variation 151.a — Toed-In Foot Position
BENEFIT (Weight Training Truth #1):
To specifically target the medial calf region (PA-L) for strengthening and thickening when performing exercises 145 to 150, turn your toes in (as shown in figure 279) and widen your stance slightly.

RISK (Weight Training Truth #2):
All R/B values remain as in the original exercise to which this variation is applied.

ALL CALF EXERCISES Execution Variations (cont'd)

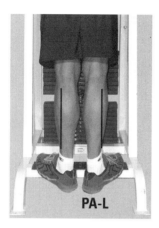

Fig. 280:
Toed-Out Foot Position
for All Calf Exercises

PA-L

Variation 151.b — Toed-Out Foot Position
BENEFIT (Weight Training Truth #1):
To specifically target the lateral calf region (PA-L) for strengthening and thickening when performing exercises 145 to 150, turn your toes outward (as shown in figure 280) and narrow your stance slightly.

RISK (Weight Training Truth #2):
All R/B values remain as in the original exercise to which this variation is applied.

ALL STANDING CALF EXERCISES: Variation 151.c — Toe Support Only

Fig. 281:
Toe Support Only
Variation

BENEFIT (Weight Training Truth #1):
A deeper stretch of your gastrocnemius and soleus muscles (and therefore your Achilles tendons) is accomplished by placing only your toes on the edge of the foot supports rather than the entire ball of your foot. This allows your heels to drop down further, but does increase the risks of injury. This variation can be applied to exercises 145 to 149.

RISK (Weight Training Truth #2):

R/B	Injury Site
(+) 7	"Other" (Zone II — Foot/Ankle)
(+) 3	"Other" (Zone III — Achilles)
(+) 3	Hamstrings

SEATED CALF RAISE Variation 151.d — Toe Support Only

Fig. 282:
Toe Support
Only
Variation

BENEFIT (Weight Training Truth #1):
A deeper stretch of your soleus muscles and your Achilles tendons (PA-L) is accomplished while in the seated/bent-knee position by placing only your toes on the edge of the foot supports, rather than the entire ball of your foot. This allows your heels to drop down further, but does increase the risks of injury.

RISK (Weight Training Truth #2):

R/B	Injury Site
(+) 7	"Other" (Zone II — Foot/Ankle)
(+) 3	"Other" (Zone III — Achilles)

All other R/B values remain unchanged for that exercise.

Exercise 152: SEATED, FRONT-FOOT RAISES

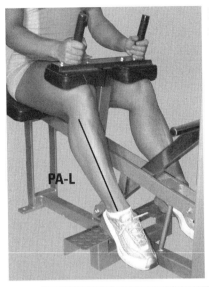

Fig. 283.1: Start/Finish

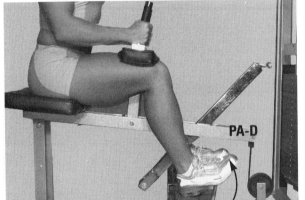

Fig. 283.2: Mid-Phase

BENEFIT (Weight Training Truth #1):

This exercise strengthens the front shin muscles, which maintain functional balance with the calf muscles; the primary target is the group of muscles that dorsi-flex (lift up) the ankle and foot (PA-L).

HOW:

- Sitting at a calf-raise machine adjusted so that the press pads touch the tops of your legs and your feet are flat on the foot-support bar, place your knees under the pads and your heels on the support bar, parallel to each other.

- Release the safety bar, and allow your toes to drop as low as possible; this is the start/finish position (figure 283.1).

- Following the plane of action (PA-D), smoothly raise your feet as far as possible — pause briefly; this is the mid-phase position (figure 283.2).

- Smoothly return to the start/finish position.

RISK (Weight Training Truth #2):

R/B	Injury Site
3	"Other" (Zone III- Achilles)
4	"Other" (Zone II — Foot/Ankle)

Exercise 153: CABLE, FRONT-FOOT RAISES

Fig. 284.1:
Start/Finish

PA-D

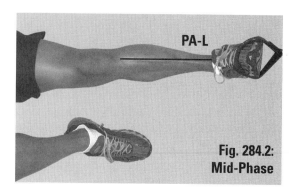

PA-L

Fig. 284.2:
Mid-Phase

BENEFIT (Weight Training Truth #1):
This exercise strengthens the front shin muscles, maintaining functional balance with the calf muscles; the primary target is the group of muscles that dorsi-flex (i.e., lift up) the ankle or foot (PA-L).

HOW:

• Sit on the floor in front of a cable crossover machine with one knee bent and the other leg flat on the floor in line with the bottom cable.

• Moving far enough away so there is tension in the cable, hook a strap across the top of your foot and point your foot downward; this is the start/finish position (figure 284.1).

• Following the plane of action (PA-D), smoothly raise your foot as far as possible — pause briefly; this is the mid-phase position (figure 284.2).

• Smoothly return to the start/finish position.

RISK (Weight Training Truth #2):

R/B	Injury Site
3	"Other" (Zone III — Achilles)

Chapter 4

Integration of the F.I.T.S. Concepts

I. WORKOUT PROGRAM PARAMETERS

The final stage of your workout-creation process is to apply implementation parameters to the workout goals you have already established. Weight-training is a journey, and like any road trip, it has many components. Remember that you made a list of your objectives in Chapter 3? That's your destination. Now the implementation parameters will give you the vehicle to get there. And of course, the R/B values help you get there safely.

The components and parameters listed below are what are required to build a customized and accurately planned weight-training program. Once implemented, the body improvement journey begins. Some of these have been dealt with in other chapters, as noted.

(1) Injury Avoidance (discussed in Chapter 2)

(2) Exercise Selection (discussed in Chapter 3)

(3) Exercise Execution (discussed in Chapter 3)

(4) Exercises per Body Part (discussed briefly in Chapter 3)

(5) Body Parts per Workout

(6) Sets per Exercise

(7) Repetitions per Set

(8) Rate of Repetition Execution

(9) Range of Motion per Repetition

(10) Workout Intensity

(11) Workout Frequency

For beginners, here are some definitions:

- *Frequency* describes the quantity and pattern of workout days in a given time frame.

- One *repetition* refers to the complete execution of an exercise from start to mid-phase to finish. (This is what is described for each exercise in Chapter 3).

- A *set* is a series of successive repetitions (non-stop) followed by a rest period.

- The *range of motion* refers to the total amount of motion between the start position and the mid-phase position (full range, or 100 per cent, is what is described for each exercise in Chapter 3).

- The *intensity* is the net effect of the number of repetitions, the number of sets, and the duration of rest periods between the sets, such that

  - *high* intensity involves many reps, many sets, and short rests
  - *low* intensity involves few reps, few sets, and long rests.

Weight Training Status

Appropriate implementation parameters depend on your weight-training status, which will fall somewhere among the four categories below. The categories are based on past weight-training experience and current weight-training goals.

- *Injured* — anyone recuperating from a sports injury or surgery, or who has suffered an injury during the course of their weight-training program.

- *Beginner* — anyone with less than one full year of weight-training experience, or anyone who weight-trains as a secondary part of an overall fitness program.

- *Intermediate* — anyone who has more than one full year of weight-training experience but has no desire to be a competitive weight-training athlete.

- *Advanced* — anyone who has at least two full years of weight-training experience and intends to compete in Olympic lifting, bodybuilding, power-lifting, or any other strength-oriented sport — or is just plain "serious" about long-term weight-training.

Important Notes

(1) If you have been weight-training at the intermediate or advanced level but are currently injured, you must backtrack to the *injured* status for all exercises that use the injured body part. You may otherwise train according to your pre-injury status. As the pain of your injury subsides, gradually move toward your pre-injury status by progressing through the stages two weeks at a time until you reach the appropriate pre-injury level.

(2) If your status is *injured* then the one exercise you

YOUR WEIGHT-TRAINING "STATUS"

Parameter	Injured	Beginner	Intermediate	Advanced
Body Parts per Workout	same as your pre-injury status	All	4–5	2–3
Exercises per Body Part	1 replacement for each body part affected by injury; all other body parts as per pre-injury status	1	2–3	3–4
Sets per Exercise	2–3	4	4	4–6
Repetitions	12–25 for replacement exer.	10–12 for all exer.*	Power/Size: 4–8; Define/Tone: 8–15*	Power/Size: 1–8; Define/Tone: 8–20*
Rate of Repetitions	For replacement: 3 sec. up + 4 sec. down	2 sec. up, 3 sec. down	2 sec. up, 3 sec. down	Variable
Range of Motion	Central 80%	100%	100%	100%
Intensity	Low	Moderate	Moderate to High	Low to High
Frequency	1 day on, 1 day off	1 day on, 1 day off	2–3 days on, 1 day off	3–5 days on, 1 day off
Rest Period between Sets	90 sec. for replacements	60–90 sec.	30–90 sec.	30–120 sec.

Exceptions are abdominals, lower back, and calves — 25–100 reps.

select per injured area must have an R/B value of less than 5.

(3) If you are injured, all body parts that are not affected by your injury can be trained at your pre-injury status.

(4) The combination of slow repetition rhythm (i.e., longer rest periods between sets), light weight, high repetition and central eighty per cent range of motion is the best tactic for "training around" your injury, in the early phase of your recovery.

(5) In the transition from *injured* to *beginner* status (i.e., when ache or tenderness is no longer present), first change your range of motion to 100 per cent, then begin to quicken your rep rhythm, and only then should you begin to add new exercises, and ultimately, go heavier.

(6) Only with *intermediate* or *advanced* status is it advisable to vary the number of reps per set, depending on your muscle objectives. Specifically, sets of eight or fewer reps (usually with concurrent increases in the weight being used) are for building size and power, while sets of fifteen or more reps are for toning or defining the target muscle. Such specific targeting is unnecessary, ill-advised and usually impossible, when *injured* or a *beginner*.

(7) The first, and simplest, way to increase the intensity of your workouts is to shorten the rest period between sets.

(8) When in a power- and strength-building mode with your workouts (i.e., *advanced* status), there are times when exceptionally long rest periods are needed between sets to enable the performance of very heavy and low-rep sets.

(9) The use of a very slow repetition rhythm can help you find the "weak zone" or "sticking point" of a power-building exercise. When found, make use of the partial range of motion tactic at that point in the exercise to overcome it.

(10) The amount of resistance (weight) to use for any exercise is dependant on the number of repetitions you intend to perform per set. At first, some trial and error will be necessary to find the resistance that has you mildly struggle to complete the last one or two reps of your intended total. When that struggle is no longer present for that number of reps, it is appropriate to increase the resistance.

(11) Remember, if an exercise that you intend to use is not as **F**ree of **I**njury as you require — *do not use it*. If an exercise that you intend to use is not **T**arget-**S**pecific — *do not use it*.

Be sure your workout truly "F.I.T.S."!

II. SAMPLES: MYTHOLOGICAL VERSUS F.I.T.S. WORKOUT PROGRAMS

As discussed in Chapter 1, the dilemma of weight training is that every conceivable weight-training program contains a balance between (+) and (−) outcomes. Luckily, this balance is virtually pre-determined by the exercises you choose. This implies, at least in theory, that there is a *best* routine, a *worst* routine, and a countless number of moderately good weight-training routines, in terms of injury causation. If you put together a workout program following the ideas of this book, your routine will be at the low end of this risk-of-injury spectrum.

This section illustrates the extremes of the risk-of-injury spectrum by presenting an example of the *worst* myth-based workout routine, followed by a sample replacement workout routine. This "F.I.T.S.-ed" routine can be looked upon as an example of an *enlightened* workout routine — one that provides all the same muscle benefits as the myth-based workout but with the added advantage of an acceptably low risk of injury for *all* exercises, at *all* potential injury sites.

Perhaps the myth-based workout routine I use below is deliberately extreme but there is no doubt that every component of it is used routinely in weight-training facilities everywhere. Further, most experienced weight-training athletes will recognize many of their typical workout choices in the routine.

Please note that the myth-based workout is presented strictly as an illustration in order to lead you to more enlightened workouts. *Do not use the myth-based workout!*

Some things to keep in mind when reviewing the "F.I.T.S.-ed" workout routine that follows the myth-based one:

- the "F.I.T.S.-ed" workout exercises offer all the same muscle benefits as those in the myth-based workout;

- all of the R/B values have been reduced to acceptable levels (in this instance, 6 and under);

- exercises with this R/B limitation are highly unlikely to create new injuries but can still aggravate a pre-existing condition, so people with a pre-existing condition or posture problem should further tailor their exercise R/B values (based upon their personal R/B values, from Chapter 2);

- as presented, the "F.I.T.S-ed" workout is for athletes at an intermediate or advanced level but can be reduced to a beginner status program by using only the exercises marked with the symbol ** (i.e., 1.a, 4, 5, 7, 9, 10, 11, 15, 17, 21, 24, 27, 28, and 29).

A Sample "Mythological" Workout (*Do Not Use!*)

Exercise	Item No.	R/B Values per Injury Site (see key opposite)															
		A	B	C	D	E	F	G	H	I	J	K	L	M	N	O	P
1. Squats (bodybuilding: narrow stance and deep hips)	117.a/117.d	10			4							8					
2. Leg Press (deep)	135	10										7					
3. Side Lunges	143	4										7					7
4. Thigh Extensions	126											2					
5. "Donkey" Calf Raises (toe support only)	146/151.c	4											9		7	6	
6. Seated Calf Raises (toe support only)	150/151.d														7	6	
7. Hamstring Curls (knee hyperext.)	132/134	3											5				
8. Straight Leg Deadlift (on platform)	128/129	10++		9				3						10+			
9. Lower Back Extensions (hyperext.)	42	7											6				
10. Behind Head Pulldowns	54		6		6	5	3	7	4								
11. Seated Cable Rowing (straight bar, narrow, to neck, locked knees and round out)	46/ 50.a, 50.b, 50.h, 50.i	10+	10+	8			3	5	4				8				
12. Shrugs (with shoulder roll)	60/61.e		7				3										
13. Upright Rowing	36		5	10	8		6	6		6							
14. Dumbbell Lateral Raises (upright, elev. elbows)	26/31.f(i)			9	8			5									
15. Behind Head Shoulder Press (standing, cheat, locked elbows, wrist ext.)	21/111.a, 31.i(i), 31.b	7	6	4	9	5				8	8						
16. Incline Bench Press (to neck, wrists ext., neck arch, elbow lock)	2/8.e, 111.a, 8.f, 3.c			8	8	7				8	8						
17. Flat Bench Press (to neck, wrist ext., neck arch, bounce cheat, elbow lock)	1/8.e, 3.a, 8.f, 3.c, 111.a	8	9	6						8	8		7				
18. Incline Dumbbell Flyes (deep)	12/17.a			3	4	9											
19. Flat Dumbbell Flyes (deep)	11/17.a			4	3	8											
20. Dumbbell Pullovers	18			7	7	7	4										
21. Standing Barbell Curls (cheat)	79/91.e	5					4		6								
22. "Preacher" Barbell Curls (wide grip)	84/91.a						6			10	10						
23. Inclined Alt. Dumbbell Curls	90						3	4		2	2						
24. Narrow Grip Bench (to neck)	96/97			10	7								5				
25. "French Press" (behind head)	102/103.b				6					9							
26. Body Dips (on bench edge)	101.b			8	8					6	8						
27. Barbell Forearm Curls (narrow grip)	112/116.b						5			6							
28. Barbell Forearm Raises (narrow grip)	114/116.b								5		8						
29. Inclined Bent-Knee Sit-Ups (neck flexion)	68/78.c	6	9														
30. Supine Straight Leg Lifts	63	7															
31. Inclined Bent-Knee Sit-Ups (torso twist, neck flexion)	68/78.a, 78.c	3	9														

A "F.I.T.S.-ed" Workout

Exercise	Item No.	R/B Values per Injury Site (see key below)															
		A	B	C	D	E	F	G	H	I	J	K	L	M	N	O	P
1a. Squats (bodybuilding)**	117.a	3			3							4					
1b. Lunges (deep)	123/124.c	4			3							6					5
2. Cable Buttock Pulls (to the Side)	139/140	3															
3. Front Cable Leg-Crossovers	144	2															2
4. Thigh Extensions**	126											2					
5. Standing Calf Raises**	145	2											2			3	
6. Seated Calf Raises	150															3	
7. Hamstring Curls (prone)**	132	3											3				
8. Bent-Leg Deadlift (bar)	39	5	6				3		4			4					
9. Lower Back Ext. (on floor)**	42/43.b	3															
10. Front Pulldowns (target-specific)	55/62.c(i)				1	3	3	4	4								
11. Seated Cable Rowing (upright torso, palms-facing, target-specific)**	46/50.c, 50.d, 50.e	2	4				3		4								
12. Shrugs (barbell)	60		4				3										
13. Replace by # 12 and 14																	
14. Barbell Shoulder Press (front, seated, wide, shallow)	24/31.a, 31.d			3	4												
15. Lateral Dumbell "Flares"**	38			6	4			5									
16. Incline Bench Press (wide grip)	2/8.a			5	3												
17. Flat Bench Press (wide grip)**	1/8.a			6	2												
18. Incline Dumbbell Flyes	12			3	4	5											
19. Flat Dumbbell Flyes	11			4	3	4											
20. Replaced by # 18 and 10																	
21. Standing, Barbell Curls**	79						4		6								
22. "Preacher" E-Z Bar Curls (part ext elbows)	85/91.c(ii)						3	3	2								
23. Seated "Concentration" Curls	89						3	4	2								
24. Upright Cable Press Downs (neutral grip)**	108.b									4	4						
25. "French Presses" (E-Z bar)	102									5							
26. Cable "Isolation" Press Downs (palm-down grip)	110.c									4							
27. Barbell Forearm Curls**	112						5				4						
28. Dumbbell Forearm Raises**	115							5			4						
29. Crunches**	73	2															
30. Reverse Crunches	76	2															
31. Standing Oblique Crunches	77	2															

***Beginners would only use these exercises in this program*

INJURY SITE KEY:

A = Back/Spine (Zone I)
B = Back/Spine (Zone II)
C = Shoulder (Zone I)
D = Shoulder (Zone II)
E = Shoulder (Zone III)
F = Elbow (Zone I)
G = Elbow (Zone II)
H = Elbow (Zone III)
I = Elbow (Zone IV)
J = Wrists
K = Knees
L = Hamstrings
M = Chest
N = Ankle/Feet
O = Achilles Tendon
P = Groin

III. WORKOUT PROGRAM CREATION

The workout creation process involves five steps in which you combine all the R/B values associated with your personal profile and objectives to develop a weight-training program. The steps are outlined with examples below, but here they are again in brief:

Step 1: Make a list of your physical objectives.

Step 2: Create a personal profile of yourself covering general factors that will affect your exercise choices.

Step 3: Calculate your maximum exercise R/B values.

Step 4: Review exercises for each body part, using the maximum exercise R/B values determined in Step 2.

Step 5: Create your exercise program, using all the information collected in Steps 1–4, plus the parameters of your weight-training status, explained earlier in this chapter.

Step 1: Your Physical Objectives

Critically evaluate your physique to determine the muscles or muscle regions to be targeted by your workouts. (See page 32, "Physique Evaluation.)

Step 2: Your Personal Profile

Make a list of all general factors that will be pertinent to creating your workout program.

Personal Profile Example

Age: 45   **Sex:** Male
Occupation: Computer Operator
Weight-Training Status: Beginner
Preferred Sleep Position: left-side, fetal-position
Muscle-Pain History:
– 20-year history of mild, episodic, low back pain;
– work-related carpal tunnel syndrome;
– pain in right knee only, going up/down stairs and no history of knee injuries.

Step 3: Your Maximum Allowable R/B Values

To calculate your maximum R/B values for each exercise, you simply subtract your R/B-personal value from the general maximum, which is seven. So, design a worksheet listing all sixteen potential injury sites, assess each body part and assign a personal R/B value based on the criteria outlined in Chapter 2. Then, just do the math. In the example that follows, based on the criteria for zone I of the back, this person must select exercises with R/B values of 4 or less.

Example of Maximum Exercise R/B Values Calculation

Potential Injury Site	R/B (Max)		R/B (Pers.)		Age		Max. Exer. R/B
Back/Spine - Zone I	7	–	2	–	1	=	4
Back/Spine - Zone II	7	–	2	–	1	=	4
Shoulder - Zone I	7	–	1	–	1	=	5
Shoulder - Zone II	7	–	1	–	1	=	5
Shoulder - Zone III	7	–	1	–	1	=	5
Elbow - Zone I	7	–	0	–	1	=	6
Elbow - Zone II	7	–	0	–	1	=	6
Elbow - Zone III	7	–	0	–	1	=	6
Elbow - Zone IV	7	–	0	–	1	=	6
Wrist	7	–	2	–	1	=	4
Knee	7	–	1	–	1	=	5
Hamstrings	7	–	0	–	1	=	6
Other - Chest	7	–	0	–	1	=	6
Other - Foot/Ankle	7	–	0	–	1	=	6
Other - Achilles Tendon	7	–	0	–	1	=	5
Other - Groin	7	–	0	–	1	=	5

Remember one final point when determining your R/B-exercise values: your age. If you are over forty, deduct one from each of your R/B-exercise values, and if you are over sixty, deduct two.

Step 4: Exercise Selection

Select the appropriate exercises for each body part based on the maximum allowable R/B values established in Step 3. Let's use the chest as an example.

(a) Look at the illustration of the chest on page 38.

(b) Select target muscles that suit your physical objectives and note their letter codes. For this example, let's pick the General Pectoralis Major (G) and the Upper Pectoralis Major (U) muscles.

(c) Look at the table on page 39. In the "Benefit (WT#)" column, we see the codes for our target muscles, "G" and "U," and their corresponding exercises.

(d) Look at the R/B values for each of these exercises in the "R/B Values (WT 32)" column on page 39.

CHEST – Physique Objectives & Corresponding Exercises

Target Muscle	Code	Apt Exer.	Exer. No.	R/B Value	R/B Approval
Upper Pec. Major	U	Incline Bench Press	2	6	No
Upper Pec. Major	U	Incline Dumbbell Press	6	5	Yes
Upper Pec. Major	U	Incline Dumbbell Flyes	12	3	Yes
General Pec. Major	G	Flat Bench Press	1	7	No
General Pec. Major	G	Flat Dumbbell Press	5	6	No
General Pec Major	G	Flat Dumbbell Flyes	11	4	Yes

(e) Compare the exercise R/B values (see table above) with the maximum R/B value for the chest as determined in Step 3 (6 in our example). If an exercise's R/B value is higher, turn to each of the execution variables (or the aggravating-replacement lists) for a modification that decreases the R/B value to fit.

This process is repeated for every body part.

Step 5: Putting It All Together

Now you can pull the information together into a workout routine by taking the "R/B approved" exercise selections from Step 4 and combining them with the implementation parameters discussed earlier in this chapter. Here's the procedure:

(a) Determine your weight-training "status", from page 239. For this example, let's use "beginner" status.

(b) Make a list of the "R/B approved" exercises, selecting one or more per body part (depending on status); also record the exercise/variation numbers.

(c) Select the implementation factors, based on their status (see page 240). For a beginner, these would be

- **Workout frequency:** one day on, one day off
- **Body parts per workout:** all
- **Rest between sets:** 60 – 90 seconds

(d) Learn, in full detail, accurate execution for each of your exercises by studying their description in this book. Take this book with you to the gym to re-enforce proper technique.

(e) Determine, for each exercise, the amount of weight you should use. This is essentially a trial and error method. The proper weight is that with which you have difficulty finishing your last two sets (at the given reps) of an exercise.

(f) After using this program routinely for about one month, review your priorities and improvements, then overhaul your program. Change as many exercise selections as your R/B approvals will allow and alter the order in which you do your exercises.

IV. A SYNOPSIS OF THE F.I.T.S. CONCEPTS

A. The weight-training status quo can be summed up as follows.

- Injuries are an accepted part of the weight-training process.
- •) The principle of *no pain — no gain* contributes to injury causation and encourages the "train through the pain" mentality.

R/B Approved Exercises and Variations

Exercise/Variation Name	No.	Sets	Reps	Weight
Flat Dumbbell Press				
—Palms Facing	13/16.3	4	10	
Seated Dumbbell Press				
—Wide Grip	32/38.1	4	10	
Low Back Extensions—Floor	47.3	4	25	
Front Chinups				
—Target Specific	53/61.31	4	10	
Seat. Cable Rows				
—Target Specific	49.1/51.	4	10	
Crunches—Supine	71.1	4	25	
Stand. Straight-Bar Curls	77	4	10	
Upright Cable Pressdown				
—Thumb-Up	102.2	4	10	
Barbell Forearm Curls	107	4	10	
Barbell Forearm Raises	109/111.1	4	10	
Bodybuilding Squats	113.1	4	10	
Prone Hamstring Curls	123.1	4	10	
Cable Butt Pulls-To Side	128.2	4	10	
Front, Cable Leg-Crossovers	133	4	10	
Standing Calf Raises	135	4	25	

- A myth-based approach to workouts is almost universal.
- The end (muscle development) justifies the means (painful injuries).

B. The F.I.T.S. way changes the status quo to reduce injuries.

- Weight-training injuries are neither necessary, nor acceptable.
- There are specific exercises that predictably cause specific injuries.
- An analytical approach reveals:
    - the duality of every exercise (risk vs benefit)
    - the exercise "see-saw"
    - the outcome "see-saw"
    - the endless loop.
- Myth-based principles can be replaced with two new weight-training truths.

C. Injury-free weight training is possible through the use of new basic ideas:

- the guiding principle of *Primum Non Nocere,*
- PEAVES to prevent weight-training injuries,
- the *ten commandments* of safe weight-training,
- the *single deadly sin* of weight-training,
- the *golden rule* of squatting.

Appendix
Replacement Exercises

AS ALREADY DISCUSSED, weight training is a journey. You may have been well on your way before you picked up this book, or you may have just begun. Either way, my hope is that this book has allowed you to build a safe and effective vehicle for your trip.

But we cannot expect miracles. Vehicles do break down — and that's what this appendix is for. It is a quick-reference guide to adjusting your exercise routine to fit your needs as they evolve. For example, while reading a weight-training magazine you may find an exercise that seems perfect for some new goal you have set for yourself. *Don't do it* without applying the principles of this book. Find the exercise in the list below and see whether it fits the *primum non nocere* principle. If not, replace it. It's that simple.

Here's how this appendix works: each injury zone has a table of exercises that involve that zone in some way. The first three columns refer to an aggravating exercise, its corresponding number so you can find it in this book, and its R/B value. The next three columns list the replacement exercise, where you can find it in this book, and the R/B value for this new, safer exercise.

Each replacement exercise has the same purpose as the aggravating exercise it replaces, and has a significantly lower R/B value regarding the injury site of concern. In some cases, under Replacement Exercise, it will say "nothing suitable," meaning that for that exercise purpose there is no exercise with a reduced R/B value regarding that injury site.

The first few exercises in each list are rated with an R/B of eight to ten and are the worst offenders. These are the ones you should *not* include in your workout. You would use these exercises only when you have a very specific reason and a great deal of experience. Otherwise, use the replacements!

HOW TO USE THIS APPENDIX
(1) The tables use the R/B rating system (where 0 is no risk and 10 is severe risk), which is based on the degree to which one of the components of execution that contribute to a risk of injury, as described in Chapter 2, is involved in the execution of a given exercise.

(2) Please note the following points when referring to the Replacement and Aggravating lists:
  (a) Every replacement exercise is virtually identical to its corresponding aggravating exercise in its purpose but has an R/B value at least two points lower for the particular injury site.
  (b) The phrase *Nothing Suitable* indicates that there is no suitable replacement matches the criteria identified in (a).
  (c) Exercise numbers divided by a forward-slash (/) indicate that the R/B value of this exercise is based on both figures, meaning that one is an execution variation of the other. For exercise *x/y*, for example, *y* is a specific exercise variation of *x*. So the R/B value for the exercise listed is calculated by adding together the R/B values of *x* and *y*,
  (d) Exercise numbers divided by a comma are to be considered separately, and have a separate R/B value.

(3) Always ensure that you know exactly how to perform every exercise in your workout — especially when adding new replacement exercises. Refer to Chapter 3 for the surprisingly large number of execution variations that must be considered.

(4) The "acid test" will be whether or not the performance of a replacement exercise, regarding a given injury site, causes any pain at that injury site. Success will primarily be painless execution. A second, but equally important, measure of success is an absence of soreness or aching one or two days after the performance of your replacement exercise(s). If your first replacement exercise selections do produce some pain upon execution, or your symptoms are aggravated one or two days following your use of the replacement exercise(s), repeat the replacement process using even lower R/B values as your guide, until painlessness is achieved.

(5) If you have followed the above procedures in order to train around an injury but still suffer pain when doing exercises of low R/B value, you must seek

knowledgeable professional attention (i.e., diagnosis, treatment, and then rehabilitation) before returning to the gym.

(6) When trying to determine the precise injury site for your pain, if the pain pattern cannot be distinguished between two zones (e.g., zones I and II of the shoulder), assume that both injury sites are involved. Simply pursue the "training around" process (as above) twice — once for each of the injury sites. This will ensure that the final "corrected" workout routine contains suitably reduced risks of injury for both injury sites. This is not an uncommon dilemma.

(7) It is very important to check all other R/B values for each of your replacement exercises. It is possible that they may have one or more R/B values for other injury sites that are beyond your acceptable limits of injury risk. In such instances, repeat the exercise replacement process until you find an exercise that suits all of your injury-prevention limits.

(8) Your execution of a low-risk-of-injury exercise can inadvertently transform that exercise into a high-risk-of-injury exercise because of either fatigue, over-zealousness, or a lack of mental focus within a given set. Maintain total attention to execution at all times.

(9) Get proper diagnosis and treatment from a knowledgeable healthcare professional for all your injuries. The "training around" procedures given here simply allow you to continue getting muscle benefit while you recover. They do not heal your injured tissues.

(10) If an exercise you intend to use is not as **F**ree of **I**njury as you require — do not use it. If an exercise that you intend to use is not **T**arget-**S**pecific, do not use it.

BE SURE THAT YOUR WORKOUT TRULY "F.I.T.S." YOU!

IMPORTANT NOTE:

As you attempt to "train around" an injury, you must first identify the exercise(s) that have been the cause of your injury. However, in order for the "F.I.T.S. Way" R/B values to be accurate and valid for you, your previous execution of any given exercise must match the "F.I.T.S. Way" description exactly. This means that you must always check all of the possible execution variations relevant to the "general" exercise. Only then can you make an accurate "Replacement Exercise" selection.

Region: Spine/Back
Zone: I — Lower

Aggravating Exercises	Exercise No.	R/B	Replacement Exercises	Exercise No.	R/B
straight-leg deadlift (on a platform)	128/129	10++	bent-leg barbell deadlift	39	5
			and prone hamstrings curls	132	3
"good mornings" (locked knees, round-out)	41/50.g + 50.i	10+	lower back ext. (hyper)	42	7
bent-over rowing (locked knees, round-out)	44, 45.a/ 50.h + 50.i	10+	bent-over rowing	44, 45.a	6
seated cable rowing (locked knees, round out)	46, 47/ 50.h + 50.i	10+	seated cable rowing (upright torso)	46/50.d	2
torso twists (standing, forward lean, round out)	71/78.e + 78.g	10+	abdominal crunches (torso twist)	73/78.b	2
dumbbell rowing (locked knees, round out)	48/50.h + 50.i	10+	dumbbell rowing	48	4
leg press (deep, high foot placement)	135/136.a	10+	leg press (shallow),	121	5
			and cable buttock pulls	139	5
straight-leg deadlift	128	10	bent-leg barbell deadlift,	39	5
			and prone hamstrings curls	132	3
bent-leg dumbbell deadlift (round out)	40/50.g	10	bent-leg dumbbell deadlift	40	6
"good mornings" (round out)	41/50.g	10	lower back extension (hyper)	42	7
bent-over rowing (round out)	44, 45.a/50.h	10	bent-over rowing	44	6

Aggravating Exercises	Exercise No.	R/B	Replacement Exercises	Exercise No.	R/B
seated cable rowing (full round out)	46, 47/50.h	10	seated cable rowing (upright torso)	46/50.d	2
torso twists (seated, forward lean, round out)	72/78.e + 78.g	10	abdominal crunches (torso twist)	73/78.b	2
squats ("bodybuilding," narrow stance/deep hips)	117.a/117.d	10	squats ("powerlifting")	117.b	7
leg press (deep)	135	10	leg press (shallow), and cable buttock pulls	121 139	5 5
leg press (deep, low foot placement)	135/136.b	10	squats ("bodybuilding") and cable buttock pulls	117.a 139	3 5
bent-leg deadlift (full round-out)	39, 40/50.h	9	bent-leg barbell deadlift	39	5
torso twists (standing, round-out)	71/78.g	9	torso twists (standing)	71	6
standing stiff-arm pulldowns (round out)	58/50.g	9	standing stiff-arm pulldowns	58	5
standing tricep pressdowns (cheating and round out)	106, 107/ 111.e + 111.f	9	cable tricep pressdowns	106, 107	0
dumbbell rowing (full round-out)	48/50.h	8	dumbbell rowing	48	4
bent-over rowing (cheating)	44, 45.a/50.f	8	bent-over rowing	44	6
torso twists (seated, round-out)	72/78.g	8	torso twists (seated)	72	5
torso twists (standing, forward lean)	71/78.e	8	torso twists (standing)	71	6
all leg-lifts	63-66	7	reverse crunches	76	2
leg lifts (pelvic crunch)	63-66/78.h	7	reverse crunches	76	2
front pulldowns (cheating)	55/62.d	7	front pulldowns	55	0
reverse-grip pulldowns (cheating)	56/62.d	7	reverse-grip pulldowns	56	0
lower back ext. (hyper)	42	7	lower back ext. (half range)	42/43.a	5
torso twists (seated, forward lean)	72/78.e	7	torso twists (seated)	72	5
"hack" squats (deep)	142	7	"hack" squats (shallow), and cable buttock pulls	119 139	3 5
standing shoulder press (cheating)	21, 22/31.i(i)	7	standing shoulder presses	21, 22	5
squats (powerlifting)	117.b	7	squats ("bodybuilding")	117.a	3
"good mornings"	41	6	lower back ext. (on floor)	43.b	3
seated cable rowing (straight bar)	46	6	seated cable rowing (straight bar, wide grip, upright torso)	46/50.d	2
bent-over rowing (barbell/T-bar)	44, 45.a	6	bent-over rowing (supported T-bar)	44/45.b	0
torso twists (standing)	71	6	crunches (torso twist)	73/78.b	2
modified hamstrings curls	137	6	modified hamstrings curls (one leg)	137/138	3
bent-leg dumbbell deadlift	40	6	lower back ext. (on floor), and cable buttock pulls (to side)	43.b 140	3 3
all bent-knee sit-ups	67, 68	6	crunches (on floor)	73	2
standing oblique crunches (round out)	77/78.g	5	standing oblique crunches	77	2
lower back ext. (half range)	42/43.a	5	lower back ext. (on floor)	43.b	3
torso twists (seated)	71/72	5	crunches (torso twist)	73/78.b	2
leg press (shallow)	121	5	"hack" squats (shallow, narrow/toed-in, or wide/toed out)	119/120.a, 120.b	3 3
standing hamstrings curls	130	5	prone hamstring curls	132	3
standing hamstring curls (toed-in)	130.1/131.2	5	prone hamstring curls (toed-in)	132/133.a	3
standing hamstring curls (toed-out)	130.1/131.b	5	prone hamstring curls (toed-out)	132/133.b	3
cable buttock pulls	139	5	cable buttock pulls (to side)	140	3
bent-leg barbell deadlift	39	5	lower back ext. (on floor), and cable buttock pulls (to side)	43.b 140	3 3
cable crossovers (round out)	14-16/17.d	5	chest cable crossovers	14-16	0
seated shoulder presses and lateral raises (round out)	23-37/31.h	5	seated shoulder presses and lateral raises	23-37	0

Aggravating Exercises	Exercise No.	R/B	Replacement Exercises	Exercise No.	R/B
standing stiff-arm pulldowns	58	5	front pulldowns	55	0
standing shoulder presses	21, 22	5	seated shoulder presses	23, 24	0
lateral raises (cheating)	26-30/31.i(ii)	5	shoulder lateral raises	26-30	0
bicep curls (cheating)	79-83, 88-90/91.e	5	bicep curls	79-83, 88-90	0
standing tricep press downs (back-arch cheating)	106, 107/111.f	5	tricep pressdowns	107	0
flat or incline bench press (cheating)	1, 2, 96/3.b	5	flat or incline bench presses	1, 2, 96	0
bent-knee V-crunches (supine)	69	5	crunches (on floor),	73	2
			and reverse crunches	76	2
all tricep exercises (round out)	98-110/111.e	4	all tricep exercises	98-110	0
dumbbell rowing	48	4	seated cable rowing (bar, wide, upright torso)	46/50.d	2
front squats	118	4	squats ("bodybuilding")	117.a	3
lunges (barbell, deep)	123/124.c	4	lunges (shallow)	123/124.b	2
side lunges	143	4	front, cable, leg-crossovers	144	2
"donkey" calf raises (including leg rotation variation)	146	4	standing one-leg calf raises (including leg rotation variation)	149	0
leg press calf raises (including leg rotation variation)	147	4	standing one-leg calf raises (including leg rotation variation)	149	0
"hack" calf raises (including leg rotation variation)	148	4	standing one-leg calf raises	149	0
Lower back ext. (machine resist.)	43.c	4	lower back ext. (on floor)	43.b	3
cable crunches	75	4	crunches (on floor)	73	2
cable crunches (torso twist)	75/78.b	4	crunches (on floor, torso twist)	73/78.b	2
bent-knee V-crunches (seated)	69/70	3	reverse crunches	76	2
"hack" squats	119	3	thigh extension	126	0
lower back ext. (on floor)	43.b	3	nothing suitable	—	—
prone hamstring curls (toed-in)	132/133.a	3	prone hamstring curls (one leg, toed-in)	133.c/133.d	1
prone hamstring curls (toed-out)	132/133.b	3	prone hamstring curls (one leg, toed-out)	133.c/133.e	1
bent-knee sit-ups (torso twist)	67, 68/78.a	3	standing oblique crunches	77	2
bent-knee V-crunches (seated)	69/70	3	crunches (on floor)	73	2
			and reverse crunches	76	2
squats ("bodybuilding")	117.a	3	"sissy squats"	125	0
lunges	123	3	lunges (shallow)	123/124.b	2
prone hamstring curls	132	3	prone hamstring curls (one leg)	132/133.c	1
cable buttock pulls (to side)	139/140	3	nothing suitable	—	—
"platform" lunges	141	3	lunges (shallow)	123/124.b	2
"modified" hamstring curls (one leg)	137/138	3	nothing suitable	—	—
dumbbell squats	117.a/117.e	3	"sissy squats"	125	0
seated cable rowing (upright torso)	46, 47/50.d	2	bent-over rowing (supported T-bar)	44/45.b	0
standing oblique crunches	77	2	nothing suitable	—	—
reverse crunches	76	2	nothing suitable	—	—
crunches (on floor)	73	2	crunches (mechanically assisted)	73/74	1
crunches (on floor, torso twist)	73/78.b	2	nothing suitable	—	—
squats ("bodybuilding")	117.a	2	thigh extension	126	0
lunges (barbell, shallow)	123/124.b	2	thigh extension	126	0
standing calf raises (including leg rotation variation)	145	2	standing one-leg calf raises (including leg rotation variation)	149	0
front cable leg-crossovers	144	2	nothing suitable	—	—
prone hamstring curls (one leg)	132/133.c	1	nothing suitable	—	—
crunches (mechanically assisted)	73/74	1	nothing suitable	—	—

Aggravating Exercises	Exercise No.	R/B	Replacement Exercises	Number	R/B
prone hamstring curls (one-leg, any rotation variation)	133.c/133.d, 133.e	1	nothing suitable	—	—

Region: Spine/Back
Zone: II — Upper

Aggravating Exercises	Exercise No.	R/B	Replacement Exercises	Exercise No.	R/B
straight-leg deadlift	128	9	prone, hamstring curls, and lower back ext. (hyper)	132 42	0 0
bent-leg deadlift (full spine round out)	39/50.h	9	bent-leg deadlift	39	6
bent-over rowing (barbell, narrow, full spine round out)	44/50.a + 50.h	9	bent-over rowing (barbell, narrow grip)	44/50.a	6
bent-over rowing (T-bar, full spine round out)	44/45.a + 50.h	9	bent-over rowing (T-bar)	44/45.a	6
seated cable rowing (full spine round out)	46, 47/50.h	9	seated cable rowing	46	6
bent-knee situps (with neck flexion)	67, 68/78.c	9	bent-knee situps	67, 68	0
crunches (with neck flexion)	73, 75/78.c	9	crunches	73, 75	0
bent-over rowing (barbell, full spine round out)	44/50.h	8	bent-over rowing (barbell)	44	5
chest presses (with neck-arch cheat)	1, 2 4–7, 96/3.c	8	chest presses	1, 2, 4–7, 96	0
behind head pull downs (narrow grip)	54/57.a	7	behind head pulldowns (narrow, target-specific)	54/57.a + 62.c(ii)	5
seated cable rowing (straight bar, narrow grip)	46/50.a	7	seated cable rowing (straight bar, wide, upright torso)	46/50.d	4
behind head chin-ups (narrow grip)	51/57.a	7	behind head chin-ups (narrow, target-specific)	51/57.a + 62.c(ii)	5
dumbbell rowing (full spine round out)	48/50.h	7	dumbbell rowing	48	4
barbell shrugs (w/shoulder rolling)	60/61.e	7	barbell shrugs	60	4
dumbbell shrugs (w/shoulder rolling)	61.d/61.e	7	dumbbell shrugs	61.d	4
bent-over rowing (T-bar, narrow grip)	44/45.a + 50.a	7	bent-over rowing (supported T-bar)	44/45.b	4
behind head pulldowns (narrow grip)	54/57.a	7	front pulldowns (narrow grip)	55/57.b	0
behind head chin-ups (narrow grip)	51/57.a	7	front chin-ups (narrow grip)	53/57.b	0
straight-leg deadlift	128	7	prone, hamstring curls, and lower back ext. ("hyper")	132 42	0 0
bent-leg deadlift	39	6	leg press-deep, and lower back ext. ("hyper")	135 42	0 0
bent-over rowing (T-bar)	44/45.a	6	seated cable rowing (straight bar, wide, upright torso)	46/50.d	4
seated cable rowing	46	6	seated cable rowing (straight bar, wide, upright torso)	46/50.d	4
behind head shoulder press	21, 23	6	front shoulder press	22, 24	0
behind head pulldowns (wide grip)	54	6	front pulldowns (wide grip)	55	0
behind head chin-ups (wide grip)	51	6	front chin-ups (wide grip)	52	0
bent-over rowing (barbell, narrow grip)	44/50.a	6	seated cable rowing (straight bar, wide, upright torso)	46/50.d	4
bent-leg dumbbell deadlift (full spine round out)	40/50.h	6	bent-leg dumbbell deadlift	40	3
bent-over rowing (barbell)	44	5	dumbbell rowing	48	4
upright rowing	36	5	barbell shrugs, and dumbbell lateral raises	60 26	4 0

Aggravating Exercises	Exercise No.	R/B	Replacement Exercises	Exercise No.	R/B
bent-over rowing (supported T-bar, narrow grip)	44/45.b + 50.a	5	dumbbell rowing	48	4
behind head pulldowns (narrow, target-specific)	54/57.a + 62.c(ii)	5	front pulldowns (narrow grip)	55/57.b	0
torso twists (head rotation)	71, 72/78.d	5	torso twists	71, 72	0
behind head chin-ups and pulldowns (target-specific)	51, 54/62.c(i)	4	front chin-ups and pulldowns (target-specific)	52, 55/62.c(i)	0
dumbbell rowing	48	4	nothing suitable	—	—
bent-over rowing (supported T-bar)	44/45.b	4	nothing suitable	—	—
dumbbell shrugs	61.d	4	nothing suitable	—	—
seated cable rowing (upright torso)	46, 47/50.d	4	nothing suitable	—	—
barbell shrugs	60	4	nothing suitable	—	—
upright rowing (target-specific)	36/37.d	3	upright rowing (partial range)	36/37.c	1
bent-leg dumbbell deadlift	40	3	prone hamstrings curls and lower back ext. ("hyper")	132 42	0 0
upright rowing (partial range)	36/37.c	1	nothing suitable	—	—

Region: Shoulder
Zone: I — Front

Aggravating Exercises	Exercise No.	R/B	Replacement Exercises	Exercise No.	R/B
upright rowing (narrow grip)	36/37.b	10++	dumbbell lateral raises (upright), and barbell shrugs	26 60	0 0
cable lateral raises (behind back, elbow elev.)	30/31.f(ii)	10+	cable lateral raises (upright)	28	0
body dips (parallel bars, elbows flared)	101.a/101.c	10	decline dumbbell press	7	7
decline bench press (toward neck)	4/8.e	10	decline dumbbell press	7	7
narrow grip bench press (toward neck)	96/97	10	narrow-grip bench press (shallow depth)	96/8.b	5
upright rowing	36	10	dumbbell lateral raises (upright), and barbell shrugs	26 60	0 0
bent-over rowing (T-bar, narrow grip, toward neck)	44/45.a + 50.a + 50.b	10	bent-over rowing (T-bar, palms facing grip)	44/45.a + 50.c	3
flat bench press (toward neck)	1/8.e	9	flat bench press	1	7
dumbbell lateral raises (elbow elev.)	26, 27/31.f(i)	9	dumbbell lateral raises	26, 27	0
cable lateral raises (elbow elev.)	28, 29/31.f(i)	9	cable lateral raises	28, 29	0
front raises (dumbbells, elbow elev.)	34/35.b	9	front raises (dumbbells)	34	6
bent-over rowing (barbell, narrow grip, toward neck)	44/50.b + 50.a	9	bent-over rowing (barbell, narrow grip)	44/50.a	7
supported T-bar row (narrow grip, toward neck)	44/45.b + 50.b + 50.a	9	bent-over rowing (supported T-bar, narrow grip)	44/45.b + 50.a	7
seated cable row (bar, narrow grip, toward neck)	46/50.b + 50.a	9	seated cable rowing (straight bar, narrow grip)	46/50.a	6
cable lateral raises (behind back)	30	9	cable lateral raises (upright)	28	0
barbell shrugs (behind back, narrow grip)	60/61.b	9	barbell shrugs	60	0
decline dumbbell press (toward neck)	7/8.e	9	decline dumbbell press	7	7
narrow grip bench press	96	8	narrow-grip bench press (shallow depth)	96/8.b	5
seated cable rowing (straight bar, narrow, toward neck)	46/50.a + 50.b	8	seated cable rowing (straight bar, target-specific)	46/50.e	0

Aggravating Exercises	Exercise No.	R/B	Replacement Exercises	Exercise No.	R/B
body dips (bench or parallel bars)	101.a, 101.b	8	tricep pressdowns	108	0
incline bench press (toward neck)	2/8.e	8	incline bench press	2	6
flat dumbbell press (toward neck)	5/8.e	8	flat dumbbell press	5	6
upright cable crossovers (thumbs facing grip)	15/17.b	8	upright cable crossovers	15	5
bent-over rowing (T-bar, toward neck)	44/45.a + 50.b	8	bent-over rowing (T-bar, palms-facing grip)	44/45.a + 50.c	3
decline bench press	4	8	decline dumbbell press (palms-facing grip)	7/8.c	5
bent-over rowing (T-bar, narrow grip)	44/45.a + 50.a	8	bent-over rowing (T-bar, palms facing grip)	44/45.a + 50.c	3
upright rowing (wide grip)	36/37.a	8	dumbbell lateral raises (upright), and barbell shrugs	26 60	0 0
front raises (barbell, narrow grip)	32/33.b	8	front raises (barbell, wide grip)	32/33.a	4
upright rowing (partial range or target-specific, narrow grip)	36/37.b + 37.c or 37.d	8	upright rowing (partial-range or target-specific, wide grip)	36/37.a + 37.c or 37.d	4
decline bench press (wide grip)	4/8.a	7	decline dumbbell press (palms-facing grip)	7/8.c	5
decline dumbbell press	7	7	decline dumbbell press (palms-facing grip)	7/8.c	5
incline dumbbell press (toward neck)	6/8.e	7	incline dumbbell press	6	5
flat bench press	1	7	flat dumbbell press (palms-facing grip)	5/8.c	4
bent-over cable crossovers (thumbs facing grip)	14/17.b	7	bent-over cable crossovers	14	4
narrow-grip bench press (toward neck and shallow depth)	96/97 + 8.b	7	tricep pressdowns	108	0
pullovers (dumbbell)	18	7	incline dumbbell flyes, and front pulldowns (narrow grip)	12 55/57.b	3 0
bent-over rowing (supported T-bar, toward neck)	44/45.b + 50.b	7	bent-over rowing (supported T-bar, target-specific)	44/45.b + 50.e	0
barbell shrugs (behind back)	60/61.a	7	barbell shrugs	60	0
bent-over rowing (barbell, narrow grip)	44/50.a	7	bent-over rowing (barbell, wide grip)	44	5
front raises (dumbbell, elbow elev., angled to side)	34/35.a + 35.b	7	dumbbell shoulder press (palms-facing, shallow)	25/31.c + 31.d	2
bent-over rowing (supported T-bar, narrow grip)	44/45.b + 50.a	7	bent-over rowing (supported T-bar, wide grip)	44/45.b	5
seated, cable rowing (bar, narrow grip)	46/50.a	7	seated cable rowing (V-grip)	46/47	3
bent-over rowing (barbell, toward neck)	44/50.b	7	bent-over rowing (barbell, target-specific)	44/50.e	0
front raises	32, 34	6	dumbbell shoulder press (palms-facing grip)	25/31.c	4
flat bench press (wide grip)	1/8.a	6	flat dumbbell press (palms-facing grip)	5/8.c	4
flat dumbbell press	5	6	flat dumbbell press (palms-facing grip)	5/8.c	4
kneeling cable crossovers (thumbs facing grip)	16/17.b	6	kneeling cable crossovers	16	3
upright rowing (partial range)	36/37.c	6	upright rowing (partial range, wide grip)	36/37.c + 37.a	4
upright rowing (target-specific)	36/37.d	6	upright rowing (target-specific, wide-grip)	36/37.d + 37.a	4
seated cable rowing (straight bar, narrow grip)	46/50.a	6	seated cable rowing (straight bar, target-specific)	46/50.e	0
seated cable rowing (straight bar, toward neck)	46/50.b	6	seated cable rowing (straight bar, target-specific)	46/50.e	0

Aggravating Exercises	Exercise No.	R/B	Replacement Exercises	Exercise No.	R/B
modified dumbbell shoulder press	20	6	incline dumbbell press (palms-facing grip)	6/8.c	3
incline bench press	2	6	incline dumbbell press (palms-facing grip)	6/8.c	3
dumbbell lateral "flares"	38	6	dumbbell lateral raises (bent-over)	27	0
bent-over rowing (T-bar)	44/45.a	6	bent-over rowing (T-bar, palms-facing grip)	44/45.a + 50.c	3
dumbbell kickbacks (palm backward grip)	109.a/109.c	6	cable, "isolation" pressdowns (palm-down grip)	110.a/110.c	0
bent-over cable pressdowns (high hands position)	106/107	6	bent-over cable pressdowns	106	0
incline bench press (wide grip)	2/8.a	5	incline dumbbell press (palms-facing grip)	6/8.c	3
decline bench press (shallow depth)	4/8.b	5	decline dumbbell press (palms-facing, shallow)	7/8.c + 8.d	2
incline dumbbell press	6	5	incline dumbbell press (palms-facing grip)	6/8.c	3
decline dumbbell press (palms-facing grip)	7/8.c	5	decline dumbbell press (palms-facing, shallow)	7/8.c + 8.d	2
seated cable rowing (V-grip, toward neck)	46/47 + 50.b	5	seated cable rowing (V-grip, target-specific)	46/47 + 50.e	0
decline dumbbell flyes	13	5	nothing suitable	—	—
upright cable crossovers	15	5	nothing suitable	—	—
front shoulder press (barbell)	22, 24	5	dumbbell lateral raises (upright)	26	0
dumbbell shoulder press	25	5	dumbbell lateral raises (upright)	26	0
bent-over rowing (barbell, wide grip)	44	5	bent-over rowing (barbell, target-specific)	44/50.e	0
bent-over rowing (supported T-bar, wide grip)	44/45.b	5	bent-over rowing (T-bar, target-specific)	44/45.a + 50.e	1
dumbbell rowing (elbow flared out)	48/49	5	dumbbell rowing (target-specific)	48/50.e	0
narrow-grip bench press (shallow depth)	96/8.b	5	tricep pressdowns	108	0
pullovers (barbell, narrow)	19.a	5	front pulldowns (narrow grip)	55/57.b	0
decline dumbbell press (shallow depth)	7/8.d	4	decline dumbbell press (palms-facing, shallow)	7/8.c + 8.d	2
behind head shoulder press	21, 23	4	front shoulder press (shallow depth)	22, 24/31.d	3
flat bench press (shallow depth)	1/8.b	4	flat dumbbell press (palms-facing, shallow)	5/8.c + 8.d	1
flat dumbbell press (palms-facing grip)	5/8.c	4	flat dumbbell press (palms-facing, shallow)	5/8.c + 8.d	1
pec-deck machine	9	4	nothing suitable	—	—
flat dumbbell flyes	11	4	nothing suitable	—	—
bent-over cable crossovers	14	4	nothing suitable	—	—
dumbbell shoulder press (palms-facing grip)	25/31.c	4	dumbbell shoulder press (palms-facing, shallow)	25/31.c + 31.d	2
front raises (barbell, wide grip)	32/33.a	4	dumbbell shoulder press (palms-facing, shallow)	25/31.c + 31.d	2
front raises (dumbbell, angled to the side)	34/35.a	4	dumbbell shoulder press (palms-facing, shallow)	25/31.c + 31.d	2
seated, cable row (straight bar)	46	4	seated cable rowing (target-spec.)	46/50.e	0
upright rowing (target-specific or partial range, wide grip)	36/37.a + 37.c or 37.d	4	dumbbell shoulder press (palms-facing, shallow), and barbell shrugs	25/31.c + 31.d 60	2 0

Aggravating Exercises	Exercise No.	R/B	Replacement Exercises	Exercise No.	R/B
flat dumbbell press (shallow depth)	5/8.d	3	flat dumbbell press (palms-facing, shallow)	5/8.c + 8.d	1
front shoulder press (shallow depth)	22, 24/31.d	3	dumbbell shoulder press (palms-facing, shallow)	25/31.c + 31.d	2
dumbbell shoulder press (shallow depth)	25/31.d	3	dumbbell shoulder press (palms-facing, shallow)	25/31.c + 31.d	2
incline bench press (shallow depth)	2/8.b	3	incline dumbbell press (palms-facing, shallow)	6/8.c + 8.d	0
incline dumbbell press (palms-facing grip)	6/8.c	3	incline dumbbell press (palms-facing, shallow)	6/8.c + 8.d	0
incline dumbbell flyes	12	3	nothing suitable	—	—
kneeling cable crossovers	16	3	nothing suitable	—	—
bent-over rowing (T-bar, palms facing grip)	44/45.a + 50.c	3	bent-over rowing (T-bar, target-specific)	44/45.a + 50.e	1
seated cable rowing (V-grip)	46/47	3	seated cable rowing (V-grip, target-specific)	46/47 + 50.e	0
dumbbell rowing	48	3	dumbbell rowing (target-specific)	48/50.e	0
pullovers (barbell, wide)	19.b	3	standing stiff-arm pulldowns (wide)	58	0
standing stiff-arm pulldowns (narrow)	58/59	3	standing stiff-arm pulldowns (wide)	58	0
decline dumbbell press (palms-facing, shallow)	7/8.c + 8.d	2	nothing suitable	—	—
incline dumbbell press (shallow depth)	6/8.d	2	incline dumbbell press (palms-facing, shallow)	6/8.c + 8.d	0
behind head shoulder press (shallow depth)	21, 23/31.d	2	cable lateral raises (bent-over)	29	0
dumbbell shoulder press (palms-facing, shallow)	25/31.c + 31.d	2	nothing suitable	—	—
bent-over rowing (supported T-bar, palms-facing)	44/45.b + 50.c	2	bent-over rowing (supported T-bar, target-specific)	44/45.b + 50.e	0
flat dumbbell press (palms-facing, shallow)	5/8.c + 8.d	1	nothing suitable	—	—
bent-over rowing (T-bar, target-specific)	44/45.a + 50.e	1	nothing suitable	—	—
seated cable rowing (palms-facing grip)	46/50.c	1	nothing suitable	—	—

Region: Shoulder
Zone: II — Top

Aggravating Exercises	Exercise No.	R/B	Replacement Exercises	Exercise No.	R/B
bent-over lateral raises (one arm, elbow elev.)	27, 29/31.e + 31.f(i)	10	bent-over lateral raises	27, 29	7
behind-back cable lateral raises (elbow elev.)	30/31.f(ii)	10	bent-over lateral raises	27, 29	7
upright rowing (wide grip)	36/37.a	10	upright rowing (narrow grip)	36/37.b	6
upright lateral raises (one arm, elbow elev.)	26, 28/31.e + 31.f(i)	9	upright lateral raises	26, 28	6
bent-over lateral raises (elbow elev.)	27, 29/31.f(i)	9	bent-over lateral raises	27, 29	7
behind head shoulder press	21, 23	9	front shoulder press	22, 24	7
body dips (parallel bars, elbows flared)	101.a/101.c	9	decline dumbbell press	7	3

Aggravating Exercises	Exercise No.	R/B	Replacement Exercises	Exercise No.	R/B
bent-over lateral raises (one arm)	27, 29/31.e	8	dumbbell lateral "flares"	38	4
upright lateral raises (elbow elev.)	26, 28/31.f(i)	8	front shoulder press (wide grip)	22, 24/31.a	4
cable lateral raises (behind back)	30	8	dumbbell lateral "flares"	38	4
front raises (dumbbell, to the side, elbow elev.)	34/35.a + 35.b	8	front raises	32, 34	5
behind head chin-ups (narrow grip)	51/57.a	8	behind head chin-ups (target-specific)	51/62.c(ii)	4
upright rowing	36	8	front shoulder press (wide grip), and barbell shrugs	24/31.a 60	4 0
behind head pulldowns (narrow grip)	54/57.a	8	front pulldowns (narrow grip)	55/57.a	5
body dips (parallel bars or bench)	101.a, 101.b	8	upright tricep pressdowns	108.a	0
narrow-grip bench press (toward neck)	96/97	7	upright tricep pressdowns	108.a	0
incline bench press (toward neck)	2, 6/8.e	7	incline bench or dumbbell press	2, 6	5
upright lateral raises (one arm)	26, 28/31.e	7	front shoulder press (wide grip)	22, 24/31.a	4
bent-over lateral raises	27, 29	7	dumbbell lateral "flares"	38	4
front raises (dumbbell, elbow elev.)	34/35.b	7	front raises	32, 34	5
pullovers (dumbbell)	18	7	incline dumbbell flyes, and seated cable rowing	12 46	4 0
front barbell raises (wide grip)	32/33.a	7	front shoulder press (wide grip)	22, 24/31.a	4
front dumbbell raises (angled to the side)	34/35.a	7	front shoulder press (wide grip)	22, 24/31.a	4
dumbbell shoulder press	25	7	front shoulder press (wide grip)	22, 24/31.a	4
front shoulder press	22, 24	7	front shoulder press (wide grip)	22, 24/31.a	4
incline dumbbell press (toward neck)	6/8.e	7	incline dumbbell press	6	5
behind head shoulder press (wide grip)	21, 23/31.a	6	front shoulder press (wide grip)	22, 24/31.a	4
flat bench press (toward neck)	1/8.e	6	flat bench press	1	4
flat dumbbell press (toward neck)	5/8.e	6	flat dumbbell press	5	4
modified dumbbell shoulder press	20	6	incline dumbbell press	6	5
upright lateral raises	26, 28	6	front shoulder press (wide grip)	22, 24/31.a	4
front raises (barbell, wide grip)	32/33.a	6	front raises (barbell, narrow grip)	32/33.b	4
front raises (dumbbell, to side)	34/35.a	6	front raises (barbell, narrow grip)	32/33.b	4
behind-head chin-ups (wide grip)	51	6	front chin-ups (wide grip)	52	3
behind-head pulldowns (wide grip)	54	6	front pulldowns (wide grip)	55	3
kneeling cable tricep extension (knuckles backward)	104.a	6	upright cable pressdowns (palms down)	108.a	0
kneeling cable tricep extension (thumbs backward)	104.b	6	upright cable pressdowns (thumbs up)	108.b	0
kneeling cable tricep extension (knuckles forward)	104.c	6	upright cable pressdowns (palms up)	108.c	0
inclined cable tricep extension	105	6	cable isolation pressdowns (thumb forward)	110.a/110.b	0
upright rowing (narrow grip)	36/37.b	6	front shoulder press (wide grip), and barbell shrugs	24/31.a 60	4 0
upright rowing (partial range or target-specific, wide grip)	36/37.a + 37.c or 37.d	6	upright rowing (partial range or target-specific, narrow grip)	36/37.b + 37.c or 37.d	2
standing tricep ext. (barbell)	98	6	upright cable pressdowns (palms down)	108.a	0
standing tricep ext. (E-Z bar)	99.a	6	upright cable pressdowns (thumbs up)	108.b	0
standing tricep ext. (dumbbell)	99.b	6	upright cable pressdowns (palms up)	108.c	0
one-arm dumbbell extension (palm backward)	100.a	6	upright cable pressdowns (palms up)	108.c	0

Aggravating Exercises	Exercise No.	R/B	Replacement Exercises	Exercise No.	R/B
one-arm dumbbell ext. (thumb baackward)	100.b	6	upright cable pressdowns (thumbs up)	108.b	0
one-arm dumbbell ext. (knuckles backward)	100.c	6	upright cable pressdowns (palms down)	108.a	0
"French" presses (straight bar, deep/behind head)	102, 103.a/103.b	6	"French presses"	102	0
pullovers (barbell, narrow)	19.a	6	pullovers (barbell, wide)	19.b	4
flat dumbbell press (toward neck)	5/8.e	6	flat dumbbell press	5	4
behind-head shoulder press (wide grip)	21, 23/31.a	6	dumbbell lateral "flares"	38	4
incline bench press	2	5	incline bench press (wide grip)	2/8.a	3
decline bench or dumbbell press (toward neck)	4, 7/8.e	5	decline bench or dumbbell press	4, 7	3
incline dumbbell press	6	5	incline bench press (wide grip)	2/8.a	3
narrow-grip bench press	96	5	tricep pressdowns (upright)	108.a	0
front raises	32, 34	5	front raises (barbell, narrow grip)	32/33.b	4
front chin-ups (narrow grip)	52/57.b	5	front chin-ups (narrow grip, target-specific)	52/57.a + 62.c(i)	3
front pulldowns (narrow grip)	55/57.b	5	front pulldowns (narrow grip, target-specific)	55/57.a + 62.c(i)	3
reverse grip chin-ups	53	5	reverse grip chin-ups (narrow grip)	53/57.c	3
standing stiff-arm pulldowns (narrow grip)	58/59	5	standing stiff-arm pulldowns	58	2
reverse grip pulldowns	56	5	reverse grip pulldowns (nar. grip)	56/57.c	3
decline dumbbell press (toward neck)	7/8.e	5	decline dumbbell press	7	3
incline dumbbell flyes	12	4	incline bench press (wide grip)	2/8.a	3
kneeling cable crossovers	16	4	incline bench press (wide grip)	2/8.a	3
flat bench press	1	4	flat bench press (wide grip)	1/8.a	2
flat dumbbell press	5	4	flat bench press (wide grip)	1/8.a	2
front raises (barbell, narrow grip)	32/33.b	4	nothing suitable	—	—
upright rowing (partial range)	36/37.c	4	upright rowing (target-specific, narrow grip)	36/37.b + 37.d	2
behind-head chin-ups and pulldowns (target-specific)	51, 54/62.c(ii)	4	front chin-ups (target-specific)	52/62.c(i)	1
squats ("bodybuilding" with narrow stance, deep hips)	117.a/117.d	4	"sissy" squats	125	0
dumbbell lateral "flares"	38	4	nothing suitable	—	—
upright rowing (target-specific)	36/37.d	4	upright rowing (target-specific, narrow grip)	36/37.b + 37.d	2
standing peak cable curls	95	4	"concentration" curls	89	0
squats ("powerlifting")	117.b	4	squats ("powerlifting," wide grip)	117.b/117.c	2
pullovers (barbell, wide)	19.b	4	standing stiff-arm pulldowns (wide)	58	2
pec-deck machine (high hands)	9/10.b	4	nothing suitable	—	—
front shoulder press (wide grip)	22, 24/31.a	4	nothing suitable	—	—
flat dumbbell flyes	11	3	flat bench press (wide grip)	1/8.a	2
bent-over cable crossovers	14	3	flat bench press (wide grip)	1/8.a	2
incline bench press (wide grip)	2/8.a	3	nothing suitable	—	—
decline bench press	4	3	decline bench press (wide grip)	4/8.a	1
decline dumbbell press	7	3	decline bench press (wide grip)	4/8.a	1
pec-deck machine	9	3	nothing suitable	—	—
front chin-ups (wide grip)	52	3	front chin-ups (wide grip, target-specific)	52/62.c(i)	1
reverse grip chin-ups (narrow grip)	53/57.c	3	standing, barbell curls (narrow grip)	79/91.b	0

Aggravating Exercises	Exercise No.	R/B	Replacement Exercises	Exercise No.	R/B
front pulldowns (wide grip)	55	3	front pulldowns (wide grip, target-specific)	55/62.c(i)	1
reverse grip pulldowns (narrow grip)	56/57.c	3	standing, barbell curls (narrow grip)	79/91.b	0
squats ("bodybuilding")	117.a	3	dumbbell squats	117.e	0
lunges (barbell)	123	3	lunges (dumbbell)	123/124.a	0
front chin-ups (narrow grip, target-specific)	52/57.a + 62.c(i)	3	front chin-ups (wide grip, target-specific)	52/62.c(i)	1
reverse grip chin-ups (wide grip)	53/57.b	3	standing barbell curls	79	0
front pulldowns (narrow grip, target-specific)	55/57.a + 62.c(i)	3	front pulldowns (wide grip, target-specific)	55/62.c(i)	1
flat bench press (wide grip)	1/8.a	2	nothing suitable	—	—
squats ("powerlifting," wide hand placement)	117.b/117.c	2	deep leg press	135	1
standing, stiff-arm pulldowns	58	2	nothing suitable	—	—
upright rowing (partial range or target-specific, narrow grip)	36/37.b + 37.c or 37.d	2	nothing suitable	—	—
pec-deck machine (low hands)	9/10.a	2	nothing suitable	—	—
upright cable crossovers	15	2	decline bench press (wide grip)	4/8.a	1
decline dumbbell flyes	13	2	decline bench press (wide grip)	4/8.a	1
decline bench press (wide grip)	4/8.a	1	nothing suitable	—	—
squats ("bodybuilding," wide hand placement)	117.a/117.c	1	front squats	118	0
front chin-ups (wide grip, target-specific)	52/62.c(i)	1	nothing suitable	—	—
front pulldowns (wide grip, target-specific)	55/62.c(i)	1	nothing suitable	—	—

Region: Shoulder
Zone: III — Chest

Aggravating Exercises	Exercise No.	R/B	Replacement Exercises	Exercise No.	R/B
pec-deck (high hands, excess depth)	9/10.b + 10.c	9	pec-deck (high hands)	9/10.b	5
incline dumbbell flyes (excess depth)	12/17.a	9	incline dumbbell flyes	12	5
kneeling cable crossovers (excess depth)	16/17.c	9	kneeling cable crossovers	16	5
flat dumbbell flyes (excess depth)	11/17.a	8	flat dumbbell flyes	11	4
bent-over cable crossovers (excess depth)	14/17.c	8	bent-over cable crossovers	14	4
pec-deck (excess depth)	9/10.c	8	pec-deck	9	4
upright cable crossovers (excess depth)	15/17.c	7	upright cable crossovers	15	3
decline dumbbell flyes (excess depth)	13/17.a	7	decline dumbbell flyes	13	3
pullovers (dumbbell)	18	7	incline dumbbell flyes, and front pulldowns (wide grip)	12 55	5 3
pec-deck (low hands, excess depth)	9/10.a + 10.c	7	pec-deck (low hands)	9/10.a	3
behind head shoulder press	21, 23	5	front shoulder press	22, 24	0
behind head chin-ups	51	5	behind head chin-ups (narrow grip)	51/57.a	0
behind head pulldowns	54	5	behind head pulldowns (narrow grip)	54/57.a	0
incline dumbbell flyes	12	5	incline dumbbell press	6	0
pullovers (barbell, narrow)	19.a	5	standing stiff-arm pulldowns (narrow)	59	0

Aggravating Exercises	Exercise No.	R/B	Replacement Exercises	Exercise No.	R/B
kneeling cable crossovers	16	5	incline dumbbell press	6	0
pec-deck (high hands)	9/10.b	5	incline dumbbell press	6	0
flat dumbbell flyes	11	4	flat dumbbell press	5	0
pec-deck	9	4	flat dumbbell press	5	0
bent-over cable crossovers	14	4	flat dumbbell press	5	0
decline dumbbell flyes	13	3	decline dumbbell press	7	0
front chin-ups	52	3	front chin-ups (narrow grip)	52/57.b	0
front pulldowns	55	3	front pulldowns (narrow grip)	55/57.b	0
pullovers (barbell, wide)	19.b	3	standing stiff-arm pulldowns (wide)	58	0
upright cable crossovers	15	3	decline dumbbell press	7	0
pec-deck (low hands)	9/10.a	3	decline dumbbell press	7	0

Region: Elbow
Zone: I — Inside

Aggravating Exercises	Exercise No.	R/B	Replacement Exercises	Exercise No.	R/B
"preacher" barbell curls (wrist flex)	84/91.d	9	"preacher" barbell curls	84	4
"preacher" straight-bar cable curls (wrist flex)	86/91.d	9	"preacher" straight-bar cable curls	86	4
standing barbell curls (wrist flex)	79/91.d	9	standing barbell curls	79	4
standing straight-bar cable curls (wrist flex)	81/91.d	9	standing straight-bar cable curls	81	4
"preacher" E-Z bar curls (wrist flex)	85/91.d	8	"preacher" E-Z bar curls	85	3
"preacher" dumbbell curls (wrist flex)	87/91.d	8	"preacher" dumbbell curls	87	3
seated, inclined, alt. dumbbell curls (wrist flex)	90/91.d	8	seated, inclined, alt. dumbbell curls	90	3
standing alt. dumbbell curls (wrist flex)	82/91.d	8	standing alt. dumbbell curls	82	3
standing one-arm cable curls (wrist flex)	83/91.d	8	standing alt. cable curls	83	3
seated alt. dumbbell curls (wrist flex)	88/91.d	8	seated alt. dumbbell curls	88	3
seated "concentration" curls (wrist flex)	89/91.d	8	seated "concentration" curls	89	3
standing "peak" cable curls (wrist flex)	95/91.d	8	standing "peak" cable curls	95	3
standing E-Z bar curls (wrist flex)	80/91.d	7	standing E-Z bar curls	80	2
reverse grip chin-ups	53	6	reverse grip chin-ups (straps or hook grip)	53/62.a	3
reverse grip pulldowns	56	6	reverse grip pulldowns (straps or hook grip)	56/62.a	3
upright rowing	36	6	upright rowing (target-specific)	36/37.d	2
standing barbell curls (wide grip)	79/91.a	6	standing barbell curls	79	4
standing straight-bar curls (wide grip)	81/91.a	6	standing straight-bar cable curls	81	4
"preacher" barbell cable curls (wide grip)	84/91.a	6	"preacher" barbell curls	84	4
"preacher" straight-bar cable curls (wide grip)	86/91.a	6	"preacher" straight-bar cable curls	86	4
chest flyes/cable crossovers (wrist flex)	11-16/17.e	5	chest flyes/cable crossovers	11-16	0
all forearm curls	112, 113	5	all forearm curls (partial range)	112, 113/116.c	2

Aggravating Exercises	Exercise No.	R/B	Replacement Exercises	Exercise No.	R/B
"preacher" barbell curls	84	4	"preacher" barbell curls (wrist ext)	84/91.g	0
"preacher" straight-bar cable curls	86	4	"preacher" straight-bar cable curls (wrist ext)	86/91.g	0
standing barbell curls	79	4	standing barbell curls (wrist ext)	79/91.g	0
standing barbell ext. (wrist flex)	98/111.d	4	standing barbell ext.	98	0
standing straight-bar cable curls	81	4	standing straight-bar cable curls (wrist ext)	81/91.g	0
tricep ext. (pronated hands and wrist flex)	100.c, 104.a, 106, 108.a, 109.c, 110.c/111.d	4	tricep extension (pronated grip)	100.c, 104.a, 106, 108.a, 109.c, 110.c	0
pullovers (dumbbell)	18	4	nothing suitable	—	—
pullovers (barbell)	19.a, 19.b	4	front pulldowns (narrow grip, straps/hook grip)	55/57.b + 62.a	0
standing stiff-arm pulldowns	58	4	standing stiff-arm pulldowns (straps/hook grip)	58/62.a	1
behind-head chin-ups	51	3	behind head chin-ups (straps/hook grip)	51/62.a	0
front chin-ups	51	3	front chin-ups (straps/hook grip)	52/62.a	0
behind-head pulldowns	54	3	behind head pulldowns (straps/hook grip)	54/62.a	0
front pulldowns	55	3	front pulldowns (straps/hook grip)	55/62.a	0
reverse grip chin-ups (straps or hook grip)	53/62.a	3	nothing suitable	—	—
reverse grip pulldowns (straps or hook grip)	56/62.a	3	nothing suitable	—	—
shrugs (barbell or dumbbell)	60, 61.d	3	shrugs (bar or dumbbell, straps/hook grip)	60, 61.d/62.a	0
all rowing exercises	44, 46, 48	3	all rowing exer. (straps/hook grip)	44, 46, 48/62.a	0
all deadlifts	39, 40, 128	3	all deadlifts (straps/hook grip)	39, 40, 128/62.a	0
"preacher" E-Z bar curls	85	3	nothing suitable		
"preacher" dumbbell curls	87	3	"preacher" dumbbell curls (wrist extension)	87/91.g	0
seated, inclined, alt. dumbbell curls	90	3	seated inclined alternating dumbbell curls (wrist extension)	90/91.g	0
standing one-arm cable curls	83	3	standing one-arm cable curls (wrist extension)	83/91.g	0
seated alt. dumbbell curls	88	3	seated alt. dumbbell curls (wrist ext)	88/91.g	0
seated "concentration" curls	89	3	seated "concentration" curls (wrist extension)	89/91.g	0
standing "peak" cable curls	95	3	standing "peak" cable curls (wrist ext)	95/91.g	0
all forearm curls (partial range)	112, 113/116.c	2	nothing suitable	—	—
upright rowing (partial range or target-specific)	36/37.c or 37.d	2	nothing suitable	—	—
all forearm raises (partial range)	114, 115/116.d	2	nothing suitable	—	—
standing E-Z bar curls	80	2	nothing suitable	—	—
standing stiff-arm pulldowns (straps or hook grip)	58/62.a	1	nothing suitable	—	—

Region: Elbow
Zone: II — Outside

Aggravating Exercises	Exercise No.	R/B	Replacement Exercises	Exercise No.	R/B
upright rowing (wide grip)	36/37.a	7	upright rowing (narrow grip)	36/37.b	5
seated cable rowing (straight bar)	46	7	seated cable rowing (straight bar, narrow grip)	46/50.a	5
bent-over rowing	44	7	bent-over rowing (straight bar, narrow grip)	44/50.a	5
all palms-forward chin-ups	51, 52	7	palms-forward pulldowns (target-specific)	55/62.c(i)	4
all palms-forward pulldowns	54, 55	7	palms-forward chinups (target-specific)	52/62.c(i)	4
"reverse" bicep curls (preacher)	92/93.c	7	"reverse" bicep curls (E-Z bar)	92/93.b	3
front shoulder raises (barbell)	32	7	front shoulder press	22, 24	0
upright rowing	36	6	upright rowing (partial range)	36/37.c	2
seated cable rowing (V-grip)	46/47	6	seated cable rowing (V-grip, target-specific)	46/47 + 50.e	0
bent-over rowing (T-bar)	44/45.a or 45.b	6	bent-over rowing (T-bar, target-specific)	44/45.a + 50.e	0
chin-ups (narrow grip)	51/57.a, 52/57.b	6	chin-ups (target-specific)	51/62.c(ii), 52/62.c(i)	4
pulldowns (narrow grip)	54/57.a, 55/57.b	6	pulldowns (target-specific)	54/62.c(ii), 55/62.c(i)	4
front shoulder raises (dumbbells)	34	6	dumbbell shoulder press	25	0
cable lateral raises (behind back)	30	6	cable lateral raises (behind, wrist strap)	30/31.g	3
upright rowing (narrow grip)	36/37.b	5	upright rowing (partial range)	36/37.c	2
seated cable rowing (straight bar, narrow grip)	46/50.a	5	seated cable rowing (V-grip, target-specific)	46/47 + 50.e	0
bent-over rowing (straight bar, narrow grip)	44/50.a	5	bent-over rowing (barbell, target-specific)	44/50.e	0
seated cable rowing (palms-facing grip)	46/50.c	5	seated cable rowing (straight bar, target-specific)	46/50.e	0
"reverse" bicep curls	92	5	"reverse" bicep curls (E-Z bar)	92/93.b	3
"reverse" bicep curls (E-Z bar, preacher)	92/93.b + 93.c	5	"reverse" bicep curls (E-Z bar)	92/93.b	3
dumbbell lateral raises (upright)	26	5	cable lateral raises (upright, wrist strap)	28/31.g	1
dumbbell lateral raises (bent-over)	27	5	cable lateral raises (bent-over, wrist strap)	29/31.g	1
dumbbell lateral "flares"	38	5	behind head shoulder press	21, 23	0
all forearm raises	114, 115	5	all forearm raises (partial range)	114, 115/116.d	2
bent-over rowing (T-bar, palms-facing)	44/50.c + 45.a or 45.b	4	bent-over rowing (T-bar, palms-facing and target-specific)	44/45.a + 50.c + 50.e	0
all palms-forward chin-ups (target-specific)	51/62.c(ii), 52/62.c(i)	4	standing stiff-arm pulldowns	58	0
all palms-forward pulldowns (target-specific)	54/62.c(ii), 55/62.c(i)	4	standing stiff-arm pulldowns	58	0
dumbbell rowing	48	4	dumbbell rowing (target-specific)	48/50.e	0
bent-over rowing (T-bar, narrow grip)	44/45.b + 50.a	4	bent-over rowing (T-bar, target-specific)	44/45.a + 50.e	0
cable lateral raises (upright torso)	28	4	cable lateral raises (upright, wrist strap)	28/31.g	1

Aggravating Exercises	Exercise No.	R/B	Replacement Exercises	Exercise No.	R/B
cable lateral raises (bent-over torso)	29	4	cable lateral raises (bent-over, wrist strap)	29/31.g	1
dumbbell, or one-hand cable, curls	82, 83, 87, 88, 89, 90	4	dumbbell or one-hand cable curls (palm up)	82, 83, 87, 88, 89, 90/91.f	0
supinated-hand tricep exercises	100.a, 104.c, 108.c, 109.a, 110.a	4	supinated-hand tricep exer. exercises (wrist flex)	100.a, 104.c, 108.c,109.a, 110.a, 111.d(ii)	0
"reverse" bicep curls (E-Z bar)	92/93.b	3	nothing suitable	—	—
standing, or "preacher," E-Z bar curls	80, 85	3	standing or "preacher" straight bar curls	79, 84	0
upright rowing (partial range or target-specific, wide grip)	36/37.a + 37.c or 37.d	3	upright rowing (partial range or target-specific, narrow grip)	36/37.b + 37.c or 37.d	1
cable lateral raises (behind, wrist strap)	30/31.g	3	behind head shoulder press	21, 23	0
"hammer" curls	94	2	nothing suitable	—	—
upright rowing (partial range or target-specific)	36/37.c or 37.d	2	front shoulder press, and barbell shrugs	24 60	0 0
all forearm raises (partial range)	114, 115/116.d	2	nothing suitable	—	—
upright rowing (partial range or target-specific, narrow grip)	36/37.b + 37.c or 37.d	1	front shoulder press, and barbell shrugs	24 60	0 0
cable lateral raises (upright, wrist strap)	28/31.g	1	front shoulder press	22, 24	0
cable lateral raises (bent-over, wrist strap)	36/31.g	1	behind head shoulder press	21, 23	0

Region: Elbow
Zone: III — Front

Aggravating Exercises	Exercise No.	R/B	Replacement Exercises	Exercise No.	R/B
standing "peak" cable curls (palms-up)	95/91.f	10	standing "peak" cable curls	95	6
"preacher" straight-bar, curls	84, 86	10	"preacher" straight-bar curls (partial elbow ext)	84, 86/91.c(ii)	6
"preacher" dumbbell curls (palm-up)	87/91.f	10	"preacher" dumbbell curls	87	6
standing straight-bar curls (full elbow ext)	79, 81/91.c(i)	8	standing straight-bar curls	79, 81	6
chest flyes or crossovers (full elbow ext)	11-16/17.f	8	chest flyes or crossovers	11-16	0
dumbbell or one-hand cable curls (palm-up, full elbow ext)	82, 83, 88, 89, 90/91.f + 91.c(i)	8	dumbbell or one-hand cable curls (palm-up)	82, 83, 88, 89, 90/91.f	6
"preacher" straight-bar curls (partial elbow ext)	84, 86/91.c(ii)	6	"preacher" E-Z bar curls (partial elbow ext)	85/91.c(ii)	2
"preacher" curls (E-Z bar or dumbbell)	85, 87	6	"preacher" curls (E-Z bar or dumbbell, partial elbow ext)	85, 87/91.c(ii)	2
standing straight-bar curls	79, 81	6	standing E-Z bar curls	80	2
standing "peak" cable curls	95	6	standing "peak" cable curls (partial elbow ext)	95/91.c(ii)	2
dumbbell or one-hand cable curls (palm-up)	82, 83, 88, 89, 90/91.f	6	dumbbell or cable curls	82, 83, 88, 89, 90	2
reverse-grip chin-ups	53	6	reverse grip chin-ups (elbow flex)	53/62.b	2
reverse-grip pulldowns	56	6	reverse grip pulldowns (elbow flex)	56/62.b	2

Aggravating Exercises	Exercise No.	R/B	Replacement Exercises	Exercise No.	R/B
"preacher" dumbbell curls (partial elbow ext and palm-up)	87/91.c(ii) + 91.f	6	"preacher" dumbbell curls (partial elbow ext)	87/91.c(ii)	2
seated inclined alt. curls (palms-up)	90/91.f	4	seated inclined alt. curls	90	0
bent-leg barbell deadlifts	39	4	bent-leg barbell deadlifts (elbow flex)	39/62.b	0
all rowing exercises	44, 46, 48	4	all rowing exercises (elbow flex)	44, 46, 48/62.b	0
barbell shrugs (1 palm up/1 palm down)	60/61.c	4	barbell shrugs (1 palm up/ 1 palm down, elbow flex)	60/61.c + 62.b	0
all pulldowns and chin-ups	51, 52, 54, 55	4	all pulldowns and chin-ups (elbow flex)	51, 52, 54, 55/62.b	0
standing "peak" cable curls (partial elbow ext)	95/91.c(ii)	2	seated alt. curls (partial elbow ext)	88/91.c(ii)	0
dumbbell or one-hand cable curls	82, 83, 88, 89,90	2	seated "concentration" curls (partial elbow ext)	89/91.c(ii)	0
"preacher" curls (E-Z bar or dumbbell, partial elbow ext)	85, 87/91.c(ii)	2	seated "concentration" curls (partial elbow ext)	89/91.c(ii)	0
standing E-Z bar curls	80	2	seated alt. curls (partial elbow ext)	88/91.c(ii)	0
seated dumbbell curls (palm-up and partial elbow ext)	88, 89/91.f + 91.c(ii)	2	seated dumbbell curls (partial elbow ext)	88, 89/91.c(ii)	0
reverse-grip chin-ups (elbow flex)	53/62.b	2	seated "concentration" curls (partial elbow ext), and standing stiff-arm pulldowns	89/91.c(ii) 58	0 0
reverse-grip pulldowns (elbow flex)	56/62.b	2	seated "concentration" curls (partial elbow ext), and standing stiff-arm pulldowns	89/91.c(ii) 58	0 0

Region: Elbow
Zone: IV — Rear

Aggravating Exercises	Exercise No.	R/B	Replacement Exercises	Exercise No.	R/B
"preacher" barbell curls	84	10	"preacher" barbell curls (partial elbow ext)	84/91.c(ii)	2
"preacher" straight bar cable curls	86	10	"preacher" straight bar cable curls (partial elbow ext)	86/91.c(ii)	2
"preacher" dumbbell curls (palm-up)	87/91.f	10	"preacher" dumbbell curls (palm-up and partial elbow ext)	87, 91.f + 91.c(ii)	2
seated alt. inclined dumbbell curls (palm-up, full elbow ext.)	90/91.f + 91.c(i)	10	seated, alt., inclined dumbbell curls	90	2
"French presses" (deep, behind head at start/finish)	102, 103.a/103.b	9	"French presses" (at start/finish)	102, 103.a	5
standing barbell tricep ext. (at start/finish)	98	8	upright cable pressdowns (palms-down grip)	108.a	4
standing E-Z bar tricep ext. (at start/finish)	99.a	8	upright cable pressdowns (thumbs-up grip)	108.a/108.b	4
standing dumbbell tricep ext. (at start/finish)	99.b	8	upright cable pressdowns (palms-up grip)	108.a/108.c	4
standing one-arm dumbbell tricep ext. (palm backward at start/finish)	100.a	8	upright cable pressdowns (palms-up grip)	108.a/108.c	4
standing alt. dumbbell tricep ext. (thumb downward at start/finish)	100.a/100.b	8	upright cable pressdowns (thumbs-up grip)	108.a/108.b	4
standing alt. dumbbell tricep ext. (knuckles backward at start/finish)	100.a/100.c	8	upright cable pressdowns (palms-down grip)	108.a	4

Aggravating Exercises	Exercise No.	R/B	Replacement Exercises	Exercise No.	R/B
flat bench press (elbow hyperext.)	1/111.a	8	flat bench press	1	0
incline bench press (elbow hyperext.)	2/111.a	8	incline bench press	2	0
decline bench press (elbow hyperext.)	4/111.a	8	decline bench press	4	0
narrow-grip bench press (elbow hyperext.)	96/111.a	8	narrow-grip bench press	96	0
flat dumbbell press (elbow hyperext.)	5/111.a	8	flat dumbbell press	5	0
incline dumbbell press (elbow hyperext.)	6/111.a	8	incline dumbbell press	6	0
decline dumbbell press (elbow hyperext.)	7/111.a	8	decline dumbbell press	7	0
front shoulder press (elbow hyperext.)	22, 24/111.a	8	front shoulder press	22, 24	0
behind head shoulder press (elbow hyperext.)	21, 23/111.a	8	behind head shoulder press	21, 23	0
dumbbell shoulder press (elbow hyperext.)	25/111.a	8	dumbbell shoulder press	25	0
standing tricep ext. (elbow hyperext. at mid-phase)	98, 100/111.a	8	upright cable pressdowns	108	4
body dips (elbow hyperext., at mid-phase)	101/111.a	8	body dips (at start/finish)	101	6
"French presses" (elbow hyperext. at mid-phase)	102/111.a	8	"French presses" (at start/finish)	102	5
kneeling or inclined cable tricep ext. (elbow hyperext. at mid-phase)	104, 105/111.a	8	upright cable pressdowns	108	4
bent-over cable pressdowns (elbow hyperext. at mid-phase)	106/111.a	8	bent-over cable pressdowns (at start/finish)	106	3
upright cable pressdowns (elbow hyperext. at mid-phase)	108/111.a	8	upright cable pressdowns (at start/finish)	108	4
dumbbell "kickbacks" (elbow hyperext. at mid-phase)	109/111.a	8	dumbbell "kickbacks" (at start/finish)	109	3
cable isolation pressdowns (elbow hyperext. at mid-phase)	110/111.a	8	cable "isolation" pressdowns (at start/finish)	110	4
"preacher" E-Z bar curls	85	8	"preacher" E-Z bar curls (partial elbow ext.)	85/91.c(ii)	0
"preacher" dumbbell curls	87	8	"preacher" dumbbell curls (partial elbow extension)	87/91.c(ii)	0
dumbbell or alt. cable curls (palm-up and full elbow ext.)	82, 83, 88, 89/91.f + 91.c(i)	8	dumbbell or one-hand cable curls (palm-up)	82, 83, 88, 89/91.f	2
standing "peak" cable curls	95	8	standing peak cable curls (partial elbow extension)	95/91.c(ii)	0
kneeling cable tricep ext. (knuckles backward at start/finish)	104.a	7	upright cable pressdowns (palms-down grip)	108.a	4
kneeling cable tricep ext. (thumbs backward at start/finish)	104.a/104.b	7	upright cable pressdowns (thumbs-up grip)	108.a/108.b	4
kneeling cable tricep ext. (knuckles forward at start/finish)	104.a/104.c	7	upright cable pressdowns (palms-up grip)	108.a/108.c	4
inclined cable tricep ext. (at start/finish)	105	7	bent-over cable pressdowns	106	3
standing barbell or straight-bar cable curls (full elbow ext)	79, 81/91.c(i)	6	standing barbell or straight-bar cable curls	79, 81	0
body dips (parallel bars at start/finish)	101.a	6	upright cable pressdowns (thumbs-up grip)	108.a/108.b	4
body dips (between benches at start/finish)	101.a/101.b	6	upright cable pressdowns (palms-down grip)	108.a	4

Aggravating Exercises	Exercise No.	R/B	Replacement Exercises	Exercise No.	R/B
body dips (elbows flared at start/finish)	101.a/101.c	6	decline dumbbell press, and upright cable pressdowns (thumbs-up grip)	7 108.a/108.b	0 4
bent-over cable pressdowns (high hands at start/finish)	106/107	6	bent-over cable pressdowns	106	3
"French presses" (E-Z bar, at start/finish)	102	5	bent-over cable pressdowns	106	3
"French presses" (straight bar, at start/finish)	102/103.a	5	dumbbell tricep "kickbacks" (palm-backward grip)	109.a/109.c	3
upright cable tricep pressdowns (palms down at start/finish)	108.a	4	dumbbell tricep "kickbacks" (palm-backward grip)	109.a/109.c	3
upright cable tricep pressdowns (thumbs up at start/finish)	108.a/108.b	4	dumbbell tricep "kickbacks" (thumb-forward grip)	109.a/109.b	3
upright cable tricep pressdowns (palms up at start/finish)	108.a/108.c	4	dumbbell tricep "kickbacks" (palm-forward grip)	109.a	3
cable "isolation" pressdowns (palms up at start/finish)	110.a	4	dumbbell tricep "kickbacks" (palm-forward grip)	109.a	3
cable "isolation" pressdowns (thumbs up at start/finish)	110.a/110.b	4	dumbbell tricep "kickbacks" (thumb-forward grip)	109.a/109.b	3
cable "isolation" pressdowns (palms down at start/finish	110.a/110.c	4	dumbbell tricep "kickbacks (palm-backward grip)	109.a/109.c	3
seated alt. inclined dumbbell curls (palms up)	90/91.f	4	seated, inclined, alternate dumbbell curls	90	2
dumbbell tricep "kickbacks" (palm forward at start/finish)	109.a	3	nothing suitable		
dumbbell tricep "kickbacks" (thumb forward at start/finish)	109.a/109.b	3	nothing suitable		
dumbbell tricep "kickbacks" (palm backward grip)	109.a/109.c	3	nothing suitable		
bent-over cable pressdowns (at start/finish)	106	3	nothing suitable		
seated alt. inclined dumbbell curls	90	2	seated, "concentration" curls	89	0
dumbbell or alt. cable curls (palm-up)	82, 83, 88, 89/91.f	2	dumbbell, or one-hand cable, curls	82, 83, 88, 89	0
"preacher" dumbbell curls (palm-up and partial elbow ext)	87/91.f + 91.c(ii)	2	"preacher" dumbbell curls (partial elbow ext)	87/91.c(ii)	0
"preacher" straight bar curls (partial elbow ext)	84, 86/91.c(ii)	2	nothing suitable		

Region: Wrist

Aggravating Exercises	Exercise No.	R/B	Replacement Exercises	Exercise No.	R/B
bent-over cable pressdowns (high hands, excess. narrow grip, wrists hyperext)	106/107 + 111.b + 111.c	10	bent-over cable pressdowns	106	4
narrow-grip bench press (excessive wrists hyperext)	96/8.f	9	narrow-grip bench press	96	4
upright cable pressdowns (excess. narrow grip, wrists hyperext)	108.a/111.b + 111.c	9	upright cable pressdowns	108.a	4
bent-over cable pressdowns (excess. narrow grip, wrists hyperext)	106/111.b + 111.c	9	bent-over cable pressdowns	106	4

Aggravating Exercises	Exercise No.	R/B	Replacement Exercises	Exercise No.	R/B
bent-over cable pressdowns (high hands, wrists hyperext)	106/107 + 111.b	8	bent-over cable pressdowns	106	4
body dips (between benches)	101.b	8	body dips (parallel bars)	101.a	0
chest presses (wrists hyperext)	1, 2, 4-7/8.f	8	chest presses	1, 2, 4-7	0
shoulder press (wrists hyperext)	21-25/31.b	8	shoulder presses	21-25	0
upright rowing (narrow grip)	36/37.b	8	upright rowing (partial range)	36/37.c	2
barbell forearm raises (narrow grip)	114/116.b	8	barbell forearm raises	114	6
bent-over cable pressdowns (high hands, excess. narrow grip)	106/107 + 111.c	7	bent-over cable pressdowns	106	4
bent-over cable pressdowns (wrists hyperext)	106/111.b	7	bent-over cable pressdowns	106	4
upright cable pressdowns (palms down, wrists hyperext)	108.a/111.b	7	upright cable pressdowns	108.a	4
"reverse" bicep curls (narrow grip)	92/93.a	7	"reverse" bicep curls	92	4
narrow-grip bench press (wrists hyperextended)	96/111.b	7	narrow-grip bench press	96	4
bent-over cable pressdowns (excess. narrow grip)	106/111.c	6	bent-over cable pressdowns	106	4
upright cable pressdowns (palms down, narrow grip)	108.a/111.c	6	upright cable pressdowns	108.a	4
upright rowing	36	6	upright rowing (target-specific)	36/37.d	2
barbell forearm curls (narrow grip)	112/116.b	6	barbell forearm curls	112	4
barbell forearm raises	114	6	dumbbell forearm raises	115	4
narrow-grip bench press (excessively narrow grip)	96/111.c	6	narrow-grip bench press	96	4
straight-bar pronated tricep exer. (excess. narrow grip, wrists hyperext.)	98, 103.a, 104.a/111.b + 111.c	5	straight-bar pronated tricep exercises	98, 103.a, 104.a	0
bent-over cable pressdowns (high hands)	106/107	5	straight-bar pronated tricep exercises	98, 103.a, 104.a	0
narrow-grip bench press	96	4	straight-bar pronated tricep exercises	98, 103.a, 104.a	0
upright cable pressdowns (palms down)	108.a	4	dumbbell "kickbacks" (palm-backward grip)	109.c	0
upright cable pressdowns (thumbs-up grip)	108.b	4	dumbbell "kickbacks" (thumb-forward grip)	109.b	0
upright cable pressdowns (palms-up grip)	108.c	4	dumbbell "kickbacks" (palm-forward grip)	109.a	0
upright rowing (wide grip)	36/37.a	4	upright rowing (target-specific)	36/37.d	2
upright rowing (partial range or target-specific, narrow grip)	36/37.b + 37.c or 37.d	4	upright rowing (target-specific or partial range)	36/37.d or 37.c	2
dumbbell forearm raises	115	4	dumbbell forearm raises (partial range)	115/116.d	0
"preacher" straight-bar curls (narrow grip)	84, 86/91.b	4	"preacher" straight-bar curls	84, 86	0
barbell forearm raises (wide grip)	114/116.a	4	dumbbell forearm raises (partial range)	115/116.d	0
barbell forearm curls	112	4	barbell forearm curls (part. range)	112/116.c	2
standing barbell or straight-bar cable curls (narrow-grip)	79, 81/91.b	4	standing barbell or straight-bar cable curls	79, 81	0
"reverse" bicep curls	92	4	"reverse" curls (E-Z bar)	92/93.b	0
bent-over cable pressdowns	106	4	straight-bar pronated tricep exer.	98, 103.a, 104.a	0
straight-bar pronated tricep exercises (wrists hyperext)	98, 103.a, 104.a/111.b	3	straight-bar pronated tricep exercises	98, 103.a, 104.a	0
dumbbell tricep extensions (knuckles backward, wrist hyperext)	100.a/100.c + 111.b	3	dumbbell tricep extensions (knuckles backward)	100.a/100.c	0

Aggravating Exercises	Exercise No.	R/B	Replacement Exercises	Exercise No.	R/B
straight-bar pronated tricep exercises (excess. narrow grip)	98, 103.a, 104.a/111.c	2	straight-bar pronated tricep exercises	98, 103.a, 104.a	0
dumbbell forearm curls	113	2	dumbbell forearm curls (part. rng.)	113/116.c	0
barbell forearm curls (wide grip)	112/116.a	2	barbell forearm curls (wide grip, partial range)	112/116.a +116.c	0
upright rowing (partial range)	36/37.c	2	upright rowing (partial range, wide grip)	36/37.a + 37.c	0
upright rowing (target-specific)	36/37.d	2	upright rowing (target-specific, wide grip)	36/37.a + 37.d	0
barbell forearm raises (partial range)	114/116.d	2	dumbbell forearm raises (partial range)	115/116.d	0
barbell forearm curls (partial range)	112/116.c	2	dumbbell forearm curls (partial range)	113/116.c	0

Region: Knee

Aggravating Exercises	Exercise No.	R/B	Replacement Exercises	Exercise No.	R/B
"hack" squats (deep)	142	10+	squats ("powerlifting")	117.b	7
"hack" squats (narrow, toed in)	119/120.a	10	leg press (toed in)	121/122.a	7
"hack" squats (wide, toed out)	119/120.b	10	leg press (toed-out position)	121/122.b	7
leg press (deep, low foot placement)	135/136.b	9	leg press (shallow), and cable buttock pulls (to rear)	121, 139	5, 0
"hack" squats	119	9	squats ("bodybuilding")	117.a	4
squats ("bodybuilding," narrow stance, deep hips)	117.a/117.d	8	"sissy" squats	125	3
squats ("powerlifting")	117.b	7	leg press (shallow)	121	5
leg press (deep)	135	7	leg press (shallow)	121	5
"platform" lunges	141	7	lunges (shallow depth), and cable buttock pull (to rear)	123/124.b, 139	3, 0
leg press (narrow, toed in)	121/122.a	7	lunges (shallow depth)	123/124.b	3
leg press (wide, toed out)	121/122.b	7	lunges (shallow depth)	123/124.b	3
side lunges	143	7	front cable leg-crossovers	144	0
front squats	118	6	"sissy" squats	125	3
lunges (barbell, deep)	123/124.c	6	lunges (shallow depth), and cable buttock pulls (to rear)	123/124.b, 139	3, 0
leg press (shallow depth)	121	5	"sissy" squats	125	3
lunges	123	5	lunges (shallow depth)	123/124.b	3
prone hamstring curls (leg rotation variations)	132/133.a, 133.b	5	prone hamstring curls (one-leg, toes in or out)	132/133.d, 133.e	0
squats ("bodybuilding")	117.a	4	"sissy" squats	125	3
dumbbell squats	117.a/117.e	4	"sissy" squats	125	3
bent leg deadlifts	39, 40	4	lower back extensions (on floor), and cable buttock pulls (to rear)	42/43.b, 139	0, 0
lunges (barbell, shallow)	123/124.b	3	thigh extensions	126	2
"sissy" squats	125	3	thigh extensions	126	2
thigh extensions	126	2	nothing suitable	—	—

Region: Hamstrings

Aggravating Exercises	Exercise No.	R/B	Replacement Exercises	Exercise No.	R/B
straight-leg deadlift (on a platform)	128/129	10+	bent-leg deadlift	39	0
straight-leg deadlift	128	10	bent-leg deadlift	39	0
"good mornings" (locked knees, round out)	41/50.g + 50.i	10	"good mornings"	41	0
bent-over rowing (straight-bar, locked knees, round out)	44/50.h + 50.i	10	bent-over barbell rowing	44	0
T-bar rowing (locked knees, round out)	44/45.a + 50.h + 50.i	10	T-bar rowing	44/45.a	0
seated cable rowing (locked knees, round out)	46, 47/50.h + 50.i	10	seated cable rowing	46, 47	0
dumbbell rowing (locked knee, round out)	48/50.h + 50.i	10	dumbbell rowing	48	0
"donkey" calf raises (toe support only)	146/151.c	9	"donkey" calf raises	146	6
leg press calf raises (toe support only)	147/151.c	9	leg press calf raises	147	6
"good mornings" (locked knees)	41/50.i	8	"good mornings"	41	0
bent-over rowing (straight bar, locked knees)	44/50.i	8	bent-over barbell rowing	44	0
T-bar rowing (locked knees)	44/45.a + 50.i	8	T-bar rowing	44/45.a	0
seated cable rowing (locked knees)	46, 47/50.i	8	seated cable rowing	46, 47	0
dumbbell rowing (locked knees)	48/50.i	8	dumbbell rowing	48	0
"donkey" calf raises (including leg-rotation var.)	146	6	standing calf raises (including leg-rotation var.)	145	2
calf-raises (on leg press) (including leg-rotation var.)	147	6	standing calf raises (including leg-rotation var.)	145	2
lower back extensions (hyper and half range)	42, 43.a	6	lower back extensions (on floor)	42/43.b	0
torso twists (standing, forward lean, locked knees)	71/78.e + 78.f	6	torso twists (standing, forward lean)	71/78.e	2
prone hamstring curls (hyperext knees)	132/134	5	prone hamstring curls	132	3
leg press (deep, high foot placement)	135/136.a	5	deep leg press, and prone hamstring curls	135 / 132	0 / 3
standing alt. hamstring curl (knee hyperext)	130/134	5	standing alt. hamstring curls	130	3
standing calf raises (toe support only, including leg-rotation var.)	145/151.c	5	standing calf raises (including leg-rotation var.)	145	2
"hack" calf raises (toe support only, including leg-rotation var.)	148/151.c	5	"hack" calf raises (including leg-rotation var.)	148	2
standing alt. calf raises (toe support only)	149/151.c	5	standing alt. calf raises (including leg-rotation var.)	149	2
torso twists (standing, locked knees)	71/78.f	4	torso twists (standing)	71	0
prone hamstring curls (all var.)	132	3	nothing suitable	—	—
standing alt. hamstring curls (including leg-rotation var.)	130	3	nothing suitable	—	—
standing calf raises (including leg-rotation var.)	145	2	seated calf raises (including leg-rotation var.)	150	0
calf raises (on "hack" machine) (including leg-rotation var.)	148	2	seated calf raises (including leg-rotation var.)	150	0
standing alt. calf raises (including leg-rotation var.)	149	2	seated calf raises (including leg-rotation var.)	150	0
torso twists (forward lean)	71, 72/78.e	2	torso twists (standing)	71	0

Region: "Other"
Zone: I — Chest/Breast Bone

Aggravating Exercises	Exercise No.	R/B	Replacement Exercises	Exercise No.	R/B
all barbell bench presses (bouncing cheat)	1, 2, 4/3.a	7	all barbell bench presses	1, 2, 4	0

Zone: II — Foot/Ankle

Aggravating Exercises	Exercise No.	R/B	Replacement Exercises	Exercise No.	R/B
calf raises (toe support only)	145-150/151.c	7	calf raises	145-150	0
seated front-foot raises	152	4	cable front-foot raises	153	0

Zone: III — Achilles Heel

Aggravating Exercises	Exercise No.	R/B	Replacement Exercises	Exercise No.	R/B
calf raises (toe support only)	145-150/151.c	6	calf raises	145-150	3
calf raises	145-150	3	nothing suitable	—	—
seated front-foot raises	152	3	nothing suitable	—	—
cable front-foot raises	153	3	nothing suitable	—	—

Zone: IV — Groin

Aggravating Exercises	Exercise No.	R/B	Replacement Exercises	Exercise No.	R/B
side lunges	143	7	front cable leg-crossovers	144	2
squats (powerlifting)	117.b	6	squats (bodybuilding)	117.a	0
lunges (barbell, deep)	123/124.c	5	lunges (barbell)	123	3
lunges (barbell)	123	3	lunges (barbell, shallow)	123/124.b	0
front cable leg-crossovers	144	2	nothing suitable	—	—

ABDUCTION - movement of an arm or leg away from the midline of the body.

A.C.E. - American Council on Exercise.

ACROMIO-CLAVICULAR JOINT - the joint of the shoulder formed between the end of the collar bone and the outer/upper projection of the shoulder blade.

ADDUCTION - movement of an arm or a leg toward the mid-line of the body.

ARTICULAR CARTILAGE - the smooth, resilient tissue located at the ends of bone; the actual joint surfaces that glide across each other to create joint motion.

BAD PAIN - soft tissue pain made apparent by weight training, even when using light weights or just warming up; this indicates injury; in contrast to "good pain."

BICIPITAL GROOVE AND TENDON – of the two upper tendons of the biceps muscle, the one that lies lengthwise in the groove in the bone of the upper arm (i.e., the humerus).

BURSA - a thin, fluid-filled sac that sits between a bony prominence and the skin; it acts as a cushion or shock absorber.

CALCANEAL PERIOSTEUM - the thin layer of tissue that wraps around, and is attached to, the heel bone.

CARPALS - the eight small bones, located between the hand and forearm, that constitute the wrist.

CERVICAL SPINE - the vertebrae of the neck.

CHEATING - the use of torso muscles to lift a weight heavier than the target muscles could lift using proper technique; believed to speed up development of the target muscles.

CLOSE-PACKED POSITION - the alignment of bones, in either of the hand/wrist or the foot/ankle regions, that is locked and stable, thus inflexible.

CONCENTRIC MUSCLE ACTIVITY - forceful shortening of a muscle to move a weight; occurs from the start/finish to the mid-phase position of a rep.

CONNECTIVE TISSUE - any soft tissue that holds the body together; includes tendons, ligaments, joint capsules, cartilage, bursae, and various fasciae.

CONTRACTURE - a chronic shortening of a muscle, making it unable to properly relax; usually has a tight, knotted texture and is tender to touch.

COSTOCHONDRAL JUNCTION - the cartilage region, at the front of the ribs, that connects the ribs to the sternum.

COSTO TRANSVERSE JOINT - the joint between the end of a rib and the transverse process of a vertebra.

COSTOVERTEBRAL JOINT - the joint between the end of a rib and the body of a vertebra.

DEAD LIFT - the act of picking a weight up from the floor (by bending over at the waist) and finishing in a fully upright position.

DECLINE - angled down, below the horizontal plane.

DEPTH (OF MUSCLE) - the total thickness, or height, of a muscle in a perpendicular-to-the-bone dimension.

DONKEY CALF RAISE - a calf exercise performed while being ridden (like a donkey) by another person.

DORSI-FLEXION - the act of lifting the front part of the foot up; as in walking on your heels.

ECCENTRIC MUSCLE ACTIVITY - controlled lengthening of a muscle to move a weight; occurs from the mid-phase to the start/finish position.

ENDLESS LOOP - part of the weight-trainer's flow-chart; it is a perpetual cycle of bad exercise choices in a workout — injuries — rest — pain eases — resume workouts with same bad exercise choices — injuries — and so on; cycle can only be broken by correcting the exercise choices and execution.

EXECUTION VARIATIONS - different body positions that are available for the performance of a given exercise; a change in benefit and/or risks usually results from each different position.

EXTENSION - movement that straightens a joint from a bent position.

E-Z BAR - a barbell with two "Z"-like angulations in it; provides hand grip position options.

FACET JOINTS - the name of the joints that lie between adjacent spinal vertebrae; responsible for spinal motion.

FASCIA - a type of connective tissue; very thin and sheet-like as it encases other connective tissues and muscles.

FLEXION - movement that bends a joint from a straight position.

FORCED REPS - the reps of a set that require a spotter to help the lifter continue to perform positive reps beyond the lifter's capacity to perform the exercise alone.

FOSSA - an indentation or cavity-like shape.

FUNCTIONAL BALANCE - the ideal state of proportional muscle strength for muscles that create opposing movements, at a given joint.

GASTROCNEMIUS - the large, visible muscle of the calf region.

GOOD MORNING - a standing bend-forward at the waist with a weight held across the shoulders.

GOOD PAIN - muscle soreness found either late in a workout from hard exertion or one to two days after a workout; it represents controlled muscle breakdown that leads to muscle growth; in contrast to "bad pain".

HACK MACHINE - a leg exercise machine that glides up and down on a backward leaning angle.

HYPEREXTENSION - the straightening of a joint, or spine, from a bent position, beyond the fully straight, neutral position.

I.F.B.B. - International Federation of Body Builders.

IMPLEMENTATION FACTORS - features of a workout that convert an exercise and its benefit into a specific workout goal; such factors include reps, sets, frequency, rest periods, rate of motion, etc.

INCLINE - angled up, above the horizontal plane.

INTER-OSSEOUS MUSCLES - deep, small muscles that lie between, and attach, adjacent bones of the fingers and toes, within the palm of the hand and the ball of the foot, respectively.

INTER-SEGMENTAL MUSCLES - deep, small muscles that attach a given vertebra to each of the vertebrae above and below it.

INTERVERTEBRAL JOINTS - the joints that attach, and allow movement between, two adjacent vertebrae; includes a pair of facet joints and the spinal disc.

ISOMETRIC MUSCLE CONTRACTION - hard muscle exertion, but against such resistance that no joint motion occurs.

I.S.S.A. - International Sports Sciences Association.

JOINT CAPSULES - the fluid-filled, balloon-like tissues that completely enclose each joint.

LIGAMENTS - connective tissues that attach one bone to another, in support of the joint within.

LOOSE-PACKED POSITION - the alignment of bones, in either of the hand/wrist or the foot/ankle regions, that is relaxed and essentially unstable.

LUMBAR SPINE - the vertebrae of the lower back.

MENISCUS - the cartilage found deep inside the knee that serves shock absorption and gliding capacities.

METATARSAL HEAD - the part of each toe bone, within the foot, that collectively creates the ball of the foot.

MID-PHASE POSITION - the exercise position at which the muscle activity changes from concentric to eccentric; the half-way point of a rep.

MUSCLE BURN - the intense heat-like feeling of muscles engorged with blood as a result of intense exertion.

MUSCLE FIBERS - the microscopic, functional units that together constitute a muscle; protein molecules arranged longitudinally.

MUSCLE INSERTION POINTS - the location, on bones, at which muscles attach (via their tendon); the end of the muscle at which the movement occurs.

MUSCLE PUMP - the look and feel of muscles swollen with blood following intense exertion.

MYOTENDINOUS - the transition zone between muscle fibers and tendon fibers; the most vulnerable region for injury within any given muscle.

MYTHOLOGY - a belief system that defines a culture or group of people; usually based on unproven assumptions.

NEGATIVE REP/PHASE - the return of a weight from the mid-phase position to the start/finish position; also called an eccentric muscle contraction; it requires a spotter to lift the weight to the mid-phase position if used after exhausting the lifter's capacity to perform the positive reps.

OLECRANON PROCESS - the hook-like process at the elbow that projects into the fossa of the humerus, thus creating the elbow joint.

PATELLA - the kneecap.

PEAK BICEPS CURL - the hard, extra muscle contraction at the end of the full range of motion intended to add depth to the muscle.

PEAVES - an acronym created as a means to prevent weight-training injuries; **P**erfect Execution, **A**voidance of high-risk exercise, **V**ariety of **E**xercise **S**election.

PERIPATELLAR SOFT TISSUE - any of the varied connective tissues that surround the knee cap.

PERSONAL PREDISPOSITION - an individual's likelihood of sustaining an injury via weight training; it is based upon old injuries, posture habits/errors, and occupation/sport activities.

PLANTAR FLEXION - the movement created by contraction of the calf muscles; downward pointing of the foot/toes.

POSITIVE REP/PHASE - the movement of weight from the start/finish position to the mid-phase position, also called a concentric muscle contraction.

PRESS - a forceful movement of weight in a straight line, perpendicular to, and away from the body.

PRONATION - (1) of the hand: palm facing downward position; (2) of the foot/ankle: the rolling inward (toward the body-midline) position.

PROTRACTION OF SCAPULA - the forward glide of the shoulder blades, along the rib cage, that in essence separates the shoulder blades from each other.

RACKING/UNRACKING OF WEIGHTS - the act of returning or removing weights to/from their support or storage racks before and after a set is performed.

R/B (EXERCISE) - the amount of injury risk (regarding a specific injury-site) associated with a given exercise.

R/B (PERSONAL) - the amount of injury risk (regarding a specific injury site) present within a given individual.

R/B RATIO - a risk-of-injury rating system (using a scale of one (low risk) to ten (high risk)) that indicates the degree of risk posed by a specific exercise toward causing a specific-site injury.

R/B (TOTAL) - the sum total of R/B (EXERCISE) and R/B (PERSONAL); this aids an individual's decision whether or not a given exercise is safe to use, regarding the risks-of-injury inherent to that exercise.

REP - the movement of the weight from the start/finish position to the mid-phase position and back to the start/finish position; multiple sequential reps constitute a set.

REPETITION MAGNIFICATION - the capacity (for a consistently used exercise to create an injury via the sheer number of repetitions) increases steadily over months and years; it converts low risk exercises into high risk.

REPETITIVE STRAIN INJURIES - soft tissue injuries that occur not through a single traumatic event, but by the performance of the same exercise frequently and vigorously over time.

RETRACTION OF SCAPULA - the reverse glide of the shoulder blades, along the rib cage, that essentially draws the shoulder blades together.

SCAPULA - the shoulder blade.

SET - a series of multiple, sequential reps of an exercise.

SHRUG - the straight-up squeezing of the shoulders, toward the ears.

S.I.T.S. TENDONS - the acronym given to the rotator cuff tendon names.

SPOTTER - a person who assists the lifter by helping the racking, positioning, and unracking of weights; also assists in forced reps and negative reps execution.

START/FINISH POSITION - the exercise position from which concentric muscle work occurs; the beginning and end positions of a rep.

STERNOCOSTAL JOINTS - the joints between the front ends of the upper ribs and the sternum (i.e., the breast bone).

SUPINE - the position of lying flat on one's back.

SUPINATION - (1) of the hand: palm facing upward position; (2) of the foot/ankle: the rolling outward (away from the body-midline) position.

SYNOVIAL MEMBRANE - equivalent to the joint capsule.

T-BAR - the shape of a bar for rowing exercises; creates a thumbs-facing grip.

TENDONS - the connective tissue that attaches muscles to bones.

THORACIC SPINE - the vertebrae of the mid back.

TIE-IN EXERCISE - an exercise that uses two adjacent muscle groups, as almost equal primary movers, to "blend" both function and appearance.

TRAIN AROUND PAIN - choosing exercises that allow painless workouts when an injury is present; prior to this book, a random search was necessary.

TRAIN THROUGH PAIN - disregarding an injury pain and continuing to perform the same old exercises, despite the pain experienced during the exertion.

VALGUS POSITION - a forced joint angulation away from the mid-line of the body.

VARUS POSITION - a forced joint angulation toward the mid-line of the body.

WEIGHT-TRAINING STATUS - a rating system that determines an individual's proper workout implementation factors.

INDEX

Numerals in italics indicate pages with images. Numerals in parentheses are exercise/variation numbers.

BOB WEATHERILL

Bob has obviously had tremendous success as a bodybuilder, but more surprisingly he has been very successful in quite a variety of other sports, as well. For instance, he has won numerous awards in motocross racing in Ontario, Michigan and Florida; he has pitched a no-hit baseball game; and he has won a provincial championship in junior hockey. He has even been awarded two certificates for personal achievement, from a Canadian prime minister and from a provincial premier. His body-building achievements include Southern Ontario Champion (1987); Eastern Canada Champion, Harbourfront Classic Champion, and Overall Ontario Champion (1989); North American Champion (1992); Overall Canadian (1993); Toronto Pro Invitational, 5th; and Texas Southwest Pro, 10th (2002). He has been a carded I.F.B.B. professional bodybuilder since 1993 and currently works as a personal trainer (both A.C.E.- and I.S.S.A.-certified) at Gold's Gym, Mississauga, Ontario. He also participates in seminars, physique modeling and guest posing.

LORNE KING

Lorne is accomplished in both athletics (professional football for the B.C. Lions and Toronto Argonauts) and in academics (Bachelor of Physical & Health Education from the University of Toronto). He owns and operates Real Fitness Personal Training in Markham, Ontario, and can be reached via e-mail at realfitness@hotmail.com.

CHRISTINE ROTH

Christine has risen through the ranks of amateur bodybuilding, having held the 2002 Ms. Ontario title and finishing third in the Ms. Canada competition. In 2003, she earned her I.F.B.B. professional card. She works full time as a personal trainer in Toronto, Ontario, and is becoming increasingly busy as a magazine fitness model. She can be reached via e-mail at christineroth@rogers.com.

ABOUT THE AUTHOR
Bruce Comstock, B.Sc., D.C.

DOCTOR COMSTOCK RECEIVED his Honors Bachelor of Science degree (in Physiology and Pharmacology) from the University of Western Ontario in 1979 and his Doctor of Chiropractic from the Canadian Memorial Chiropractic College, Toronto, in 1983. He has been in private practice ever since. It was during his first eight years of practice, at the injury clinic of Gold's Gym, Toronto, that he developed a particularly keen interest in the biomechanical causes of weight-training injuries. His efforts to delineate the biomechanical features of both the performance of weight-training exercises and the causes of weight-training injuries were steadily advanced by, not only, the several thousand injured weight-training participants who attended the clinic, but also through his own weight training injuries. The specific cause-and-effect relationships between weight-training exercises and injuries that he identified have become the foundation for this book. He continues to practice in Toronto, Ontario, and resides in Richmond Hill, Ontario, with his wife and two children. He can be reached at FITSWAY@sympatico.ca.